Published by Straight Talk Books
P.O. Box 301, Milwaukee, WI 53201
800.661.3311 • timeofgrace.org

Cover image: welcomia/iStock

Printed in the United States of America
ISBN: 978-1-949488-04-3

GROWING
stronger

BUILDING FAITH ONE DAY AT A TIME

Introduction

Growing in spiritual wisdom is a lot like building your family's financial assets. It just doesn't happen all at once, no matter how much you crave it. Proverbs 13:11 teaches financial patience and focus: **"Whoever gathers money little by little makes it grow."**

You could say the same thing about a weight-loss plan. Healthy, rapid weight loss almost never happens. Instead, when people adopt better nutritional habits and get better exercise, the weight *slowly* falls off.

There is no way to gain mastery of biblical teachings in a hurry. Your spiritual wisdom will come not from one or two big gulps, but from the accumulation of daily devotional sips and weekly messages in church; it comes from insights gained in your small group or formal Bible study.

It is my hope that these Grace Moments devotions will provide those little sips to give you slow and steady spiritual growth. If you've found benefit in them, how about passing them on to a friend who needs them?

Ready? Let's go!

Pastor Mark Jeske

january

Because of the LORD's great love
we are not consumed,
for his compassions never fail.
They are new every morning.

Lamentations 3:22,23

Finding happy in a new year

Pastor Matt Ewart

It could be said that life is a string of attempts to outweigh the unhappy with the happy. So did things balance out last year? Maybe you are just hoping to find *some* happy in this new year.

A wise man named Solomon wrestled with the concept of happiness. In the book of the Bible we call Ecclesiastes, he demonstrated how empty you'll become if you try to outweigh the unhappy with the happy. He tested and observed everything that promised happiness, and he found nothing but frustration.

So he concluded his book with these words: **"Now all has been heard; here is the conclusion of the matter: Fear God and keep his commandments, for this is the duty of all mankind"** (12:13).

Translation: your purpose is not to seek happiness. Your purpose is to seek God, to know God, and to obey him. Which, I admit, might sound like the opposite of happiness. But hear me out.

The more your heart depends on finding happiness, the more you will be heartbroken when you can't find it. But the more your heart depends on seeking God, the more your heart will be filled up by what you find.

Unhappiness and emptiness are a consequence of living in a broken world. But Jesus came to redeem you from your brokenness. Seek him and follow him this new year, and you will find all the happy that your heart needs.

Where did I come from?

Pastor Mark Jeske

It's always a little irritating, isn't it, to hear someone described as a "self-made man"? No successful or well-to-do people ever did everything on their own. Even the most brilliant were helped and assisted by many, many others along the way.

In the same way it must infuriate God to hear bright and influential people deny that there is intelligent design in the origin of the human race. Only those who want no divine authority over them would find persuasive the arguments that the incredible complexity of a human being simply evolved over millions of years by completely random mutations, i.e., essentially by self-synthesis.

We are not self-made. Every man, woman, and child who ever lived is a stunning example of God's imagination, design skill, and biological engineering and construction: **"It is he who made us, and we are his; we are his people, the sheep of his pasture"** (Psalm 100:3). The second half of that marvelous passage is the logical implication of the first half. If God really did invest all that energy and skill into creating us, he must have plans for us, and we need to pay attention to those plans *because we belong to him.*

Divine design and creation of the human race is not demeaning. In fact, it is ennobling, because it signifies that we mean a great deal to the Great Power above.

You are precious. Beautiful. Wanted.

Called by name
Jason Nelson

I did this thing in the classroom if I couldn't remember a young man's name. I would just call him Maynard. I called one boy Maynard so often everyone else started calling him Maynard too. I think even his mom started calling him Maynard. No one knew his real name until he graduated from high school and the principal called him by his given name to present him with his diploma. His classmates looked at each other in disbelief. I feel a little bad about it now.

If someone calls us by the wrong name, it's like a reflex to correct him or her. It's important to set the record straight. Bad things can happen if our identity is mistaken, especially by the computers that keep big data on all of us. I had to prove I wasn't Jason Nelson Jr. to one of the credit bureaus. I don't know that person, but I knew it would be a mess if his debts got commingled with mine.

God keeps us all straight. He knows our names and the stories that go with them because they are his stories too. **"Do not fear, for I have redeemed you; I have summoned you by name; you are mine"** (Isaiah 43:1). He will graciously gather us to himself in his name. **"Bring my sons from afar and my daughters from the ends of the earth—everyone who is called by my name"** (Isaiah 43:6,7).

God's heart hurts when we suffer

Pastor Mark Jeske

It is one of the painful aspects of parenthood that sometimes we have to stand by and let our children struggle. We instinctively want to rush in and fix everything for them and spare them any pain. But sometimes it is necessary that they suffer consequences of bad decisions they have made. If we intervene too soon, we will ruin the educational aspects of their experience.

But our hearts still hurt while we watch and wait. So does God's. He loves his children even more than we do ours. His heart is thrilled when we are doing well and gloomy when we are rebelling and creating messes. And when he judges that the time is right, he will come to help, just as he did for the Israelites as they were being assaulted from both east and west: **"Then they got rid of the foreign gods among them and served the Lord. And he could bear Israel's misery no longer"** (Judges 10:16).

Some Christians visualize God as reigning serene and undisturbed over all things in his heaven, emotionlessly moving his chess pieces around. They reason that since he has already seen the past, present, and future, nothing can surprise or delight him. Not true. Scripture describes his intense and emotional engagement in how we are doing. How he grieves when we run away from him! How he rejoices when we repent and return!

That's what love is like, you know.

Audience to the King
Pastor Matt Ewart

It will break a king's heart if there is an injustice within his kingdom that he doesn't know about. King David knew that. He could only help the people whose voices he could hear. He dreaded the idea that there were many cries for help that never made it within earshot of his throne.

A king can only help when he hears the requests for help. Which makes Psalm 18 interesting.

This is a psalm in which David gives thanks that God heard him crying for help. David had been running for his life from King Saul. While David was on the run, he wasn't exactly a model of what it looks like to trust God. He failed more than once. He tried taking matters into his own hands. But he kept crying out for help along the way. Here's how David put it in this psalm: **"In my distress I called to the Lord; I cried to my God for help. From his temple he heard my voice; my cry came before him, into his ears"** (verse 6).

Maybe today you'll feel like something in your life is being threatened. Maybe you'll experience distress. And when that happens, you might not be a perfect model of what it looks like to trust God. But the good news is that no matter where you are or where you've been, your King can hear you. Your King wants to hear from you.

Epiphany glory

Pastor David Scharf

You might have expected the people of Jerusalem to have remembered the shepherds' message about Jesus' birth, but it appears they did not. If they knew that the "King of the Jews" was born in Bethlehem, you might have expected the religious leaders to have paid him a visit. But they did not.

And yet, Jesus' glory shined for the Magi. **"We saw his star when it rose and have come to worship him"** (Matthew 2:2). Jesus did not leave them in the dark. Jesus gave them an *epiphany* (which means "to make known" or "reveal"). The festival of Epiphany is a festival older than Christmas, only exceeded in age by the festival of Easter. Epiphany is especially important for non-Jews because through the account of the wise men (i.e., non-Jews) coming to worship the baby Jesus from the East, God shows that Jesus is the Savior for all people—including us! That's why this festival is known as the "Gentile Christmas."

In the cathedral of Cologne, you can see the Shrine of the Three Kings. Visitors are told that their number was three and that their names were Caspar of Tarsus, Balthazar of Ethiopia, and Melchior of Arabia. But the Bible doesn't mention any of that—no number, no names, no place of origin. Why? Because none of that really matters. Instead Scripture records what really matters. These Gentiles came to worship Jesus as their Savior—Jesus is for all people!

Let's worship him too!

The main thing
Pastor Matt Ewart

Just think about all the things you would need to do if you had a special guest come into your home. Think of all the cleaning, cooking, and perhaps shopping that you'd need to do. Special guests deserve the best.

Mary and Martha were welcoming a most special guest—Jesus himself. What would you do to get your home ready for that? Yikes. Apparently they were a little behind on their preparations.

While Jesus was with them, Luke records that Mary was sitting with the guest while Martha was still preparing for the guest. Martha was busy working while Mary was busy sitting. We can relate to why Martha was irate—Mary wasn't pulling her weight.

Taking care of guests is important. Martha was working on good things. . . . **"But Martha was distracted by all the preparations that had to be made"** (Luke 10:40).

There are plenty of good things that you can do today. But any good thing can become a distraction if it becomes the main thing.

For Mary the main thing wasn't the state of the house. It was the One who sat in the house. This focus on "the one thing needed" would eventually give these sisters incredible resiliency when they dealt with the death of their brother, Lazarus.

You've got lots of good things you can do today, but don't let those good things distract you from the main thing. Jesus wants time with you today to prepare you for your years on earth and your eternity with him.

Time is short

Pastor Mark Jeske

Time continually slips into the future. Rock musician Steve Miller will not go down as one of America's greatest philosophers, but he's right on that point. Our lives are evaporating with frightening speed, and the older you get, the faster time seems to go.

It's hard to teach the shortness of time to children and teens. Their lives seem to stretch on ahead into infinity; they assume that they have plenty of time to do anything they want. Add to that the addictive quality of all the computer and video games available to them. I hasten to add that older people also find ways to waste huge amounts of time. Are you convinced that all the time you spend on social media is a good investment?

Frittering away time is nothing new—Paul encouraged the Christians in Ephesus to make their time count: **"Be very careful, then, how you live—not as unwise but as wise, making the most of every opportunity** (literally 'redeeming the time'), **because the days are evil"** (Ephesians 5:15,16). Are there important tasks awaiting you that you are avoiding or delaying because you're frittering away time on activities that don't really matter much?

Quick check: Are there unresolved conflicts in your family where you could break the logjam? Is someone you know ready for an invitation to go to church with you? What is your ratio of time spent on video games versus prayer?

What time can you redeem for Jesus today?

Facing Goliath
Pastor David Scharf

David wouldn't have been our pick. His brothers seemed to be more physically impressive. They were the kind of guys who probably starred as wide receivers for the Bethlehem High School football program and made the All-Judean All-Star team each year. David was just their little brother. And yet, the brothers were afraid of Goliath, but David was confident.

He knew he'd win against Goliath, not because of his strength but because his God was with him. David said, **"I come against you in the name of the LORD Almighty. . . . This day the LORD will deliver you into my hands . . . and the whole world will know that there is a God in Israel"** (1 Samuel 17:45,46). Everyone would see the box score in the next day's papers and know that there is a God, a real God, in Israel!

You and I don't have the promise to defeat Goliath. But you do have the promise of God's presence. Go forward confidently today, relying on the promises he does give you in his Word. He loves you. He forgives you. He's with you. He will never forsake you. Remember that the hero in the David and Goliath story isn't David; it's God. This is the same God who is the hero of your story as well. Jesus defeated death to give you life. With Jesus on your side, face your "Goliaths" with the same confidence as David and trust that God will deliver you in the way he knows is best!

Can I lose my salvation?

Pastor Mark Jeske

There has been an argument for centuries between Christians as to whether or not it is possible to lose your salvation. People who answer that it is not possible put their emphasis on God's grace—that if God has named someone his child, he could never go back on his word. His grace is unconditional; his forgiveness is total.

Scripture presents a more complicated picture—that we are saved by grace *through faith*. God's grace is indeed unconditional, but our faith, once given to us by God, now becomes part of our choice and obedience. Scripture gives us the solemn warning that those who have received the knowledge of the gospel truth and then throw it away will experience an even more frightful eternity than those who never knew: **"If we deliberately keep on sinning after we have received the knowledge of the truth, no sacrifice for sins is left, but only a fearful expectation of judgment and of raging fire that will consume the enemies of God"** (Hebrews 10:26,27).

There are life choices that you can make that will keep you from that horrible spiritual suicide. You can respect Satan's cunning counterattacks, knowing that he will try even harder to seduce you. You can choose to go to church, to be fed by the Lord's Supper, to read your Bible, and to pray by yourself and in community.

You can choose the path of daily repentance and daily embracing the cross of Christ as your lifeline to God's favor.

A battle that ends in triumph

Pastor David Scharf

Agree or Disagree: Life is a battle that you never quite win.

Look at the last ten years of your life. Maybe you've lost someone you love . . . battle. Maybe you've fought sickness, perhaps many times . . . battle. Maybe you've struggled to stay motivated at work and at home, struggled to keep up with life's demands, struggled with the energy needed to make it through this life . . . battle. One battle is certain for each one of us: struggling with sin . . . battle, battle, battle!

Look at the last ten years of your life again. Remember that God was at your side . . . triumph. Remember how God gives you a glimpse of the rest you will enjoy in heaven every time you worship him and listen to him through his Word. He gives rest to your weary soul . . . triumph. Remember how in the Lord's Supper he gives you a sweet foretaste of the wedding feast of heaven . . . triumph. And because of Jesus and his cross, what comfort do you have for those who have died in the Lord and for yourself one day? Triumph!

Someone once said that the Christian will in some way lose every battle but still win the war. That's so true. Jesus has already defeated all of the enemies that stand against us. Is life a battle? Yes, but for the Christian—for you—it is a battle that ends in triumph!

"Blessed are those who are invited to the wedding supper of the Lamb!" (Revelation 19:9).

Wish not

Pastor Matt Ewart

On several occasions Jesus instructed people on the issue of worry. **"Do not worry about tomorrow, for tomorrow will worry about itself"** (Matthew 6:34). He warned people that worrying about life is a form of not trusting God. That makes sense. The warning to not worry is easy to keep on the radar.

What often goes missed is a danger that is similar yet opposite. While we shouldn't waste all of our energy *worrying about* tomorrow, it is also true that we shouldn't waste all of our energy *wishing for* tomorrow.

Sometimes we can put so much hope in what tomorrow might bring that we spend all of the present wishing to be in the future. What is it that grabs your heart's attention so much that you spend your energy wishing for tomorrow? James brought up a good point: **"Why, you do not even know what will happen tomorrow. What is your life? You are a mist that appears for a little while and then vanishes. Instead, you ought to say, 'If it is the Lord's will, we will live and do this or that'"** (James 4:14,15).

We have an idea of what tomorrow might bring, and maybe it's even exciting. Don't let wishing for tomorrow's possibilities divert you from the purpose God intends for today. Your Savior doesn't just promise you a better future. He is active right now with you today, empowering you to live out your purpose as a redeemed child of God.

The ruminators
Jason Nelson

This one is for all the farm girls and boys out there. Y'all know that cattle are ruminators. Cows kill time lying around chewing on what they have already eaten but haven't completely digested. Much more seriously, this one is also for the rest of us who spend lots of time brooding over what has been happening to us that we just can't make sense of.

Reflecting leads to insight, repentance, and redirecting our lives. But we can't do it perfectly, and sometimes dwelling on disappointments and failures paralyzes us. Ruminating feeds anxiety and depression. It drains our energy because it messes up our brain chemistry. Activity is the antidote. Activity jostles our endorphins out of hiding and we feel better. Doing life is a great distraction from worrying about life. Focusing on what we can accomplish keeps us from obsessing over where we have failed.

I would never want to make this sound easy because it isn't. Telling someone who is bogged down to "buck up" is insensitive and gives them one more inadequacy to dwell on. And we can't live a productive life in someone's behalf. But we can show up when they need to get moving. We can bolster their confidence. We can suggest better things to think about. We can point them in the right direction. We can do some constructive prodding. **"Rise up; this matter is in your hands. We will support you, so take courage and do it"** (Ezra 10:4).

Does God really love me?

Pastor Mark Jeske

If you are a believer in God, I can assume that you believe in God's power, control, ambitious plans, sovereignty, holiness, eternity, and command of 10,000 times 10,000 angels. You know that he made the universe, holds the hounds of hell at bay, protects his children, and will ultimately crush all evil.

But here's the thing: does he *love* me? Am I just a microscopic chess piece on his insanely large chessboard, or is he really my *Father*? Am I just a thing he has made, a tiny, tiny cog in an immense machine, or do I *matter*? Does he care how I'm doing? how I feel? what I have to deal with each day? Does my success or failure matter to him?

St. Paul ached to know these things too, and the Spirit of the Lord gave him this confidence: **"I am convinced that neither death nor life, neither angels nor demons, neither the present nor the future, nor any powers, neither height nor depth, nor anything else in all creation, will be able to separate us from *the love of God* that is in Christ Jesus our Lord"** (Romans 8:38,39).

Christmas, Good Friday, and Easter clinched it for Paul. If God's Son, divine and holy from all eternity, would take on human flesh for me, obey the commandments for me, suffer and die for me, and rise again to guarantee my forgiveness and resurrection, there can be no doubt.

He loves me.

Can people change?

Pastor David Scharf

I ask couples in premarriage counseling this question: "Who do you want to marry: the person you are marrying or the person you hope they become?" There's a right answer, you know. It's the person you're marrying! It's dangerous to enter into a marriage thinking that you can change the other person. Many have tried and been disappointed. Change is hard!

Jesus told a parable about a man who had a fig tree. Year after year he went out to look for fruit but did not find any. He wanted to cut the tree down. It's a stern warning to us. God is not looking for the superficial leaves of religion; he is looking for real fruit that comes from following him. And too often, the fruit I produce is paltry.

But this story filled with warning also has a hero. The caretaker of the vineyard jumped in between the owner and the fig tree and said, **"Sir . . . leave it alone for one more year, and I'll dig around it and fertilize it"** (Luke 13:8).

Do you know who the caretaker is? It's Jesus. On the cross he stood between us and the ax of God. Jesus was cut down so that we could live.

Now he tends you with his Word, and he fertilizes you with the Lord's Supper because as our caretaker, he knows, "I can put fruit on that tree."

With the right Caretaker, people really can change!

What's wrong with our world?

Pastor Mark Jeske

God made people to be bright, ambitious, creative, and restless. It's only natural that people would invest huge amounts of energy into making their lives better by controlling their environment. For a while people can sustain the illusion that the world is getting better and better all the time. Technological innovation brings greater personal comfort, wealth, and speed of travel and communication.

So why aren't people evolving into better human beings? Why is there so much violence, racism, crime, abuse, and hatred? What's wrong with our world? The Bible helps us see the terribly corrosive power of sin as it is transmitted from one generation to another. We are not evolving into better people. We are devolving: **"For the creation waits in eager expectation for the children of God to be revealed. For the creation was subjected to frustration, not by its own choice, but by the will of the one who subjected it, in hope that the creation itself will be liberated from its bondage to decay and brought into the freedom and glory of the children of God"** (Romans 8:19-21).

You and I can't stop that universal bondage to decay. But Jesus did. By his amazing incarnation and work, he reconnected God and humanity. All who trust and believe in him will enjoy personal forgiveness and restoration, first in part, then fully.

What a thrill it will be for all who have experienced that bondage to decay to be allowed to see Christ's astonishing re-creation of a new heaven and new earth.

Take it back

Jason Nelson

I was wandering around Walmart while my wife was shopping. I was in one of the aisles of Christmas decorations. A young mom was there with her little girl. They were looking at outdoor decorations. The little girl was begging for a Santa or a snowman. Mom was impatient and firm. She snatched up a Nativity and said, "If we get anything, we are getting this because this is what Christmas is about." I thought, "Good for you! You are taking Christmas back for your family."

That mom became my hero. She was young enough to never know a Christmas that wasn't commercialized, but it didn't faze her. I bet she never thought it was Walmart's job to keep Christ in Christmas. It was hers. Without hesitation, she took Christmas back for her daughter.

Could we follow her example? Do you think we could join forces and take back a couple hours on Sunday morning? We gave them up without much of a fight. Does youth soccer really need Sunday morning? Is it really the only gym time available for junior high basketball? I think we should take Sunday morning back and tell school and community leaders that we are. They can have our kids at other times, but on Sunday morning they belong to Jesus. It would be good for kids. **"Start children off on the way they should go, and even when they are old they will not turn from it"** (Proverbs 22:6). In the end, it will be good for everyone.

He feeds the world

Pastor Mark Jeske

One of the most endearing features of the acclaimed *Blue Bloods* television show is the family Sunday dinner. Four generations of Irish Catholic Reagans sit around a big table, and the cameras always record the family's meal prayer: "Bless us, O Lord, and these thy gifts, which we are about to receive from thy bounty, through Christ our Lord. Amen." What a pleasure it is to see Christians acknowledging God's gracious providing on national television.

Do you "say grace" before (and after) you eat? Do you make up a prayer for the occasion, or do you recite a treasured family tradition? Here's one our family has used for decades: **"The eyes of all look to you, and you give them their food at the proper time. You open your hand and satisfy the desire of every living thing"** (Psalm 145:15,16). What a great moment to reflect on the goodness of a God who feeds the world—believers and unbelievers, people and animals alike.

Farmers get this better than anybody. Their crops are at the mercy of the weather, so they are always looking at the sky to see what God is giving. They see directly God's blessing of fertility on their animals and crops, so they may have a slight advantage over city folks in the intensity with which they pray for good weather.

Can you imagine the pleasure God must feel when his grateful children notice his work and thank him?

Balance sheets and resumes
Pastor Mark Jeske

How can you tell if people think of themselves as successful?

Look at what's on their resume: educational attainments, advanced degrees and certifications, positions held (always higher and higher in rank), and special honors and awards. Look what's on their personal balance sheets: market investments, real estate, business ownership, trusts, and cash. Look at their presence on social media—are pics of them eagerly consumed because of their beauty, abs, or clothes?

What is your self-image? **"Let not the wise boast of their wisdom or the strong boast of their strength or the rich boast of their riches, but let the one who boasts boast about this: that they have the understanding to know me, that I am the Lord, who exercises kindness, justice and righteousness on earth"** (Jeremiah 9:23,24). Wealth, fame, beauty, and strength are all temporary and will soon fade away.

Is your relationship with the Lord the highest-ranked item on your personal balance sheet? Are you proud to know him? Is that on your personal resume? Is your self-worth based on your personal achievements? Or the opposite—do you suffer from low self-esteem because you see more failures than triumphs in your life?

All this pride and fear melt away when the Father's love, the Savior's forgiveness, and the Spirit's wisdom and strength are the features of your life that give you the most satisfaction and peace.

The truth test

Jason Nelson

I'd like you to take this little test about truth. The answers are below, but don't peek now.

1. *T or F   Truth is truth no matter who says it.*
2. *T or F   All truth is from God.*
3. *T or F   If something rings like truth, it has a biblical foundation.*

Early in my educational experiences, I saw that most ideas I found appealing also reflected the Bible's teaching no matter who said them. I encourage you to get to know your Bible well enough so that you can apply this truth test to everything you hear. Our ability to do that makes us modern-day Bereans. **"The people of Berea were more open-minded than the people of Thessalonica. They were very willing to receive God's message, and every day they carefully examined the Scriptures to see if what Paul said was true"** (Acts 17:11 GW).

We tend to prefer our truth from people we like or people like us. But that is a narrow range and filters out a lot of other truth tellers. Truth seekers are generally curious, listen to many ideas, and apply the truth test to everything they hear. And *voila!* God shows us there is more truth available than we thought. Recognizing it makes us able to **"run in the path of** [his] **commands, for** [he] **has broadened** [our] **understanding"** (Psalm 119:32).

Now it is up to you to decide whether what I wrote here passes the truth test or not.

Answers: 1-T, 2-T, 3-T

God's grace is universal

Pastor Mark Jeske

One of the sad characteristics of life on this planet in the 21st century is that we have all gotten more tribal. Under stress, we shrink backward into groups just like us. This is bad news for America's eternally strained racial environment.

The Black Lives Matter movement cannot imagine why anyone could disagree with them or oppose them. Those who advocate All Lives Matter or Blue Lives Matter too see their position as more universally moral. Neither side has much empathy for the other, and so the shouting goes on.

Christians have an important role here. We can affirm the unconditional universality of God's grace. We can teach and live the truth that God wants all to be saved and that all nations and tribes will be represented in the throng around the throne in heaven. We can show the world how to love, respect, and appreciate people not like us for Jesus' sake.

We can live out the beautiful relationship that took place in a chariot in Gaza along the Mediterranean coast long ago. The evangelist Philip was led to an African government official who was puzzling over a Bible. Philip sat with him and revealed the gospel of Christ to him. The Ethiopian said, **"Look, here is water. What can stand in the way of my being baptized?"** Philip baptized him, and the African **"went on his way rejoicing"** (Acts 8:36,39).

Two very different men became brothers that day.

This is only a test

Pastor Mark Jeske

The Israelites and their great leader Joshua had conquered the central portion of the land of Canaan. But they didn't finish the job. The upshot was that the new nation was surrounded on all sides by intensely hostile enemies: Tyre and Sidon (Phoenicians) to their northwest; Aram (Syria) to the northeast; Ammonites to the east; Moabites, Amalekites, and Midianites to the southeast and south; and the dreaded Philistines to the southwest.

God decided to make the presence of those hostile nations work for him: **"'I will use them to test Israel and see whether they will keep the way of the LORD and walk in it as their ancestors did.' The LORD had allowed those nations to remain; he did not drive them out at once by giving them into the hands of Joshua"** (Judges 2:22,23). When the Israelites lost interest in the Lord, he let them be harassed by their enemies.

The entire biblical book of Judges shows how God successfully used Israel's crises to lead them to repentance and to return to him. He then came to their rescue again and again to bring them security and peace.

You know, it may be that God has chosen not to take away all of our troubles and threats for the very same reason. Sometimes foolish sinners like us need his two-by-four upside the head to get our attention. But it's not punitive. It's *corrective* when our troubles lead us back to him.

He does it for our good, you know. He loves us.

Coexist

Pastor Mark Jeske

It is your destiny to live in a world where educated people don't think there is absolute truth anymore. Nobody can say anybody else is right or wrong. The greatest social sins are being judgmental and intolerant.

A prime example is the "Coexist" bumper sticker. The Christian faith is viewed as just another set of unprovable and personal religious opinions, and its cross is lumped together with symbols for Islam, pacifism, gay rights, Judaism, paganism, and Taoism. In today's world, you can have your opinions and I can have mine, but don't you dare ever say I'm wrong, and don't you dare ever say that your religion is the only right one.

Well. I guess it all depends on the basis for your convictions. Christianity is *inclusive*—Christ Jesus died for all, to bring forgiveness and life to all, and all those who believe it freely have it. But it is *exclusive* too: **"Thomas said to him, 'Lord, we don't know where you are going, so how can we know the way?' Jesus answered, 'I am *the* way and *the* truth and *the* life. *No one* comes to the Father except through me'"** (John 14:5,6).

Don't shoot the messengers. Christians proclaim the exclusivity of Christ, not because they are better than anybody else or enjoy feeling smug and superior but because there is only *one way* out of the grave and hell.

Behind the tongue

Pastor Matt Ewart

Words are extremely powerful things. Nations have rallied together because of a single speech. Top-level leaders of huge companies have fallen because of what they said in a single sentence. Relationships have thrived and failed over words that were said.

The Creator used words to speak this creation into existence, and ever since then on a much smaller scale our words have had the power to shape things. Words have the power to shape lives. But the apostle James explained the danger in that: **"No human being can tame the tongue. It is a restless evil, full of deadly poison"** (James 3:8).

In modern terms, he might have compared it to a fire hose with no nozzle to control it. The more you try to control it, the more you realize you can't. The only thing you can do is stop the source. And the fire hydrant that feeds your mouth is none other than your heart. Whatever is in your heart is eventually going to come out in the form of words.

God is not content to teach you how to filter your language, and he gives no classes on how to choose your words carefully. Jesus came not to tame your tongue but to address your heart.

So when the Word of God became flesh and dwelled among us, he spoke some powerful words that transform you from within:

It is finished. I forgive you. I am with you always. Peace I leave with you.

Giving and sharing
Jason Nelson

By definition, giving is a sacrifice. It is taking something we value and presenting it to someone we value even more, expecting nothing in return. In Leviticus, God taught Old Testament believers to love him like that by insisting they make significant sacrifices. They burned up animals that took effort and expense to raise. They poured out wine that took time to ferment. When it was over, those things were gone.

We give when we help our neighbor dig her car out of a snowbank. That's a couple hours of our lives we will never get back. We accept no payment because she is our neighbor. Giving is love with no returns. When I gave my daughter's hand in marriage, I whispered in my son-in-law's ear, "No givsies backsies."

Sharing is loving with mutual benefits. There is an expected reward. We get satisfaction in what we have offered to others. God wanted Old Testament believers to share the Passover meal. Family and friends got together to enjoy food and drink. They expressed their faith in the Lamb of God whose blood redeemed them. The older folks told stories of their unique experiences as God's people. And younger folks discovered their heritage.

Sharing is love where nothing is lost. Everyone is enriched. Faith and life mean more to us because they are appreciated by others. And it is very appropriate for others to return the favor. Giving and sharing are nice ways to live.

No God, no joy

Pastor Mark Jeske

The original sin of the human race was to choose to believe that life independent of God, his Word and ways, would be happier and more fulfilling. Eve (and Adam) became convinced that eating the forbidden fruit would open their eyes to new beauties, open their minds to new wisdom, and open their hearts to exciting new experiences. They saw submission to God and acceptance of his authority and value system as slavery. They wanted control. The rush of excitement as they bit into the fruit seemed to validate Satan's whispered promises.

But then the joy drained away. They heard their heavenly Father's bitter disappointment. They heard the predictions of misery to come. They felt the hot flush of shame and guilt. They were expelled from their garden paradise. Later on, imagine what it must have been like to look at the bloody corpse of their younger son.

The prophet Jeremiah spoke to people who were still under Adam and Eve's delusion: **"'Your wickedness will punish you; your backsliding will rebuke you. Consider then and realize how evil and bitter it is for you when you forsake the Lord your God and have no awe of me,' declares the Lord, the Lord Almighty"** (Jeremiah 2:19).

It is only through Christ that our guilt is relieved. It is only in submission to God's Word that we are free. Only when our lives are aligned with God's will do we experience satisfaction.

Fear of forgiveness?

Pastor David Scharf

Hydrophobia. That's the fear of water. It seems silly to be afraid of something you need. Frankly, it's not just silly, it's deadly. Hydrophobia is a very dangerous disease in animals because it will drive the animal wild, causing it to bite and tear, because it knows it needs something. But it dreads the "something" it needs: a drink of water.

Forgivenessphobia. Okay, I made up that word. But I didn't make up the condition. Too often people (you and me included at times) run around and take out our guilt over our own inadequacies on others. Too often we try to find satisfaction in the things of this world or the things that we do. Almost like we're afraid to accept the one thing we need: forgiveness.

St. Augustine, early Christian theologian and philosopher, said it right: "You have made us for yourself, O Lord, and our hearts are restless until they rest in you." Don't be afraid. Find rest today in Jesus' words to you, the one thing you need today: **"Your sins are forgiven"** (Mark 2:5). He won that forgiveness and freedom for you when he gave his life for yours on the cross. He assured you by making you his child in your baptism. He gives you visible forgiveness in his body and blood in the Lord's Supper. Every sin is gone.

Now don't be afraid to accept the fact of what he earned for you: forgiveness.

Why do I exist?

Pastor Mark Jeske

On his second missionary journey, St. Paul traveled to the center of the ancient city of Athens to start a conversation with the Greeks who lived there. They were an earnestly religious people, and Athens was full of monuments and temples to their gods and goddesses. Their priests taught them that the human race had sprung from stones cast behind them by a man named Deucalion and a woman named Pyrrha.

Paul did not ridicule myths like these, but he began to tell the people about the real origin of the human race. We came from the mind and will of one God, who launched the entire universe into being. **"The God who made the world and everything in it is the Lord of heaven and earth and does not live in temples built by human hands. And he is not served by human hands, as if he needed anything. Rather, he himself gives everyone life and breath and everything else"** (Acts 17:24,25).

Nobody today believes that Deucalion and Pyrrha populated the earth with stones. Instead, the academic elite in our world embrace and propagate the idea that the human race is the product of random evolution and mutation. Perhaps someday people will sneer at that idea too, realizing that there had to be intelligent design to bring about such brilliantly imagined and engineered living creatures as you and me.

In the meantime, look up to heaven and give thanks to the One who gave you life and breath.

Why did I land here?

Pastor Mark Jeske

Is there any meaning to the place of your birth, or is your arrival random and meaningless? People want answers to that aching question. That's why stories of delivery by a stork keep hanging around. People want there to be a reason why they are where they are.

St. Paul spoke to that ancient longing in the human heart when he spoke to the Greeks in Athens: **"From one man he** [i.e., God] **made all the nations, that they should inhabit the whole earth; and he marked out their appointed times in history and the boundaries of their lands"** (Acts 17:26). Paul was giving those inquiring minds great comfort—not only did they have a wise and loving Creator, but they had a *place*. They weren't just aimless dust motes or twigs floating downstream. There was a reason for their location and relationships. There was care and design in their lives. They *mattered*.

There is care and design in yours as well. "Bloom where you are planted" is a wise old saying, based, perhaps, on this Scripture verse. It doesn't mean you can't ever move somewhere else. It does mean that you can embrace your location, no matter how humble, and be useful to God right there, right now. Part of the grand adventure of life is slowly discovering God's intent in placing you where you are.

You might not figure it out right away, and that's okay. Enjoy the ride.

What is my purpose?
Pastor Mark Jeske

When the stagecoach brought you to Laramie or Cheyenne, that was the end of the line for you. The driver might have helped you get your trunk out of the boot, but then he climbed back into the driver's seat, shook the reins of the horses, and clattered off. You were on your own.

Some people might feel birthed and abandoned in life. They have not yet gotten to know their Creator, who is intensely interested in how they are doing. We weren't just made and then dumped—he wants to develop a relationship with us. St. Paul wanted his Athenian listeners to experience the hope and fulfillment that come from reconnecting with the source of life itself: **"God did this so that they would seek him and perhaps reach out for him and find him, though he is not far from any one of us. 'For in him we live and move and have our being'"** (Acts 17:27,28).

Are you a parent? Did you drive home from the hospital and leave your firstborn lying in the nursery with the other newborns? *Of course not!* You carefully nestled the babe in your arms (old school) or packed him or her carefully into your brand-new car seat (present times) and proudly brought the newest member of your family home. In the same way, the meaning and purpose of your life will unfold as you come to know God through his Word.

He's not far from you. He wants you close to him.

What are my gifts?

Pastor Mark Jeske

You may have noticed that God doesn't whisk you safely up to heaven as soon as you are converted to faith. You're still here! That can mean only one thing: your work here is not completed. You're not just killing time here until death or judgment day ends it all. You are part of God's mission team to make a spiritual difference in other people's lives.

You are called to be distributors of God's Word and God's love. You have been given a place and a set of relationships by God. The only question that remains is the particular role that he needs you to play. For that you need to take a personal gifts inventory of your life. **"Each of you should use whatever gift you have received to serve others, as faithful stewards of God's grace in its various forms"** (1 Peter 4:10).

Q: So how do you know what those gifts are? A: What are you good at? Where does your spiritual passion lie? What kinds of work and service do you care about? What do other people compliment you on? Do people tell you that you are good at teaching and explaining? singing? playing a musical instrument? creating a spreadsheet? growing and arranging flowers? telling stories? writing? graphic design? caring for buildings? creating great meals? caring for children? designing websites? curating a church Facebook page? organizing care for seniors?

Using God's gifts satisfies your soul.

february

Be completely humble and gentle;
be patient, bearing with one another in love.

Ephesians 4:2

What do you have?

Pastor David Scharf

A man was visiting a Texas landowner. After dinner the landowner took the man out on the front porch to show him the view. Waving his arm toward the horizon, he said, "Everything you see belongs to me. Those oil wells on the horizon—they're mine. That grain on the hills—that's mine. Those cattle in the valley—mine. Twenty-five years ago when I came out here, I had nothing. But now I own everything you see."

The host waited for words of praise. But the visitor waved his arm toward the heavens and said, "And what do you own up there?"

Do you find yourself focused on what you have or don't have here on earth? Do you let it affect whether you're in a good mood or a bad mood? If so, chances are that you are too focused on the "down here" stuff and not focused enough on the "up there" stuff.

Sometime today, look up and realize what you have: a God who scooped you up in his arms at your baptism and said, "You are mine and I am yours." A God who loved you to death on a cross. A God who says, **"Be content with what you have, because God has said, 'Never will I leave you; never will I forsake you'"** (Hebrews 13:5).

What do you have? Turns out you have a lot!

Undeserved thankfulness
Pastor Matt Ewart

Genuine thankfulness is the byproduct of a heart that is properly aligned with God. When your thankfulness begins to slip, that's the first warning sign that something in your heart needs attention. So even though it is nowhere close to Thanksgiving, here's a simple exercise to see how thankful you are. Ready?

For the next 24 hours, be mindful of all the things you have and all the relationships you have. And as you force yourself to be aware of those things, *be thankful only for that which you don't deserve.*

Once you make a list of all the things you deserve, think twice about them. These are the things that are putting your heart out of alignment. Truth be told, this world doesn't owe you a thing, and neither does God.

The good news is that God does not give us what we deserve. Jesus took what you deserve, and it cost him his life. But here's what's amazing: God did not stop when he took care of your eternity; he takes care of you every day until you enter eternity.

Are there things that your heart thinks it deserves? Pay attention to those things today. Let Jesus take control of them to bring your heart back into the right focus with the result of genuine thankfulness.

"Sing and make music from your heart to the Lord, always giving thanks to God the Father for everything, in the name of our Lord Jesus Christ" (Ephesians 5:19,20).

My careless tongue
Pastor Mark Jeske

"Talk is cheap," goes the old saying. Alas, that old saying is a lie. Hurtful words may come cheaply and easily out of your mouth, but the damage done and the cost of repairs may be extremely expensive.

I once mouthed some very critical words about a family member to another family member, who then felt it necessary to share my words with the person. Busted! The person I smacked down and his wife have been cool to me ever since. At first I was furious for getting ratted out, but then I put the blame where it belonged—on the one who should have kept his critical opinions to himself in the first place. Here are the brakes I should have had on my tongue from the start: **"The words of the reckless pierce like swords, but the tongue of the wise brings healing"** (Proverbs 12:18).

Take a little inventory of your relationships. Are any of your relatives or friends bleeding from verbal wounds that you have given? Don't just settle for a sullen truce, or worse, run away. How might your wise tongue bring about some healing? Are you angry right now with what someone has said about you? You know, you can decide to forgive the person (if for no other reason than that Christ Jesus has unilaterally decided to forgive you your sins).

Perhaps the tongue of the wise (i.e., you) might bring about some healing.

Wrestling with the devil

Jason Nelson

"Keep your mind clear, and be alert. Your opponent the devil is prowling around like a roaring lion as he looks for someone to devour" (1 Peter 5:8 GW).

We expect Satan to come at us like a roaring lion. We expect him to be scary, noisy, and conspicuous. But he's a sneaky, sneaky lion. And he is a snake in the grass—our grass. Satan rarely comes at us with a frontal assault. He rarely makes mischief in our lives by rushing at us head-on to maul us. He doesn't want us to see it coming. He lies in the weeds and watches so he can see which way we are heading. He's a savvy wrestler. He notices how we're leaning and uses our own body weight against us. Our own momentum does us in. He slips alongside and pushes us too far in the direction we are inclined to go so he can roll us over. Then he flops on top of us and pins us down.

Satan nibbles away at us to go for just one more: one more drink, one more bet, one more flirtation with the pretty person at work, one riskier pursuit of some guilty pleasure. The first move in wrestling with Satan is pulling ourselves back. The first move in wrestling with Satan is being clearheaded and alert to the things that tempt us so that we can pull ourselves back. Then we can regain our moral balance and be faithful to our Lord.

Who's going to heaven?

Pastor David Scharf

A pastor was called on to see a man dying of a terrible disease. The man had Christian training in his youth but had turned away from it and had lived an awful life. Now on his deathbed, his thoughts returned to God. He repented of his sins, and the pastor announced God's forgiveness before the man died.

One prominent member of the church said to the pastor before the funeral, "Pastor, you're not actually going to bury that good for nothing scoundrel, are you? Because if he went to heaven, I don't want to go there!" The pastor answered, "Don't worry about that—you're not going there." "What?!" said the good church member. "This miserable man is in heaven, and I'm not going there?" The pastor said, "Not if that's the sentiment in your heart. All have sinned. No one deserves heaven. And all are forgiven through faith in Jesus. There's only one way to heaven—through Jesus!"

Take comfort in that today. It's not your good works; it's not your offering total; it's not your church service that gives you the confidence of heaven. It's because Jesus died for your sins that you are going to heaven. Remember, that's true for everyone you see today as well!

"I tell you, the tax collectors and the prostitutes are entering the kingdom of God ahead of you" (Matthew 21:31).

Do something!

Pastor Mark Jeske

Psychologists, substance abuse counselors, and social workers have a last-ditch strategy when helping someone out of destructive behaviors seems to have hit a brick wall. It's called an intervention. Friends and family members of the abuser all show up at the same time, surround him or her, and pile their testimonies and observations one upon the other to overwhelm the person's lies, dodges, and excuses. Interventions often work, because people who have made wrongdoing habitual can't break out on their own. They need an external energy source to blast them out of their ruts.

That's true of habitual spiritual sinfulness too. Jeremiah realized with shame and sadness that his nation was so far gone it couldn't change course on its own. Nothing less than a divine intervention would do, and he prayed for God's mercy: **"Although our sins testify against us, *do something,* Lord, for the sake of your name. For we have often rebelled; we have sinned against you"** (Jeremiah 14:7).

Maybe your efforts to get through to an alcoholic or drug abuser in your own circle of friends or family has stalled. Maybe you feel helpless to change your own destructive choices. Call on the Lord, not because of your own worthiness but *for the sake of the Lord's own name* and reputation. Be honest with him; accept responsibility; cry out not for a reward you think you deserve but for mercy that you have not deserved.

Lord, *do something*!

Lord, be gentle when you correct me
Pastor Mark Jeske

Jeremiah was one of God's all-time great prophets. He was given a hard message at a hard time. Everybody wanted a miraculous deliverance from the attacking Babylonian imperial army. Jeremiah was instructed to advise the people *to surrender*! He took terrible personal abuse for that seemingly collaborationist message, but in fact his words were from the Lord, who had already given victory to Babylon and had arranged the deportation and captivity for Judah's spiritual good.

And yet Jeremiah knew that he too was a sinner who needed a Savior. He knew that God is a God both of law and gospel, a God who both punishes sin and forgives sin. Just like you and me, Jeremiah prayed that God would treat him according to his grace and mercy, not the severe justice that Jeremiah knew he deserved: **"Discipline me, Lord, but only in due measure—not in your anger, or you will reduce me to nothing"** (Jeremiah 10:24).

Jeremiah was open to God's correction, even when painful. God's discipline is not punishment—it is the application of pain to bring about greater good in someone's life, like a surgeon's knife that cleans out an infected abscess or the shock of disinfectant hitting an open wound.

The time is coming soon when we will need correcting no more, when in heaven we never sin again. In the meantime, we will submit to God's correction, trusting that he will keep the hardships within our limits to bear.

Let God's love be your default

Pastor David Scharf

Sometimes my computer gets so messed up that it freezes and doesn't do what it should. Do you know how to fix that? Shut it down. Wait. Start it up. The default settings come back, and you're good to go for a while again!

Sometimes life feels so messed up that we freeze and don't feel like we do anything the way we should. Have you been there recently? Do you know how to fix that? Shut down your worries and get back to your default settings. What are those settings?

The story has it that when Michelangelo came down from the scaffolding that he had set up while painting the Sistine Chapel, he had become so accustomed to looking upward that it caused actual pain to turn his eyes to the ground. His default had become gazing on the story of God's love that he was painting.

Let it be yours too. Before there was a world, there was just God. He thought of your face . . . and he smiled. From that moment on he did everything he needed to make you his, including dying on a cross and rising from the dead. Now every day his goal is to keep you close until he spends eternity with you in heaven.

When life seems messed up, let that love of God be your default setting, **"know and rely on the love God has for** [you]**"** (1 John 4:16).

I feel so lonely

Pastor Mark Jeske

The logo for a nonprofit agency that advocates for children with autism is a puzzle piece. It's a quiet and sweet way to promote the idea that autistic children are gifted and complex people and that they are needed for the full human picture to be revealed.

It is sadly possible to be lonely, achingly lonely, even when there are plenty of people around. Some folks are natural salespeople, outgoing and aggressive. Others are shy, awkward, too inhibited to seek out others. Some are so afraid of criticism and rejection that they avoid being with anyone they don't know well. Some lose their few friends to death or moving away and never replace them with new ones.

It is one of the greatest benefits of congregational life to give people social capital. As people grow closer to Christ, they just naturally grow closer to each other. A common belief system is a marvelous bond, and it invites all those scattered puzzle pieces to interlock one by one. Congregations also are a significant labor force for Christ. There is nothing quite like the power of a group of volunteers in service to others that both brings value to the people they're serving but also to their own lonely spirits. **"Carry each other's burdens, and in this way you will fulfill the law of Christ"** (Galatians 6:2).

Go ahead. Take a chance. Get involved in some form of service and add your puzzle piece to the picture.

My sex life is my business

Pastor Mark Jeske

Of all the wrenching social changes that people have been through in the last two generations, the most traumatic have been over marriage and human sexuality. The challenges that the baby boomers launched in the 1960s came to their logical conclusion, and who knows if we're done changing yet. These changes have affected not only the secular world but the families in the Christian church as well.

Cohabiting is no longer the slightly shameful "shacking up," but it's now the new normal. Even old folks do it when they think it benefits them financially. A homosexual lifestyle no longer is something to keep quiet. TV shows have helped to make gay couples the new normal. You can't say a word or you'll be branded as homophobic. The societal consensus that marriage consists of one man and one woman blew up in a decade. There are no longer two genders, assigned by birth. You may now choose your gender identity, and one option is "neither."

The biblical way has become the new counterculture. God says: **"Flee from sexual immorality. All other sins a person commits are outside the body, but whoever sins sexually, sins against their own body. Do you not know that your bodies are temples of the Holy Spirit, who is in you, whom you have received from God? You are not your own; you were bought at a price. Therefore honor God with your bodies"** (1 Corinthians 6:18-20).

Whose approval do you seek?

February 11

The reality you will never know
Pastor David Scharf

Have you ever heard someone who is going through a tough time say, "What do people do who don't have Jesus in their lives?" By God's grace, I've never experienced that reality.

Today you will face difficulties and struggles and temptations and sins—most of it no one will know about. But there is One who does. He knows you. He knows your name. He knows your needs. He knows your failures. And because he knows you, with all that you face, he will help you. He knows you . . . and you know him.

Today you will hear a lot of voices, many of which intend you harm. But Jesus says, **"My sheep listen to my voice; I know them and they follow me"** (John 10:27). See, that's something admirable about sheep. Go to a watering hole in the desert of Palestine. You'll find multiple shepherds and their flocks all mingled together. You'd think that it would be tough to separate them all out. But it's not. All it takes is for the shepherd to call out, and instantly the sheep follow his voice. Sheep won't budge for a stranger's voice. In the midst of all the voices you hear today, pick out the soothing voice of your Shepherd and follow him. He never leads you wrong.

Aren't you glad that you'll never have to know the reality of what it's like *not* to have Jesus? Me too!

Wrestling with God

Jason Nelson

"So Jacob was left alone. Then a man wrestled with him until dawn. When the man saw that he could not win against Jacob, he touched the socket of Jacob's hip so that it was dislocated as they wrestled. Then the man said, 'Let me go; it's almost dawn.' But Jacob answered, 'I won't let you go until you bless me'" (Genesis 32:24-26 GW).

Jacob was having a restless night before a high stakes meeting with his brother, Esau. Years earlier, Jacob defrauded Esau out of the family birthright, and they hadn't seen each other since. They were finally going to meet up. Two estranged brothers would engage in a stare down at dawn. Jacob didn't know if the meeting would result in a warm embrace or violent conflict. Should he even go through with it? God came between them and wrestled with Jacob.

God kept trying to escape Jacob's hold on him. Why would God push anyone away at the turning point of a crisis? To show us we have the courage to see it through. In every crisis, we struggle with ourselves, other people, and God himself. Holding on to the Almighty for all we are worth is the only way to get through it. God pushes back so that we grab on to him more tightly. God pushes back so that we strengthen our grip. God inflicts a little short-term pain on us so that we rejoice in the blessed relief of an answer to our prayers.

Sometimes you have to wrestle with God to get a blessing.

Dishonest scales
Jason Nelson

When I step on the bathroom scale, I generally don't like the readout. I've tried pulling myself up a little with the towel bar to get a better number. But that's cheating.

"The Lord detests dishonest scales, but accurate weights find favor with him" (Proverbs 11:1). God hates any kind of fraud. Fraudulent practices have been around since he rebooted human history after he booted Adam and Eve out of the Garden of Eden. Merchants cheated people by putting their fingers on the payload side of a balance scale so they could charge more money for less product. Now cheaters try to institutionalize their advantage. Politicians gerrymander congressional districts so their voters will outnumber voters from the opposition party. They must think we won't notice.

Justice is supposed to be blind, and any kind of scale is supposed to be fairly balanced. But our commerce and politics are out of whack. We take dishonest scales for granted. We might even think treating others fairly puts us at a disadvantage.

God saw that people cheat and asked himself, **"Shall I acquit someone with dishonest scales?"** (Micah 6:11). He answered yes and unbalanced his own standards of justice for our benefit. He placed our sin and shame on Jesus like he deserved it and we didn't. That's how **"he's already made it plain how to live, what to do, what God is looking for in men and women. It's quite simple: Do what is fair and just to your neighbor"** (Micah 6:8 MSG).

God's gift of love

Pastor Matt Ewart

Valentine's Day is about giving gifts to people you love. Picking a gift can be difficult because a gift communicates what you think of someone. Perhaps there was a time when someone gave you a gift that left you shocked (good or bad) because of what it communicated.

We naturally apply this concept to God. You can look at everything that happens in your life as a gift from him. But some days you wonder what these "gifts" communicate. "Why did he allow this bad thing to happen?" "Why is he not giving me the good things I want? Does he really know me? value me? love me?"

When King David looked back at the life he had been given, he saw so much evidence of God's love for him that he put it into these terms: **"As high as the heavens are above the earth, so great is his love for those who fear him"** (Psalm 103:11).

And before you can wonder how David reached that conclusion, he points to the reason for it: **"As far as the east is from the west, so far has he removed our transgressions from us"** (verse 12).

You won't always understand why things happen to you or to others you love. But especially on Valentine's Day as people exchange gifts that communicate something, pause for a moment to reflect on the message God communicated when he gave his one and only Son for you.

No overstuffed recliner

Pastor David Scharf

Things happen in every Christian's life that make us wonder, "Where is Jesus?" A job loss, a spouse loss, a self-confidence loss, a . . . loss. I'm guessing you can relate. Where is Jesus?

When we think of Jesus' "working years," we think of the 33 years he walked on this earth, the 40 days after he rose from the dead, and his ascension into heaven. So what's he doing now? Playing checkers with the Father, biding his time until he returns? Challenging the saints to golf at the Savior's Tournament on the perfectly manicured fairways of Zion Interstellar Golf Club? Taking a nap on his overstuffed recliner throne?

Hardly! There are so many dangers facing his church! The devil, the world, and our selfish natures are constantly trying to get us to step out of the church and embrace the world. The devil knows the church's mission: make disciples. The devil knows that if he can get the church to join the world, then there is no need for the world to join the church!

And so Jesus prays for you today and works every loss in your life out so that you might gain heaven. Isn't that a cool thing to think about? Jesus prays to the Father . . . for you. He constantly rules everything . . . for you. Jesus' throne is no overstuffed recliner!

"My prayer is not that you take them out of the world but that you protect them from the evil one" (John 17:15).

The stakes are higher now

Pastor Mark Jeske

Jesus told his disciples once that those to whom much had been given, from them much would be expected and even demanded. God's self-revelation did not come all at once, and he cut people slack when their available information was thinner. He didn't drop the entire Bible on Adam and Eve. Over the centuries he slowly released more and more information about himself, his plans, and his work, some verbal and some in writing. Over the centuries he steadily left a clear track record of his interactions with both righteous and unrighteous people.

Over the centuries the portrait of the coming Messiah came increasingly into focus, with more and more detail and explanation. Over the centuries the dreadful consequences of sinful rejection of the gospel became clearer and clearer. The human race is increasingly running out of excuses for its ignorance and apathy.

You know far more about God and his agenda than Old Testament believers ever knew, and that raises the stakes (and the risks). **"We must pay the most careful attention, therefore, to what we have heard, so that we do not drift away. For since the message spoken through angels was binding, and every violation and disobedience received its just punishment, how shall we escape if we ignore so great a salvation?"** (Hebrews 2:1-3). Don't complain about the increased pressure. Celebrate the clarity and power of the revelation you have to work with.

Believe it. Live it. Share it.

Gluttony

Pastor Mark Jeske

My grandmother used to ask me with a grin, "Do you live to eat or eat to live?" I think that was her gentle way to encourage me not to become a glutton, though I didn't know that word back then. Though the word sounds a little antique today, the sin is real: **"A discerning son heeds instruction, but a companion of gluttons disgraces his father"** (Proverbs 28:7).

Do you like to cook? Do you like to eat? Last Thanksgiving Day did your house look like ours, where for an hour after the meal nobody moved much, stunned into a food coma? How can you tell when enjoying God's rich abundance and diversity of foods and treats becomes gluttony? When your diet is so full of rich and processed foods that you are headed for obesity . . . when your overeating is causing you major health problems . . . when God's gift of wine and other alcoholic beverages becomes an addiction and you can't stop . . . when your appetite for the high life is costing you way more money than you can afford and you're shorting your family, your debt service payments, and your offerings to the Lord.

Our appetites are always threatening to take over our lives, and satisfying them becomes our obsession. The Proverbs passage above provides a clue about how to gauge your gluttony index—listen to your family.

A discerning son heeds instruction. Eat to live; don't live to eat.

I don't need a god

Pastor Mark Jeske

"I don't need your god to be happy, and I don't want your cult putting its rules on my life."

That angry shout is what Christians and their churches are hearing from the crowd today. Perhaps this seems like a new thing. Our country did have a long run where churchgoing and a Christian viewpoint were not only socially acceptable but actually socially expected.

Not anymore. We live in a post-Christian age that actually needs to be re-evangelized, as if it were a new world mission field. But let's not kid ourselves. Denial of the existence of God, of accountability to God, and of acceptance of the Bible as his revealed will are nothing new. They have been a plague on the human race ever since Eve and her foolish husband imagined that life without God was better, that independence from him was true freedom, and that the two of them should be left alone to pursue their own happiness, thank you very much.

A sad Father in heaven surveys the wreckage that sin and Satan have left on earth. But he will not yield. Atheism may sound cool today, but God has another word for it: **"The fool says in his heart, 'There is no God'"** (Psalm 14:1).

You do people no favors when you soft-pedal the existence of God, the reality of sin and judgment day, the terror of hell, and the sweet eternity of heaven. Just tell the truth and let the power of the Word do its job.

Free lunch tomorrow
Pastor Matt Ewart

On one occasion I saw a clever sign that a restaurant had posted in its window. It read: *Free Lunch Tomorrow.*

There was a moment of excitement as I thought through my schedule for the next day and realized that lunch was wide open. And a moment later that excitement vanished when I realized that this sign was permanent. Every single day they promised free lunch *tomorrow*. And tomorrow would never be today.

Sometimes it can feel like God is the same way. We hear promises of a better future and healed relationships and hope for tomorrow. But tomorrow never seems to get here, and that can be frustrating. Tomorrow loses all hope when you think about the certainty of death.

The apostle Paul knew that frustration well. He wrote, **"If the dead are not raised, 'Let us eat and drink, for tomorrow we die'"** (1 Corinthians 15:32).

But what Paul brings out so beautifully in the rest of that chapter is that the dead are in fact raised. When Jesus entered into death, he did so to take away its claim on you. Death cannot keep you, just as it could not keep him.

So if today is one of those days when it just seems like your life isn't leading anywhere, remember that the distress over tomorrow has been taken away. And as long as your Savior gives you a today, he still has a divine purpose for you.

The gift of less to lose
Jason Nelson

One of the best gifts God ever gave me was getting to a point where I had less to lose. I am not trying to compete with Job. His losses were epic. When God vacuumed nearly every distraction from his life, he was able to declare, **"I know that my redeemer lives, and that in the end he will stand on the earth"** (Job 19:25).

Life happened. My wife and I could measure the effects. We had less income for ourselves and still had to spend money on other people. We moved to a smaller house in a poorer community, drove cars well into six digits on the odometer, and tuned in antenna TV because it was free. But as we had less to lose, we became more grateful for what we had.

Getting to the point of having less to lose is no picnic. It is very stressful. I would never recommend you start throwing things overboard unless you have a hut in a tropical paradise. But when God starts peeling away the excess in your life, pay close attention to what remains.

The journey led us to agree on a stewardship practice. Nothing new comes into our house unless something old goes out. If we get a new sweater, Goodwill gets an old one. If we update a light fixture, the Habitat ReStore gets the old one. Someone else can use them. And we don't want to squander the gift of having less to lose.

My negativity
Pastor Mark Jeske

Here are some things that drive me crazy: people who are always criticizing other people, people who are always finding fault with every event, people who never seem to be happy, people whose moods are always a drag on the group, and people who assume the worst in others. *Hmm . . .* you don't suppose other people see those things in me, do you?

If my spirit is always cramped and bitter, what does that say about my worldview? It says that I'm not sure that Jesus really won. It says that I've been cheated in the distribution of resources and gifts. It says that I can't trust anybody, that nobody really likes me, and that frankly I don't really like myself. I assume things will fail and that I will be disappointed. *Again!*

Perhaps that's why I am so drawn to positive people. They always seem to find joy wherever they go. (Is it luck? Karma? Are they too dumb to see all the obvious problems?) They seem interested in me. They seem to shed stress and have the ability to let go and let God. They have light: **"Light in a messenger's eyes brings joy to the heart, and good news gives health to the bones"** (Proverbs 15:30).

Today I'm going to look for blessings, not breakdowns. I'm going to assume that God will send some light today, and I'll be watching for it. And I am going to try to share some good news with a sad soul.

Held together in Jesus
Pastor David Scharf

"You've got it so together!" Has anyone ever said that to you? If you're like me, when you hear those words, your first thought is, "If only you could see what's going on inside of me!" Truth be told, sometimes I have things anything but "together." Is it the same for you?

The Bible says, **"For in him [Jesus] all things were created: things in heaven and on earth, visible and invisible, whether thrones or powers or rulers or authorities; all things have been created through him and for him. He is before all things, and in him *all things hold together*"** (Colossians 1:16,17).

You see, *we* can't hold *anything* together. We need only look at our frailties and insecurities and failures to realize that we can't hold "it" together. But Jesus can. He's the one who made all this. In him, it's all held together.

Have you ever heard of laminin? It's a glycoprotein that promotes cell adhesion. It's not an overstatement to say it's the glue that holds us together. Without it, we would literally fall apart. If you look at it under a microscope, you'll see that it's shaped like a cross. Isn't it cool that the protein that holds us together *physically* looks just like the cross that holds us together *spiritually*?

Feeling unraveled as you look to the future? Remember that the One through whom all things were made is also the One who loved you enough to die for your sins. He'll hold it together for you today.

Strong and weak
Pastor Mark Jeske

How great the power of sexual desire! How little we understand it. How hard it is to control. Sex has been making money for people for millennia and is a boom industry today—prostitution, pornography, escort services, and strip clubs just keep proliferating.

Sexual desire can make a man's brain into mush and his muscles weak. Samson was chosen to be a *judge* in Israel, i.e., a charismatic military and social leader who would unite the people in faithfulness to the Lord. Though gifted with incredible divine strength, he carried around also serious weakness: **"Some time later, he fell in love with a woman in the Valley of Sorek whose name was Delilah. The rulers of the Philistines went to her and said, 'See if you can lure him into showing you the secret of his great strength and how we can overpower him'"** (Judges 16:4,5).

Delilah made a puppy out of this mighty man. Entire platoons of Philistine soldiers could not subdue him, but his sexual weakness caused him to lose his powers. (Think I'm making this up? Read Judges 13–16.) Every child of God today in these troubled times needs to be alert to Satan's terrible sexual assaults. Society today no longer helps us resist adultery and respect marriage.

Guys, be aware that your desires can make you brain-dead. Women, be careful with your sexual power. Remember who gave it to you.

Restored to normal
Pastor Matt Ewart

When you look at Jesus' miracles recorded in the New Testament, they all have one thing in common. They all restored what sin had stolen.

In the Garden of Eden when sin was introduced into a perfect creation, the results were catastrophic. Yes, the creation we see today is beautiful and majestic. But this is just the broken version. Sin broke God's creation, and that brokenness extends to you too.

But this is a brokenness that our Lord Jesus has the power to heal.

People who were blind, deaf, mute, crippled, paralyzed, bleeding, diseased, and even dead were brought to Jesus. Humankind's brokenness was brought into the presence of the Son of God. And quite often when he brought healing, the Scriptures refer to it as Jesus "restoring" them. He wasn't giving them some new power. He was just restoring what sin had stolen.

What has sin stolen from you? What brokenness do you struggle with? Maybe what you need to know today is that Jesus knows about it and he knows what it is like. You see, he willingly entered sin's brokenness so that he could heal it. His resurrection proves that your sin is taken care of and your death has been undone.

And one day he will restore everything—including you—to the way it was originally created to be. On that day you'll get to witness a wide-scale miracle that begins with this declaration from heaven: **"He who was seated on the throne said, 'I am making everything new!'"** (Revelation 21:5).

Overcoming personal baggage

Pastor Mark Jeske

Some children show up for school each day with some pretty heavy life baggage: depression, sexual abuse, parental conflict, poverty, inadequate sleep and nutrition, violent talk and actions in their homes and neighborhoods, and terrible peer pressure. One of the things that great teachers do for their students is help them overcome their personal baggage. It's not that the excuses the kids bring are nothing. They are a big deal. But children from stressed backgrounds will never get anywhere in life if they habitually use their baggage as their free pass from personal responsibility.

Jephthah had a terrible family background. His mother was a prostitute. But Jephthah didn't let that shame keep him down: **"Jephthah the Gileadite was a mighty warrior. His father was Gilead; his mother was a prostitute. Gilead's wife also bore him sons, and when they were grown up, they drove Jephthah away. 'You are not going to get any inheritance in our family,' they said, 'because you are the son of another woman'"** (Judges 11:1,2).

Jephthah's talent and drive lifted him to the position of Israel's commander-in-chief. He channeled his shame into positive energy. His embarrassing personal past helped him to be comfortable around other outsiders and outcasts, and he made them feel important.

So—which pieces of your past have you used as excuses for mediocrity or failure? Which young person in your life, burdened by personal baggage, needs your encouragement?

Nine leper syndrome

Jason Nelson

Those ingrates! Isn't that how we're supposed to feel about the nine lepers who didn't say thank you? Isn't that why Jesus asked this loaded question? **"Were not ten healed? Where are the nine? Can none be found to come back and give glory to God except this outsider?"** (Luke 17:17,18 MSG). Or is Jesus doing what he always does—sending the rest of us a message through a not-so-isolated incident?

Before the healing miracle, Jesus was discussing faith with his inner circle. They wanted the right thing, didn't they? **"Give us more faith"** (Luke 17:5 MSG). But Jesus didn't just hear the question. He saw what was behind it. He knew those guys too well. He knew they wanted to be among the select few in the big faith group. So, he said, **"You don't need *more* faith. There is no 'more' or 'less' in faith"** (verse 6). Any amount can move a mountain.

And then these lepers showed up. Jesus healed them. Not because he wanted a thank-you but because they needed to be healed and they all called out for God's mercy. I'm sure they were all grateful not to be lepers anymore. But it was a recognized outsider who came back. It was the man least appreciated by everyone watching who didn't just say thank you. He adored Jesus. **"He kneeled at Jesus' feet, so grateful. He couldn't thank him enough"** (verse 16).

We all suffer from nine leper syndrome. There aren't enough ways to thank Jesus for what he has done for us.

Two things determine a gift's value to you: what it is and who gave it. It needs to either be a genuinely nice gift or come from a genuine person for the gift to be received and treasured.

Giving to God

Pastor Matt Ewart

Two things determine a gift's value to you: what it is and who gave it. It needs to either be a genuinely nice gift or come from a genuine person for the gift to be received and treasured.

A gift was given to Jesus that should have been rejected on both accounts. The gift came from a social outcast, likely a prostitute. And it seems she had used the money from her career to purchase some very rare, very expensive perfume. She probably purchased it with the hope that it would increase her clientele.

But instead it turned into a gift for Jesus. **"She began to wet his feet with her tears. Then she wiped them with her hair, kissed them and poured perfume on them"** (Luke 7:38).

The onlookers that day protested. Both the gift and the giver were inappropriate.

But the same should be true of us. Who are we to give to God? And what do we have that God should want? Both the gift and the giver are insufficient.

But the woman who poured out her perfume on Jesus wasn't promoting herself. She was celebrating Jesus. He had changed her identity from "sinful woman" to "forgiven child," and as a result she reprioritized her inventory to honor him.

To this day, genuine giving to God is not a promotion of who we are or what we have. It's a celebration. We have been given a new identity that moves us to reprioritize our inventory.

Explore your wilderness

Jason Nelson

"Can God really spread a table in the wilderness?" (Psalm 78:19). Can God provide what we desperately need when we feel lost and dead inside? We don't want to give up. Our instincts tell us if we keep going, eventually we will make our way out of our private wastelands. With God at our side, we can exit the great unknowns in better shape spiritually, physically, and emotionally than when we went in.

The largest designated wilderness in the United States is the Wrangell-St Elias Wilderness of Alaska. It covers over 9,000,000 acres. It has vast expanses where no human has set foot. But some people have gone there on purpose. They want to live off the grid. They want to depend only on the resources God places around them and discover what human resourcefulness he creates within them. There is only one way to survive. They must constantly explore the wilderness.

Those of us on the grid also face intimidating challenges. It's a jungle out there. Jesus knows all about it. He resisted evil in the wilderness and went to the wilderness to get away from it all and pray. He guides us in exploring our wilderness. He says ask the right questions and they will be answered. Seek the right things and you will find them. Knock on the right doors and they will be opened (Matthew 7:7,8). Then the wilderness becomes a land of God-given opportunity.

march

Sanctify them by the truth; your word is truth.

John 17:17

Unlikely Lenten preachers: Caiaphas

Pastor Mark Jeske

It's a basic principle of any legal justice system that people should not be convicted or suffer penalties for the offenses of others. And yet that's exactly what God built into the sacrificial worship life of his Old Testament Israelite people. Every Jew should have been well aware of the concept of substitutionary atonement, i.e., that God would accept the death of an animal in place of the guilty people who brought the sacrifice.

The high priest in Jerusalem, Caiaphas, was the ringleader of priestly hostility to Jesus and his ministry. In giving his blessing to what was basically an assassination plot, he unwittingly enunciated the heart and core of Jesus' entire mission—to be the Lamb who took away the sins of the world. Truth is truth regardless of who says it: **"One of them, named Caiaphas, who was high priest that year, spoke up, 'You know nothing at all! You do not realize that it is better for you that *one man die for the people* than that the whole nation perish'"** (John 11:49,50).

Although an unlikely Lenten preacher, Caiaphas put his finger on what the Father had worked out as the grand strategy for the redemption of the human race. Here's how God could have it both ways—both punishing sinners and forgiving sinners. The guilt of the human race was loaded upon Jesus; his holiness was transferred to the sinners.

Those who believe it have it.

Unlikely Lenten preachers: The Sanhedrin

Pastor Mark Jeske

Trial by a jury of your peers is one of the features of the American justice system of which we are most proud. In theory, an impartial group of at least a dozen men and women from your social group should be able to guarantee a fair hearing.

You would think, therefore, that the Sanhedrin, a huge assembly of 70 people, would have provided a fair trial when Jesus was arraigned before them. Not so. That group was so corrupt that they had a prearranged guilty verdict, thanks to conspiracy and bribery. Here again, however, this group inadvertently became Lenten preachers, for what they said was actually true: **"The high priest tore his clothes and said, 'He has spoken blasphemy! Why do we need any more witnesses? Look, now you have heard the blasphemy. What do you think?' 'He is worthy of death,' they answered"** (Matthew 26:65,66).

That corrupt group, sadly the highest governance allowed the Jewish people under Roman rule, actually articulated God's rescue plan for the human race. It was the Father's will to blame Jesus Christ for the evil thoughts, words, and deeds of the entire human race! God was actually using these unworthy judges to speak for him. When they (unjustly) said that Jesus was worthy of death, the Father was (mercifully) saying that he now considered Jesus Christ responsible for the world's sin. Thus he now carried all the blame.

And we do not.

Unlikely Lenten preachers: Pontius Pilate

Pastor Mark Jeske

The Romans were justifiably proud of their legal system, elements of which form the backbone of Western law today. It didn't take the Roman governor of Judea and Samaria, Pontius Pilate, very long to figure out that the bound rabbi before him had committed no crime: **"Once more Pilate came out and said to the Jews gathered there, 'Look, I am bringing him out to you to let you know that I find no basis for a charge against him'"** (John 19:4). Not only was there nothing upon which to *convict* him, there wasn't even enough of a case to *charge and hold* him.

Pilate had absolutely no way of knowing that he was uttering a powerful statement about the manner in which the almighty God was about to bring about the salvation of the world. The innocence of Jesus Christ, about which Pilate was absolutely correct, meant that Jesus completely qualified as the innocent victim, the substitute, who was at the heart of God's Old Testament system of reconciliation.

The death of Christ, which would soon take place, would have been meaningless, a terrible and bloody miscarriage of justice, but also the terrible squandering of the life of the Son of God, if he had not lived his 33 years in complete moral perfection. Jesus Christ was innocent of any sin or crime against the laws of God or Rome, and thus his death was acceptable to God the Judge as payment for the sins of the world.

He is the Lamb of God, pure and holy.

Unlikely Lenten preachers: Roman soldiers

Pastor Mark Jeske

Foreign soldiers performing garrison duty in a conquered territory that hated them knew to be on their guard at all times. They also quickly became skilled in applied cruelty to break the spirit of resistance and enforce their will in the occupied territory in which they would always be outnumbered.

The Roman soldiers on crucifixion duty that received Pilate's order on Good Friday morning were undoubtedly a tough lot. They had dealt death to others and seen their buddies killed. They carried out the punishment of crucifixion in order to terrorize the local population into submission, usually posting the charges above the unfortunate victim as a disincentive to any others who might contemplate similar crimes.

The routine execution of three Jews started off normally enough. The soldiers were hardened to the screams of two of the condemned. But it soon became apparent to these soldiers and their junior officer that something very unusual was happening. The calm and loving demeanor of the one in the middle stunned them.

The darkness that came upon the entire land, as well as the earthquakes that began to rock the surrounding area as the middle one's death approached, totally changed their thinking and their world: **"When the centurion and those with him who were guarding Jesus saw the earthquake and all that had happened, they were terrified, and exclaimed, 'Surely he was the Son of God!'"** (Matthew 27:54).

Their Lenten sermon was correct. He was. And is.

Appreciate your workers

Pastor Mark Jeske

Company managers will often say things like, "Our employees are our greatest assets," but the rank and file don't always feel the love. An annual Employee Appreciation Day can go a long way toward building a culture where the worker bees feel wanted, respected, and fairly compensated. Every company hopes that all employees will give 100 percent all the time and go that extra mile for customers. The truth is, however, that resentful employees are much more likely to do only the minimum. They can provide at best a mediocre customer experience, and their grumbling can poison the workplace atmosphere.

Jesus told a story about a boss and his expectations. He entrusted a significant amount of capital into the hands of key lieutenants and then left it to their own energy, initiative, and hard work to grow that investment. After a time the owner returned, analyzed the business results, and called in his first lieutenant: **"Well done, good and faithful servant! You have been faithful with a few things; I will put you in charge of many things. Come and share your master's happiness!"** (Matthew 25:21).

Although Jesus' parable wasn't intended primarily for business training, his story nevertheless shows good management practice: the boss trusted his workers, didn't micromanage, let them do things their way, paid attention to their performance, praised them, and promoted them.

Do you manage others? What are you doing that shows that your workers are your greatest asset?

Kintsugi
Pastor Matt Ewart

In most cultures when you break something, you either hide it or you throw it away. But centuries ago, the Japanese culture decided to do something different. They developed a practice called *kintsugi*, which is best translated as "golden joinery." The idea was to take a broken dish or bowl and join the pieces back together. Rather than trying to hide or mask the imperfections, they would highlight them with gold. The result was not only a broken object made whole again but also an object that significantly increased in value.

Ever since the Garden of Eden we have been trying to hide our brokenness. We see our imperfections as things to be ashamed of until we can fix them or hide them well enough. We think real beauty depends on how perfect we are, and we dismiss others or even ourselves when brokenness is revealed.

But look at what Jesus did: **"It is not the healthy who need a doctor, but the sick. I have not come to call the righteous, but sinners to repentance"** (Luke 5:31,32).

He came to collect all the broken pieces of what sin has done to you and to make you whole again. When sinners repent and welcome Jesus to address the brokenness, the result is amazing. People are made whole again, and by virtue of Jesus' righteousness, their value is infinitely increased.

Keep in mind today that Jesus views brokenness as an opportunity to add beauty and value.

Prodigalish

Jason Nelson

In his book the *Prodigal God,* Timothy Keller takes another look at Jesus' well-known parable of Luke 15. The heading someone put in our Bibles perpetuates the idea that this is a heartwarming story about the departure and return of an immature and self-centered little brother. But it is really the complicated story of a family pulling apart because everyone is a prodigal.

Getting all of Jesus' meaning out of the story depends on understanding the definitions of *prodigal.* Most people interpret the parable with the first definition in mind: "Rashly or wastefully extravagant." That is the nature of all prodigal sons and daughters. But there is a second definition: "Giving or given in abundance; lavish or profuse." That defines the father in the story and the nature of our prodigal God.

One way or another, we are all "prodigalish." We're like the younger brother. We disrespect our heavenly Father whenever we indulge our unrighteousness and wander off to be selfish. Or we're like the older brother. We disrespect our heavenly Father when we indulge our self-righteousness by thinking we are morally superior to the people who wander off. Either way, we put our heavenly Father in a very tough spot. In order for him to accept any of us, he needs to be prodigalish too. **"See what great love the Father has lavished on us, that we should be called children of God! And that is what we are!"** (1 John 3:1).

Ask for the ancient paths
Pastor Mark Jeske

It is the conceit of the young to imagine that their age is the most enlightened in history, that technology has changed everything, that new is always and automatically better, that all old things are obsolete. Yesterday's stuff and ways are, well, you know, so yesterday. Alarm clocks, flip phones, and landlines are beneath contempt.

"Old" principles of human morality have been completely revised. Absolute standards for right and wrong are in the trash. "Tolerant" and "diverse" have replaced "judgmental" and "narrow-minded." You can choose any sexual behaviors you want. For that matter, you can choose any gender identity that suits you at the moment, and no one is allowed to tell you you're wrong.

Disrespect for historic and timeless principles of human behavior is nothing new. Six centuries before Christ, Jeremiah confronted the same conceits and had this wise counsel: **"This is what the Lord says: 'Stand at the crossroads and look; ask for the ancient paths, ask where the good way is, and walk in it, and you will find rest for your souls'"** (Jeremiah 6:16).

Committing adultery has not lost its sinful nature just because we're in the 21st century and everybody thinks it's cool now. Judgment day is coming whether you believe in it or not. Because of the conscience that God put into every human being, sin against his will brings anxiety, fear, and guilt, not peace.

Ask for the ancient path: Christ is the Way, the Truth, and the Life.

Sometimes God lets you fall

Pastor Mark Jeske

You know, all Christians, me included, really like the passages in Scripture that talk about God's rescuing activity. We adore the stories of Daniel and his lions, David and the giant Goliath, Jonah's underwater weekend, Jesus' five thousand lunch guests, and Jairus' dead sixth-grade daughter coming back to life. Personally I love passages like **"the Lᴏʀᴅ upholds all who fall and lifts up all who are bowed down"** (Psalm 145:14).

But think a minute. Those words from the Word invite the question—if God is so smart, loving, and omnipotent, why did he let you fall or get so bent over in the first place?

Fact 1: our falling is our fault. God didn't make the human race sin. We chose it, chose it against his advice and warnings. *Fact 2:* God has indeed envisioned and decreed a place where none of his children will ever again fall or be bowed down, but we're not there yet. It's called heaven. We're still on earth. *Fact 3:* Pain is not all bad. Pain is good when it cures us of our arrogance, kills our illusions that earth is a paradise, and illustrates our desperate need for divine help to survive the war we're in.

Here is hope: he catches us when we fall. He will not let us be tempted beyond our ability to bear. Here is comfort: he gives strength to those who stagger under loads that make them stoop.

Follow me

Pastor David Scharf

Then Jesus said to Peter, **"Follow me!"** (John 21:19).

Do you know the context of that verse? You might think that it was Jesus seeing the "full of life and potential" Peter at the beginning of his ministry and calling him to be one of his disciples. Jesus did do that, but that was a number of chapters before this! Check out the reference: John chapter 21 is one of the accounts of the resurrected Jesus. This is *after* . . .

After Peter was slow to believe, *after* Peter had doubted Jesus' power when walking on water, *after* Peter told Jesus that Jesus would never suffer a cross, *after* Peter had cut off Malchus' ear, *after* Peter abandoned Jesus in the garden, *after* Peter denied Jesus three times . . . you get the point. And yet, Jesus still said, "Follow me"? I don't get it.

We can only get it after we realize what else it was after . . .

After Jesus gave his life on Good Friday to pay for the sins of the world. *After* Jesus rose to life on Easter morning. *We* remember Peter's sins, but because he removed those sins forever, *Jesus* does not. That's why Jesus could say to Peter, "Follow me!"

Think you have too many "afters" to hear those words from Jesus? Think again. His cross and empty tomb assure you. It's why after all of our afters, Jesus can say, "You're forgiven—follow me!" Follow him, certain that when your final after comes, Jesus will say, "Welcome home!"

This devotion is not about sex

Jason Nelson

But I still got your attention. When I was doing seminar presentations, I would watch the audience watch me. If I was losing them, I would fabricate a transition: "Now we are going to talk about sex." Bam! It went dead quiet and every eye was on me. It worked like magic with any audience. Then I told them I made it up, and we continued with the topic I was speaking about. They seemed disappointed.

Our attention likes to go where it wants to go. God has ways of getting in front of us and directing us where he wants us to go. He's not afraid to use matters of life and death to do it.

Hezekiah was king of Judah. The world order was changing. His little kingdom was in the crosshairs. Alliances were shifting. Foreign leaders used disinformation to undermine people's faith in God and confidence in Hezekiah's leadership. What should he do?

God got his attention. Isaiah told him, **"Put your house in order, because you are going to die"** (2 Kings 20:1). It was a really bad time to come down with something. His back was already up against the wall. But, **"Hezekiah turned his face to the wall and prayed to the Lord"** (verse 2). God answered his prayer: **"I will deliver you and . . . defend this city for my sake and for the sake of my servant David"** (verse 6). It all worked out because God never gets distracted.

Plan your legacy
Pastor Mark Jeske

Death and dying freak people out. They deal with that fear in various ways. Some people can't go into a hospital to visit someone, even a close friend. Some have phobias about funeral homes. Many refuse to take even the first step in making out a will, the basic building block for preparing a legacy for those who will survive you. Surveys report that two-thirds of Americans would die without a will if today were their last day. Yikes!

Christians who read even a little of the Bible have learned that they are managers and stewards of their money and possessions. This is an *essential* feature of the Christian life to which we have been called, but it includes not only our day-to-day spending decisions. God is very interested in our legacy plans: **"A good person leaves an inheritance for their children's children"** (Proverbs 13:22).

That legacy can take various forms. One is *financial.* The older generation has had more time to accumulate some assets and give the youngsters a boost to help them out of debt, get a house, or get a business started. One aspect is *educational.* Education has always been important. In today's information-based economy, it is urgent.

The greatest of all legacies is *spiritual.* It is your greatest gift to leave behind the example of one who loved the Lord, loved his Word, loved people, loved to give, loved to serve.

Tilting the covenant

Jason Nelson

For 40-plus years God used ten core laws, peculiar ceremonies, stern warnings, and divine retribution to drag his *children* through the wilderness and into the promised land. Under Moses the deal was, "You obey me, and I will be there for you. You don't obey me, and you will have hell to pay." It was the standard agreement. But something changed with Joshua. On a hallowed plain between sacred hills, Joshua restated the agreement between God and his people. It was different this time and signaled a covenant shift. God was done with the *children* of Israel. He wanted faithful grown-ups. With the trumpets of Jericho fading from their memories and the real estate parceled out, Joshua gave people permission to go their own way if they wanted to. He spoke only for himself and tilted the covenant away from compliance toward commitment.

"If serving the Lord seems undesirable to you, then choose for yourselves this day whom you will serve, whether the gods your ancestors served beyond the Euphrates, or the gods of the Amorites, in whose land you are living. But as for me and my household, we will serve the Lord" (Joshua 24:15).

Joshua lived up to his own name. He didn't dictate terms. He delivered on promises. In Hebrew his name is *Yeshua.* In Greek his name is *Yesous.* In English his name is *Jesus.* And it means, "God delivers." Joshua set the example and committed himself to the promise of a namesake who would come to deliver all people from their sins.

What people think
Pastor Matt Ewart

People around you will form opinions about you based on how you live your life. Some will think highly of you. Others won't. Rarely is someone loved by everyone.

There was a high-ranking Roman soldier in the first century who lived his life in such a way that everyone had very high opinions about him. So much so that when this man's beloved servant was on the brink of death, his friends were more than happy to seek out Jesus on his behalf. Here's what they said to him: **"This man deserves to have you do this, because he loves our nation and has built our synagogue"** (Luke 7:4,5).

Some people might have similar opinions about you, saying that you're such a good person you deserve to have God do anything for you. And it's tempting to agree with them. But when this Roman soldier heard what his friends had done, he quickly sent another entourage with a direct message to Jesus: **"Lord, don't trouble yourself, for I do not deserve to have you come under my roof"** (verse 6).

Jesus was impressed by this Roman soldier, but not because he built a temple. He was impressed by this man's faith. The soldier knew that all the great things he had done were nothing compared to the great things Jesus came to do.

Faith in Jesus does not eliminate the impact of great things you do for other people. Faith recognizes that what people think about you isn't as important as what Jesus did for you.

Is God really with us?

Pastor Mark Jeske

You can be forgiven if you think that in reading devotional literature like these Grace Moments sometimes they seem to overdo the happy talk. We want life to be like a TV show—all problems are quickly wrapped up in 60 minutes (or less if you subtract the time consumed in commercials). Life, alas, is not always like that. Sometimes we wait a long time for relief.

The Midianites, a nomadic nation to Israel's south, ravaged Israel's towns for seven years. Their raiding parties burned up the Israelites' crops, stole and slaughtered their livestock, and caused terrible poverty. **"The angel of the Lord appeared to Gideon, he said, 'The Lord is with you, mighty warrior.' 'Pardon me, my lord,' Gideon replied, 'but if the Lord is with us, why has all this happened to us? Where are all his wonders that our ancestors told us about when they said, "Did not the Lord bring us up out of Egypt?" But now the Lord has abandoned us and given us into the hand of Midian'"** (Judges 6:12,13).

What Gideon could not see was that God was completely on top of the situation for all seven of those terrible years. He was doing important spiritual things for the Israelites the whole time. What Gideon also did not know was that God had designed an extraordinary rescue plan that he would reveal at just the right time.

When you yourself cry out, "Is God really with us?" know with absolute certainty that the answer is *yes*.

I'm hungry to learn, Lord

Pastor Mark Jeske

All educators will tell you that it's never too late to learn. They love growing in knowledge and want to encourage people of all ages to adopt the posture of being lifelong learners.

This is true of the Bible as well. Perhaps you weren't blessed with a Christian school or Sunday school in your past, and other children got so far ahead of you that you gave up. It's never too late. I don't care what your age might be—cultivate a hunger for the Word and let God speak to you. **"Show me your ways, Lord; teach me your paths. Guide me in your truth and teach me, for you are God my Savior, and my hope is in you all day long"** (Psalm 25:4,5).

Don't set unrealistic expectations. Some sections are difficult and will take some work. Some things will come to you over time. Some things you may never understand. But the more you read, the more comfortable you will get with the powerful content in every chapter. Find a good teacher and soak in whatever you can. Find a home group and study together with other people . . . or form a home group of your own. Take advantage of your church's study opportunities.

The clearer your understanding of the Word, the stronger your faith will be. You will pick up on Satan's lies more quickly; you can reject his temptations and avoid his traps with the same powerful armor Jesus himself used: "This is what the Lord says . . ."

Say it with me: "I'm hungry, Lord. Speak to me."

Jesus is still in the healing business

Pastor David Scharf

You've probably heard of faith healers. They come around, demand money, and make the promise of healing you. If they can't heal you, it's your fault because you didn't have enough faith. Can you see where I'm going with this? It's a scam! Nowhere has God promised to give people the supernatural ability to heal! He could, but he doesn't promise it. So does that mean he's not in the healing business?

Not at all! In fact, I would submit to you that you have likely been healed as many times as anyone in the Bible! How can I say that? Because of the incredible way that God made you. He gave you an immune system that "heals itself" over and over, many times not even registering with your brain that you even got sick! Is that healing not from God? It certainly is!

Here's where it's good to have the humility of Galen. Galen was the most famous doctor of antiquity next to Hippocrates. He said, "I bound his wounds, but God healed him." Isn't that the truth? Jesus is still in the healing business. Feeling a cold coming on? Chances are by next month, Jesus will have healed you. Cancer not going away but getting worse? In a big sense, then even better—God has chosen you to soon join him in the place where there is no more sickness!

"Jesus healed many who had various diseases" (Mark 1:34).

Speak God's truth no matter what

Pastor Mark Jeske

Our world is a mess. People are born disconnected from their Maker. They are ignorant of the Savior, Jesus Christ. And until they come to faith, they don't have access to the Spirit's wisdom and power. People need to be *converted,* born again, regenerated, brought back into a relationship with their God.

How does that happen? By believers sharing the powerful message of the gospel with unbelievers. Does a successful conversion depend on the skill of the proclaimer? Nope. The power inheres in the Word of God. But here's the thing: though he could of course do all this proclaiming himself, God has *chosen to depend on his believers* to engage with unbelievers and bring them the message. He will wait and wait some more for us to speak.

This great honor and heavy expectation rests especially on leaders in God's church. In fact, to spur his prophet Jeremiah to get into motion, he told him that he should fear God even more than rejection: **"Get yourself ready! Stand up and say to them whatever I command you. Do not be terrified by them, or I will terrify you before them"** (Jeremiah 1:17).

What are you and your congregation doing to engage people in your community? Don't be afraid of people. When you speak words from the Bible, people are hearing not your thoughts but God's. Let him take care of the converting.

You just take care of the talking.

My impulsiveness
Pastor Mark Jeske

"Look before you leap." Ha! That's for other people, right? I know when to buy a car, buy a house, sign a contract, or move to another city to take a new job. When I leap quickly, it shows I'm decisive, self-confident, and right.

Er, maybe not. Maybe it shows that I'm too lazy to have done my homework, too deaf to have listened to other people, too impatient to have thought through the implications, and too self-centered to have considered the impact of my actions on other people.

You know, it's a lot easier to think a little more on the front end than to have to do a lot of apologizing and repairs on the back end: **"The prudent give thought to their steps"** (Proverbs 14:15). Yeah, baby. They sure do.

Where can I get some brakes for my impulsiveness? First, a little humility therapy. I need to dial down my opinion of my own brilliance. Second, more respect for others. There is huge value in the minds and experiences of the people around me. I need to spend some energy on tapping into that wealth of wisdom. Third, I need to say out loud before I leap, "Father, is this a good idea? Does it align with your ways? Am I missing anything?"

When the pastor is reading my obituary at my funeral, would he use the adjective *prudent* to describe me?

Microscopic
Pastor Matt Ewart

The bigger our telescopes get and the farther they can see, the bigger we realize this universe is.

Every time I brush up on how big the universe around us is, it gives me the chills. If I were merely to list the measurements for how big our galaxy is (not to mention the estimated hundreds of billions of other galaxies out there), the editor of this book wouldn't be happy with all the zeros I would have to enter. I would exceed the word limit immediately. This universe is too massive for us to comprehend.

David knew that three thousand years ago, even without high-tech telescopes. As he looked up into the sky, he made this observation: **"The heavens declare the glory of God; the skies proclaim the work of his hands"** (Psalm 19:1).

This universe was designed to be a testimony to how big God is. But you were designed to be a testimony to how loving God is. The sky is doing its job. But a lot of times we don't.

It can be startling to consider that in the grand scheme of this universe, we are not fulfilling the purpose for which we were designed. We don't belong here, and we definitely don't belong with God.

But that's where his love becomes even greater. The Son of God was willing to enter his own creation so that he could save the part of it that he loved the most—you. The size of this universe is microscopic in comparison to that kind of love.

Memorial stones

Pastor Mark Jeske

I'm a visual person, and I bet you are too. When I receive a gift from a friend, I like to display it where I can see it so that I think about that person. Our fridge at home is full of special magnets, photos, and children's coloring sheets.

After the entire Israelite nation had crossed over the miraculously dry Jordan riverbed, the Lord instructed Joshua to have the tribal elders carry out one stone for each of the 12 tribes and create a memorial on dry ground. **"In the future, when your children ask you, 'What do these stones mean?' tell them that the flow of the Jordan was cut off before the ark of the covenant of the Lord. When it crossed the Jordan, the waters of the Jordan were cut off"** (Joshua 4:6,7). What a stimulus for retelling that story over and over! No Israelite child should ever have been ignorant of the miracle river crossing.

Do you have "memorial stones" in your church? I don't mean literal river stones. I mean visual reminders of God's great acts of salvation in our lives. Your church undoubtedly displays the cross of Calvary somewhere. Perhaps there are paintings or stained-glass windows celebrating and teaching God's works. Perhaps there are colorful and artistic symbols of the life of Christ.

What kind of "memorial stones" could you place around your home to show visitors (and your family) that Jesus is the most important person in your life?

Find joy in little things
Pastor Mark Jeske

Those of us who own old houses have a maxim: "Never say you'll be happy when the house is all fixed up, because then you'll never be happy." Old houses always have something that isn't right. You have to love the process and decide to be happy with your house *right now*, or else you'll pretty much be miserable all the time.

Did your mother have a perfectionist streak? Do you? Are you unable to relax until everything in your life is just right? A spiritual gift that I crave for myself and pray for you to have is the serenity of spirit to find joy in little things. Jesus wants that for you too. **"Rejoice always, pray continually, give thanks in all circumstances; for this is God's will for you in Christ Jesus"** (1 Thessalonians 5:16-18).

Are you so focused on big schemes and dreams that you don't notice the spectacular flowers at your feet? Did you miss yesterday's stunning sunset because you were in a funk over your frustrating day? As you yearn for diaper emancipation and are so disappointed that you're not there yet, did you miss your toddler's toothy smile and merry eyes? You know, the people I most love hanging out with, the ones I slide over to in a room, are the ones who seem to have learned how to rejoice always.

I want them to teach me how to do that.

march 23

When leaders go first, people will follow
Pastor Mark Jeske

Five friends are wasting time trying to decide where to have lunch. One wants speed, one wants ambience, one wants a particular cuisine, yada yada. Finally the one with the loudest voice and best common sense figures out a compromise and ends the dithering: All right! We're going *there*!

The Israelites who lived in the northern part of the country in the 13th century B.C. were coming under great stress on one occasion because of an aggressive army of Canaanites led by King Jabin. God's prophet Deborah commissioned Barak as the Israelite commander and urged Israel to rally against the threat. The Lord gave a great victory to Israel, and peace returned to the land. **"On that day Deborah and Barak son of Abinoam sang this song: 'When the princes in Israel take the lead, when the people willingly offer themselves—praise the Lord!'"** (Judges 5:1,2).

If you have military service in your background, you need no persuading about the tremendous value of leadership in a group endeavor. But all of us, civilians included, benefit from good leadership in our government, businesses, churches, and families. It's much more fun to follow when a gifted individual provides clear direction, encouragement, and job assignments. Good leaders listen well, assess the path ahead, inventory resources, and come up with a plan. Good followers know when to be quiet and join the team.

Would you choose an important leader in your life and pray for that person right now?

He's just waiting to be asked
Pastor Mark Jeske

"Why should I bother praying? If God is as omniscient as you Christians say, he should know what I need and just give it. If I have to tell him, then he doesn't really know everything. If he knows my needs and doesn't help me, then he's either powerless or cruel or both."

Whew. Did you ever hear talk like that? I have. The skeptic who uttered those blasphemies completely missed the point that God's ultimate desire is to have a relationship with us, not bring heaven on earth. We will experience heaven in heaven. In the meantime, the faith-bond that links us to God is of paramount importance. It is everything.

When God's children experience hardships, of course he sees. Of course he cares. The one who sent his Son to the cross for us couldn't love us more. But he usually waits—first, to see if we can handle the problems with the skills and resources he's already given us, and second, *to be asked*: **"The Lord is near to all who call on him, to all who call on him in truth"** (Psalm 145:18). The whole point of his answers to our prayers is not merely to reduce our pain but to build up our faith in him.

What do you need from him right now? Say a prayer that acknowledges his awesome love, his unbelievable power, and his steady wisdom. Then ask.

Show of force

Pastor Matt Ewart

When tensions rise among nations and their differences are not settled, what can often happen is they resort to a show of force. It could be a military exercise in the region. It could be a missile test. The idea is to intimidate the other side into capitulating.

This doesn't just happen on a national level—you do this too. The time you raised your voice at someone (or gave him the silent treatment), that was a show of force. In little ways and big ways you can try to manipulate others.

But manipulation is not how God handles things, and Palm Sunday is the proof. During holy week Jesus would face the unrighteous anger of the jealous Jewish leaders. He would endure an unfair death sentence from Rome. He would face torture and death. So on Palm Sunday, before it all, he made a show of force in a way that you'd never expect.

His force was humility. Do you know why? Because in a way, the real enemy was you. It was humankind who brought sin into this world long ago, and your life is a constant testimony that sin remains.

Divine strength would have destroyed you. But it was his righteous humility that allowed him to take your place and redeem you.

"Rejoice greatly, Daughter Zion! Shout, Daughter Jerusalem! See, your king comes to you, righteous and victorious, lowly and riding on a donkey, on a colt, the foal of a donkey" (Zechariah 9:9).

Two words to avoid

Jason Nelson

There are two words I suggest we avoid in describing Christianity. The words are *liberal* and *conservative*. At face value, a liberal is "marked by generosity, broad-minded." A conservative is "marked by moderation or caution." I have been called both, and at face value I can be.

But each word has been bundled with other ideas that can be inconsistent with the essence of Christianity. Many people associate these terms with the political continuum. *Liberal* describes those a little left of center, and *conservative* describes those a little right of center. Historically, those were two sides of the same coin in a democracy. History also documents that when either position is taken to an extreme, it ends in totalitarianism, which is "centralized control by an autocratic authority." Meaning, you better accept the whole bundle or else.

When people describe their faith orientation as conservative or liberal, it makes me wonder. Are they stereotyping themselves? Are they the stone-cold law-and-order types? Or are they the bleeding-heart, anything-goes types? It also makes me wonder: would I fit in with them or not and do they tolerate dissenting points of view?

Christian values are broad and deep. Jesus is the nonpartisan Savior of all people. We seek to express our faith in a diverse society. The Christians I know are a mix of people who love the stability God's Word produces and the generosity his grace inspires. Those convictions defy a one-word description.

Special treatment
Pastor Matt Ewart

I've noticed something interesting that happens whenever I get a new smartphone (which isn't all that often). As soon as it enters my possession, that phone gets special attention. I am careful with the way I handle it. I take special care to keep it clean. I am gentle when I pick it up and put it down. And alarms go off if the kids get anywhere near it.

A few months later it's a different story. The phone doesn't get as much care as it used to. It isn't as clean as it was. And while I don't throw it across the room, I do toss it around fairly liberally.

It's interesting how things we once cared for greatly can depreciate so quickly.

How well do you care for yourself? And while we're at it, how well do you care for the people around you? How you treat people—including yourself—communicates how valuable they are.

So as you think about yourself and the people around you, consider what John wrote: **"See what great love the Father has lavished on us, that we should be called children of God! And that is what we are!"** (1 John 3:1).

God paid a big price so that he could take sinful people and make them his adopted children, loved and completely forgiven by him. Through Christ's holiness he sees you and those around you as priceless. Therefore, what God identifies as holy, treat and use as holy.

You have too many men

Pastor Mark Jeske

If you would ever perform a "prayer audit" on the content of your communications with God, especially of those prayers that request help, it should come as no surprise that 100 percent of them involve prayers for more—better health, more money, better job, better home. God always loves to hear from us, appreciates the trust and respect we show him, and actually gives us as much as he thinks we can handle.

But—sometimes he thinks we have too much, that he can do more for us by subtraction rather than addition. Seriously! When the crisis with the Midianite attacks was reaching an intolerable point, God announced his rescue plan to a hero named Gideon: **"You have too many men. I cannot deliver Midian into their hands, or Israel would boast against me, 'My own strength has saved me'"** (Judges 7:2).

This is the balancing act with our faith lives that God constantly works at. He loves to give us things, but the risk is that we grow proud, that we forget the true cause and effect of solving our problems. He had to prune down Gideon's army so that Israel would give him glory for the victory.

Here are two challenges for you: when you accomplish something significant with your own mind and resources, humbly give God credit. And when you experience subtractions from your life, assume that God is going to do great things through your weakness.

Jesus, the servant

Pastor David Scharf

"If I had all-power, what would I do with it?" Have you ever mused as to what it would be like if God were to make you in charge of all things?

Well, Jesus was in charge: **"Jesus knew that the Father had put all things under his power. . . . So he got up from the meal, took off his outer clothing, and wrapped a towel around his waist"** (John 13:3,4).

And how did Jesus use that power?

He used that power to . . . wash his disciples' feet. Washing feet was a job for the most menial servant. But who is washing feet here? Jesus, the Lord of all things, and he is serving in the humblest of ways. Well, maybe not the humblest—that would come less than 24 hours later as he served you by giving himself for you on the cross.

Marvel at the Savior you have. He's a Savior who is willing to serve not just disciples, but you. Jesus served the disciples his body and blood for their forgiveness in the Lord's Supper. Jesus wants to continue to take off his outer coat, wrap a towel around his waist, and serve you with that same comfort. Come and let him wash your feet. Let Jesus, the servant, empower you to be "_(your name)_, the servant" for others in your life.

Love it when Satan loses

Pastor Mark Jeske

I am really sick of seeing and hearing how often Satan wins. I grieve over persecutions of Christians, destruction of Christian churches, and the inevitable refugees of the world's constant wars. I grieve for children abused by the adults who were supposed to care for them. I grieve over how malicious hackers attack and ruin businesses, how Ponzi scheme sellers dupe people and destroy their savings.

I love it when Satan loses and loses big. The high priest Jehoiada was an outstanding advisor to the young king Josiah. His leadership was so compelling that Josiah followed him and the two launched a spiritual reformation that severely reduced Baal worship in Judah: **"Jehoiada then made a covenant that he, the people and the king would be the Lord's people. All the people went to the temple of Baal and tore it down. They smashed the altars and idols and killed Mattan the priest of Baal in front of the altars"** (2 Chronicles 23:16,17). Jehoiada's leadership brought an era of peace and blessing upon little Judah, its last. After he died, the wheels came off and the misery started again.

Satan is going to keep winning some of the battles, but Christ has already won the war. The really big things are safe and secure. The captives have been released, our sins have been forgiven, debts paid, and immortality guaranteed. Satan can't steal anything from us that our eternal Father can't and won't restore many times over.

Satan, I love it when you lose.

Who sends the rain?

Pastor Mark Jeske

If you are not connected in faith to the Creator, if your mind is not informed by the Word of God, if Scripture has not helped you to see and understand the stories of our origins, then you will have to come up with other explanations of cause and effect in our world. Magazine articles, blogs, and TV shows stay away from any suggestion that there could be intelligent design in our world, unless they attribute brilliant engineering to "Mother Nature."

Nobody today worships Baal or Asherah anymore, but people when pressed will find all kinds of explanations for natural phenomena. But only one explanation aligns with reality: **"Do any of the worthless idols of the nations bring rain? Do the skies themselves send down showers? No, it is you, Lord our God. Therefore our hope is in you, for you are the one who does all this"** (Jeremiah 14:22).

One of the great benefits of getting out of town on your vacation is to give you a fresh look at God's natural world. There is no wise and omnipotent Mother Nature, but there is a kind, wise heavenly Father who made the natural wonders you are looking at. It is part of your worship life not just to go to church and sing and pray your praises. You worship God outdoors when you give him the glory he deserves for what he has made.

You worship him also when you ask him for things in nature that only he can do.

april

They found the stone rolled away
from the tomb, but when they entered,
they did not find the body of the Lord Jesus.

Luke 24:2,3

april 1

I'm blessed

Pastor Mark Jeske

Christians can be forgiven if they overuse the word *bless*, even if outsiders aren't sure what they mean. When we do it for God, when we *bless* his holy name, we are praising him for his mighty works. When he does it for us, when he *blesses* our lives, it means that he is intervening in the "natural order of things" to bring some kind of good thing—relief from a painful problem, an extra burst of financial resources, employment, a raise, a spouse, a child, a new friend.

God created us to be independent. He wants us to do for ourselves what he has equipped us to be able to do. He created us to be interdependent, helping other people and letting other people help us. But he also loves to deal directly with us and give us more than the minimum, even spoil us a little. He loves to answer our prayers *just because we asked.* He loves to make our lives better: **"The Lord will open the heavens, the storehouse of his bounty, to send rain on your land in season and to bless all the work of your hands. You will lend to many nations but will borrow from none"** (Deuteronomy 28:12).

One of many clichés we have for greeting one another is to say, "How are you?" Often the mumbled and often insincere answer is, "I'm good." I have a friend who upon being asked how she is always responds, "I'm blessed."

I am too.

Impossible to win

Pastor Daron Lindemann

Have you ever played a carnival game and lost? Yup. Here's why. They're rigged so that you lose. Basketball free throw? Sorry, the rims are shrunk and then bent into an oblong shape to appear larger in front.

Carnies know that when we fail, we'll pay for another game. And another. That's how they win.

God makes the Ten Commandments impossible to win, but for opposite reasons. God wants us to stop trying to win his forgiveness or pay for eternal life with our performances. When we fail, he wants us convinced that we can't be perfect on our own.

Once Jesus told his disciples, **"'It is easier for a camel to go through the eye of a needle than for someone who is rich to enter the kingdom of God.' When the disciples heard this, they were greatly astonished and asked, 'Who then can be saved?' Jesus looked at them and said, 'With man this is impossible, but with God all things are possible'"** (Matthew 19:24-26).

Jesus did the impossible for us. Jesus made it through the eye of the needle. How could Jesus, bigger than creation and world empires and sin and death, fit through the eye of a needle? By becoming small. By giving up bigness and beauty. By giving in to the curse of sin and death, which he didn't deserve. And he won forgiveness for you. Now it is possible for you to follow him. And to obey the Ten Commandments.

Abide with me
Pastor Mark Jeske

The risen Lord Jesus gave an extraordinary gift to two disciples from his wider acquaintance, to a man named Cleopas and his friend. Without revealing who he was, he caught up to them as they were walking a few miles outside Jerusalem to the little town of Emmaus. He drew them into conversation about the tumultuous events of the last three days, and seeing their confusion gave them a private Easter Day lesson in Old Testament interpretation that they would never forget.

As they drew near their destination, they implored him: **"Stay with us, for it is nearly evening; the day is almost over"** (Luke 24:29). And he did.

All Christians resonate with that impassioned plea. We need Jesus in our homes and in our lives too. We are lost without him; we have everything when we have him. His presence brings hope, comfort, and passion for our mission. Henry Lyte was an Anglican priest who was profoundly moved as he attended the deathbed of a fellow pastor. The hymn he wrote based on that experience has brought inspiration and peace to millions of Christians all over the world as we contemplate the swift passage of time:

Abide with me; fast falls the eventide.
The darkness deepens; Lord, with me abide.
When other helpers fail and comforts flee,
Help of the helpless, oh, abide with me!

There's only one thing to do with a bell

Jason Nelson

I had an epiphany one Easter morning. There's only one thing to do with a bell.

The children were invited to be in a bell choir. Dozens streamed to the front of church, including three of my grandchildren. They picked up different colored handbells. My little Addison knew exactly what to do with hers. When you get your hands on a bell, you ring that thing. For at least 45 seconds, there was uncensored Easter joy.

Eventually, the adults in charge herded everyone in place. Most little ringers followed the cue cards and chimed along nicely with the music in the background. My grandson tried helping his little brother keep time. Noah kept shouting "Now!" in Sawyer's ear whenever Sawyer's color came up. His color came up a lot. Sawyer didn't care and just kept ringing his bell. I was laughing and crying. Alleluia! There is one reason to celebrate like this. Jesus lives!

> *Ring out, wild bells, to the wild sky,*
> *The flying cloud, the frosty light:*
> *The year is dying in the night;*
> *Ring out, wild bells, and let him die.*
>
> *Ring in the valiant man and free,*
> *The larger heart, the kindlier hand;*
> *Ring out the darkness of the land,*
> *Ring in the Christ that is to be.*

Lord Alfred Tennyson

There is only one thing to do with a bell. If you can get your hands on one, ring it. Now!

I believe in the resurrection: Christ's body

Pastor Mark Jeske

Christians have been reciting the Apostles' Creed in its various forms for at least 1,700 years. This Easter season, when you have a chance to use these venerable words to state what you believe in, put a little extra oomph into the phrase, "I believe in the resurrection of the body." It's a big deal.

In fact, the physical resurrection of Christ is the culmination of God's great work of rescuing the human race. The actual revivification of the Savior's corpse demonstrates the Father's approval of the Son's splendid work on our behalf. God's favor and forgiveness now rest upon us, and those who believe it have it. The rising of Christ's body from the tomb also guarantees ours.

Easter celebrates not only the spirit of Christ coming back to life but his *body* as well. The risen Jesus told his disciples, **"Why are you troubled, and why do doubts rise in your minds? Look at my hands and my feet. It is I myself! Touch me and see; a ghost does not have flesh and bones, as you see I have"** (Luke 24:38,39).

The magnificent Easter story is for believing and for telling. Let it drive away the troubles and doubts in your mind as it once did for Jesus' disciples. And let this magnificent triumph always be the heart and core of the church's message to the world. He's alive! We are too! He lives forever! We will too!

I believe in the resurrection: My body

Pastor Mark Jeske

A brilliant and imaginative young woman named Mary Shelley wrote what is considered by some to be the first science fiction novel in the year 1818. She was only 20 at the time. The story of *Frankenstein* describes the use of the electricity in lightning to revivify a fresh corpse. Such a procedure, though scientifically impossible, is just barely believable enough to carry the story.

Only God could promise that he can and will bring your body back to life, no matter how many years have passed, no matter how far the decomposition process has progressed, no matter how thoroughly earth and insects and bacteria and animals and water have caused it to disintegrate.

When a believer dies, his or her soul/spirit is taken to the joy of God's presence. When Christ returns to judge the earth, he will call your body forth. Thus your life in heaven will be both spiritual *and* physical.

A man named Job who had known terrible suffering of mind and body found great comfort in the guarantee of the physical resurrection. He eagerly looked forward to praising his God face-to-face—literally: **"I know that my redeemer lives, and that in the end he will stand on the earth. And after my skin has been destroyed, yet in my flesh I will see God; I myself will see him with my own eyes—I, and not another. How my heart yearns within me!"** (Job 19:25-27).

Mine does too, Job.

I believe in the resurrection: Every believer's body

Pastor Mark Jeske

In a sense, forest fires are ordinary. They've been happening "naturally," through lightning strikes, for instance, for millennia. Forestry professionals will point out the positive "recharging" effects to the whole ecosystem of the big burn.

Except when there are homes, people, and animals in the way. People who build their homes in the forests of the mountain West are taking a risk, hoping that one of these wildfires won't incinerate their places. Can you imagine the misery of the people who have to come back to pick through the ashes of a burned-down home? Almost everything tangible in their lives went up in smoke.

The day of our deaths will also take all possessions out of our hands. More—a day is coming when God will return to this earth, melt it down, and re-create a dazzling new universe. Everything tangible in people's former lives will perish—except for the people. On the day of Christ's return, we will trade in our stuff for the people we "lost" through death. Every believer's body will rise, be publically acquitted in God's court, and be gathered together for the Grand Reunion: **"Multitudes who sleep in the dust of the earth will awake: some to everlasting life"** (Daniel 12:2).

In the new world that God will create, death will never separate us again. We will get back all of our loved ones who died in the Lord. All of them. Seriously. All of them.

I believe in the resurrection: Every unbeliever's body

Pastor Mark Jeske

Satan inspires people every which way to minimize and marginalize the reality of hell. Some atheists stoutly deny both the existence of God and the idea of life after death. "When I die, I rot," snorted British philosopher Bertrand Russell. Some imagine that the worst that can happen is that the wicked will be vaporized instantaneously. It will hurt for only a second and then—nothingness. Some borrow ideas from the Asian subcontinent and imagine that they will be reincarnated for another and then another go at life until they get it right. Some imagine that hell could only be for the worst of earth's monsters, like Adolf Hitler or Charles Manson.

Are you interested in God's message about what he is going to do? Here it is: **"Multitudes who sleep in the dust of the earth will awake: some to everlasting life, others to shame and everlasting contempt"** (Daniel 12:2). Yes—the bodies of unbelievers will rise from the dead, but they will be separated for final judgment and eternal punishment. It will never end.

Along with the physical torment of hell come mental and psychological agony. The shame that the condemned will feel about themselves will never end. The contempt of God for them will never end. Their self-loathing and intense regrets and aggrieved blaming and revenge fantasies will never end.

Now you know.

Options for hard times
Diana Kerr

Ever have one of those situations in which your friend is going through a hard time and you just don't know what to say? Yeah, me too. (And I'm even a life coach.) Sometimes I say dumb things and then regret it later.

After reading the story of Job in the Bible, it's safe to say that Job's friends were in a tough spot. Job had nearly every possible horrible thing happen to him *all at once*. When his three friends showed up to comfort him, they began weeping, and then maybe they experienced that awkward moment I've felt so many times where they thought, "What on earth do we say?!"

Here's what they decided to do: **"Then they sat on the ground with him for seven days and seven nights. No one said a word to him, because they saw how great his suffering was"** (Job 2:13).

When a friend is going through something tough, you don't have to talk a lot or give advice. You've got other options. You can choose to just listen instead— maybe ask some questions to encourage him or her to open up. You can ask them what they need—"Do you want to talk about it or totally avoid the subject? What do you need today?" You can admit you're not sure what to say. You can admit you can't relate to their pain, but you know Jesus does. Or you can sit in total silence. Your presence makes a difference.

Where do I go with my anger?

Pastor Mark Jeske

How do you get angry? Are you the kind who flares up intensely, unleashes an outburst, and then calms down quickly and a day later can't even remember the argument? Or do you passively get angry inside and let it build and build and build? Well, neither is healthy or helpful: **"My dear brothers and sisters, take note of this: Everyone should be quick to listen, slow to speak and slow to become angry, because human anger does not produce the righteousness that God desires"** (James 1:19,20).

Anger is not bad in and of itself—God himself gets angry. Our problem is that our sinful perceptions, reasoning, judgment, and brakes are faulty. We sometimes take offense at things that aren't offenses, brood over wrongs and refuse to forgive, enjoy feeling smug and righteous, and grossly overestimate our wisdom in meting out punishments.

Is there anger in your heart right now? Be honest. Where do you go with it? Don't store it up! Don't explode and vent it out! In your mind and heart, go to the cross of Christ and drain it out on the ground, right there, on the sacred ground where his blood dripped. Let it go. Let God take care of judging and punishing. If you've been victimized, pray for God to straighten the person out. If you are in the wrong, let the forgiveness of Christ wash over you and heal you.

You are not God's agent of wrath in the world. You are his agent of mercy.

Grace versus truth?

Diana Kerr

A lot of Christians struggle with the tension of grace and truth. We want people to know that Jesus loves them. On the other hand, we know the Bible says you can't do whatever you want. God makes the rules.

Christians cover a wide spectrum. On one end of the extreme, you find judgy, finger-pointing lovers of the law. They're not afraid to proclaim their disgust of society's sin, even with megaphones at sporting events. On the other end, you find the arms-open, "live-however-you-want" Christians. They're perfectly content with lifestyles that are not God's will for his people. It's shocking that both groups somehow believe in the same God and read the same Bible.

You may not fall on one extreme or the other. Maybe you flop back and forth like me. I can be judgmental and unloving in one conversation, and in the next conversation I sacrifice God's truth to avoid discomfort.

John 1:14 says, **"The Word became flesh and made his dwelling among us. We have seen his glory, the glory of the one and only Son, who came from the Father, full of grace and truth."**

Jesus embodied grace and truth simultaneously. In order to walk in grace and truth like Jesus did, we must realize they aren't separate or contradictory. Truth flows from grace, and vice versa. Grace makes truth more beautiful and meaningful, and vice versa.

And not ironically, in order to keep growing in your ability to exude both grace and truth, you yourself are going to need continual grace and truth.

God's homework
Jason Nelson

One thing I didn't like about teaching was correcting homework. The more I assigned, the more I had to correct. And I usually assigned a lot. The more meaningful I tried to make it for my students, the more difficult it was for me to evaluate. It was tempting to use lots of true or false questions because they were easy to correct. But every time I thought of a creative way for my students to show me what they learned, it was a challenge for me to grade.

Every day of our lives we get homework from Jesus. He assigns interesting ways for us to demonstrate we love him and understand what he did for us by dying on that cross and exploding from that grave. You can hear him whispering in the background when we face unexpected challenges: "So, show me what you've learned." The homework is individualized for each of us. Christ always makes us think hard and work hard to put into practice what he taught us. Doing our homework well is never a matter of guilt but is always a matter of conscience and an expression of our love for him.

Jesus isn't an easy grader, but he is a very gracious one. That gives us confidence in the final analysis. We who believe in him will be passing on to glory. His added comment will bring a smile to our faces: **"Good job . . . faithful servant!"** (Matthew 25:21 GW).

Buried in Jesus' jersey

Linda Buxa

A while back, Carson Wentz, the quarterback for the Philadelphia Eagles, left people in tears. A video went viral of Lukas, a ten-year-old boy with terminal cancer who loved the Eagles. Wentz sent him a video, then brought Lukas to the Eagles' stadium, introduced him to teammates, and made him a smoothie. When Lukas died 13 days later, he was buried in Wentz' uniform.

Carson Wentz, a regular human, was brought to tears with the immensity of that knowledge. Here he was, only a 24-year-old man at the time, so beloved that a family buried their young son in Wentz' jersey.

We've been buried with a jersey too—Jesus' jersey of righteousness. (Some people call it a robe. Po-*tay*-to. Po-*tah*-to.)

"We were therefore buried with him through baptism into death in order that, just as Christ was raised from the dead through the glory of the Father, we too may live a new life" (Romans 6:4).

When we were baptized, Jesus not only forgave our sins, but he also put his jersey on us. We are on his team. We walk around knowing that—even though we will all die—because Jesus defeated death, we live a new life here on earth. And we will live a perfect life in a new heaven and a new earth where there is no more sickness, mourning, pain, or death. For ten-year-olds. For quarterbacks. For us.

For now, until we live in the place with no more crying, it brings us to tears with the immensity of that knowledge.

Lord, give me patience with myself

Pastor Mark Jeske

"The mass of men lead lives of quiet desperation." Henry David Thoreau said that, and I fear he's right. It may look to us in our weaker moments that everybody around us has it together, but that is not so. We are all balls of insecurities, fears, frailties, guilt, and regrets. We are all poseurs and fakes. We are all works in progress, and most days progress is slow.

Everyone who has ever been a leader in the work of the church has stood in awe of the apostle Paul. What a hero! He spent his life traveling throughout the eastern Mediterranean world, took a terrific amount of rejection and abuse, forewent wife and family, spent years in prison, and died a martyr's death, viewed as an enemy of the state. What a mighty man of God!

Paul knew the real truth: **"What a wretched man I am! Who will rescue me from this body that is subject to death?"** (Romans 7:24). He was painfully aware of his shortcomings. He carried with him the memories of being a persecutor of Christians. He was a sinner all his days, just like you and me, which means that his words and life always fell short of God's holy standards.

Who rescued him from his dilemma? Christ did. The steady words of assurance of the gospel enable us to live with our shortcomings, knowing that our sins are forgiven. The gospel releases God's gifts in us and helps us to be patient with ourselves.

Where do I go with my disappointments?

Pastor Mark Jeske

There is great resilience in human nature. People know how to take a lickin' and keep on tickin'. We get knocked down and we get up again. Every athletic coach spends a lot of time with the attitude of his or her players, pushing and pushing so that they won't ever quit, no matter how daunting the odds.

But we do have limits to how much we can take. We all hit some experiences that become dream crushers. After your fourth exploitative and selfish boyfriend, you start to doubt that there are any decent men anywhere. You're 40 years old and realize that you have never felt true approval from your perfectionist mother. Your spouse stops doing the wonderful things that made you take the risk and get married in the first place, and your marriage becomes a dull endurance march.

Where do you go when you're in an emotional hole like that? Why, to your Father, who loves you unconditionally and always has a listening ear: **"Why, my soul, are you downcast? Why so disturbed within me? Put your hope in God, for I will yet praise him, my Savior and my God"** (Psalm 42:5). You are not going to experience heaven until you get to heaven, but the God who lives there gives you little tastes and insights that your best life is still to come. He thinks you're beautiful and wonderful and can't wait to enjoy you in his Paradise.

In the meantime, give him all your disappointments and dreams and then watch for his answer.

Christ Jesus sets murderers free
Pastor Daron Lindemann

The list is long for sins prohibited by the Fifth Commandment. They include murder, physically harming another person or recklessly endangering another's life, abortion, needlessly ending a person's life for whom death is near (euthanasia), and suicide. Sins against the Fifth Commandment even include treating our bodies in harmful, unhealthy ways.

What a wicked world! Stained with the blood of abortion, domestic abuse, and gang fights. Terrorized by our hatred, bigotry, ethnic cleansing, and racism. Hurt by our angry words. But Jesus came. Here. He offers his mercy to a world of murderers and sinners. **"Christ Jesus came into the world to save sinners—of whom I am the worst"** (1 Timothy 1:15).

Thirty years ago the Brazilian government turned a high security prison over to two Christians to run it on Christian principles: the love of God and love for each other. Chuck Colson, a well-known advocate of prison ministry, visited the prison and was taken on a tour. His guide escorted him to a notorious prison cell once used for torture. Inside was a crucifix, beautifully carved by the inmates, depicting the prisoner Jesus, hanging on a cross.

"He's doing time for the rest of us," the guide said softly (Max Lucado, *In the Grip of Grace*). Jesus sets murderers free. Jesus saves us even from sins against the Fifth Commandment. Even the worst. Now live!

Keep your clothes on for sexual purity

Pastor Daron Lindemann

Joseph kept his clothes on. It's that simple. Here's the story. His brothers hated him and sold him as a slave, and eventually he ended up serving a man in Egypt named Potiphar. **"Now Joseph was well-built and handsome, and after a while his master's wife took notice of Joseph and said, 'Come to bed with me!'"**

Joseph said no. **"How then could I do such a wicked thing and sin against God?"** (Genesis 39:6,7,9). Potiphar's wife grabbed his outer cloak and he ran. Frustrated by his lack of promiscuity, she framed Joseph, and Potiphar tossed him in prison.

But Joseph kept his clothes on. Not just his regular clothes (the ones he still had on). He maintained his true identity: the righteousness of God. That kept him sexually pure.

Your identity is not tied to sexual fulfillment or frustration, gender identity or confusion, or fantasizing with porn. That is not who you are, as much as Joseph's cloak in a woman's lustful possession wasn't his identity. The grace and mercy of a faithful God made Joseph strong against temptation.

Your identity in Christ is not broken or hurt; it is not lonely or misunderstood; it is not unfulfilled or weak. Clothed with Christ you are whole and complete. Clothed with Christ you are loved and known. Clothed with Christ you are beautiful and accepted. You don't need sexual sin. Keep those clothes on for sexual purity.

Impressive attention to detail
Pastor Mark Jeske

We all love to hear our names spoken out loud. Every person who works in sales who's worth a dime knows how important it is to remember people's names. The more they can remember about their customer's life, the better the relationship (and probably the greater the sales). You get points for asking about spouse, children, and personal achievements. Remembering a birthday is a home run.

But that knowledge is still pretty superficial. Jesus Christ, your Savior, wants you to know the scale of the passion and depth of the attention that God pays to his children. He makes it his business to know *everything* about you. Why go to such extreme lengths? Because he cares so much for you. So what's included in "everything"? **"Even the very hairs of your head are all numbered"** (Matthew 10:30). Unbelievable! God has both the capacity and the interest to keep that kind of data.

The important conclusion is not that God wastes his divine time on nonessential trivia like hair follicles. What that means is that he sees all of your struggles, hears all of your prayers, feels all of your pain, tracks all of your health issues, senses all your fears, claps for all of your triumphs, grieves with you in every setback, beams a smile on all your acts of generosity, and tracks every minute of your life until you are safe in his arms.

Now that is what I call impressive attention to detail.

They felt it

Jason Nelson

These poor fellas never got past Saturday. Maybe it was Monday when they were walking back to Emmaus, but they were feeling like it was Saturday. They saw what happened on Friday and were in a Saturday state of mind. On that particular Saturday, all the hosts of heaven and people around Jerusalem agreed on one thing. Jesus was dead. These guys were so depressed. **"They just stood there, long-faced, like they had lost their best friend"** (Luke 24:18 MSG). Because on Friday they did. They heard something unusual happened on Sunday. But they were feeling like it was still Saturday.

As they were walking, they didn't know Jesus because the Bible says they were **"kept from recognizing him"** (Luke 24:16). They had been impressed by Jesus and were hoping he was the one who would restore Israel to its former glory and get them out from under Roman oppression. They were hoping Jesus would give Jews better standing in the world. That hope was dashed on Friday, and they were feeling like it would always be Saturday for them.

So Jesus started from the beginning. He pointed out everything Moses and the prophets said about him. When they invited him for dinner, he showed them it would be Sunday forever in the way he broke bread and handed it to them. When they took the bread, it hit them. **"Didn't we feel on fire as he conversed with us on the road, as he opened up the Scriptures for us?"** (Luke 24:32). Jesus lives, and they could feel it.

The world is going crazy

Pastor Mark Jeske

By some measures our world is getting less violent. By others, it's going crazy. What is certain is that instantaneous digital media has so shortened the news cycle that we are all wired into all news all the time. Everybody knows everything that is happening when it's happening. We are all informed on the myriad ways that cruel and murderous people have found to take the lives of others—trucks driving up on sidewalks and slaughtering pedestrians and angry, suicidal gunmen with automatic weapons shooting up churches, schools, and malls.

Sigh. In reality, the world has always been crazy. Ever since Adam and Eve stopped trusting in God and went off to try things their own way, life on earth has often been like life in hell. Hatred. Crime. Violence. Racism. Murder. War. What are we to do? If there ever was a time when this world needed God's intervention and protection, that time is now: **"For your sake we face death all day long; we are considered as sheep to be slaughtered. Awake, Lord! Why do you sleep? Rouse yourself! Do not reject us forever"** (Psalm 44:22,23).

Indeed, awake, Lord, and help us! We need you now. Protect our children. They are so small and vulnerable. Send more angels, please. Protect your churches—the world needs more worship and witness. Protect schools, especially Christian schools. Your gospel of hope must be transmitted to the hopeless.

Whenever you're ready, come and take us home.

Deadly sins new and old: Gambling
Pastor Mark Jeske

Okay, Okay, gambling in and of itself does not belong in a list of deadly sins. You can search the Bible from cover to cover and not find a divine prohibition of gambling. But it is a risky human behavior that easily becomes sinful, and if you choose to gamble, you had better beware of the temptations. It can quickly go from amusement to addiction.

Questions to ask: Can you afford it? Is your gambling money coming from funds that should be saved for the mortgage payment, credit card bills, and your kids' college fund? Can the other people you're gambling with afford it (you are your brother's keeper, you know)? Has gambling become an exciting wealth-building strategy for you that makes you hate your job? Can you afford the time spent in front of the slots or at a table? Do you find yourself lying to cover your activities? Are you still in control of the behavior, or is it controlling you?

If you want to check yourself on the above points, don't trust your own judgment completely. See how your activities are playing with the other people in your family. How do they view the time you spend? the money you've lost? You know, seeking to build wealth is actually encouraged in the Bible, but the preferred method is by working and saving: **"Dishonest money dwindles away, but whoever gathers money little by little makes it grow"** (Proverbs 13:11).

God doesn't wash your mouth with soap

Pastor Daron Lindemann

Naughty words. We hear them. We read them. We say them. We write them.

Back when I was a kid, naughty words were followed by a good scolding—as in that dirty mouth being washed out with soap. Ick! The chemicals in soap make it taste like death by poison. It can sure be an effective measure of discipline (it worked on me), but it shouldn't be the only one.

Soap can't change your heart. That's where you hold your beliefs, attitudes, and priorities. That's the true source of either evil or goodness. Jesus said, **"The things that come out of a person's mouth come from the heart"** (Matthew 15:18).

So God has changed your heart. He's given you a new identity that isn't dominated by naughtiness and shameful words, but by divine grace and purity. In Baptism, God washes your heart out with soap and then looks at you, smiles, and says, "How pretty! How pure! How clean!" God praises you!

Replace the shaming names you call yourself like "failure" and "loser" and "dirty" with names that God calls you. Wake up each morning and go to sleep each night living in God's peace, no matter what anyone else thinks about you.

God praises you even before you perform better because Jesus performed his work of saving you. God praises you even when you still make mistakes because his grace knows your heart and your identity better than you do.

Who should you listen to?

Diana Kerr

At age 18, Katie Davis moved to Uganda for a year to do mission work. Her parents and others didn't exactly want her to, but she said she had to obey God even above her own parents. She ultimately decided to stay in Uganda permanently, started a nonprofit that's changed countless lives, and adopted 13 orphaned girls. What if she'd let family discourage her from ever going to Uganda?

You've probably heard the story of David and Goliath, but did you know that David faced discouragement from family too?

"When Eliab, David's oldest brother, heard him speaking with the men, he burned with anger at him and asked, 'Why have you come down here? And with whom did you leave those few sheep in the wilderness? I know how conceited you are and how wicked your heart is; you came down only to watch the battle'" (1 Samuel 17:28).

What if David had listened to his brother rather than trusting God to help him fight Goliath? What if he had gone home back to the sheep?

Friends and even your own family might not always support the ways you try to serve God. The Bible tells us to honor our parents and to love others, but God also makes it clear that he is the ultimate truth and that he comes first. Whether you're doing big things like moving to Uganda or living out your faith in smaller displays of obedience and trust, don't let people sway you from following God and his Word.

Where do I go with my fears?
Pastor Mark Jeske

What a blessing digital media is! I can share information instantaneously with my friends and family and coworkers with a few mouse clicks. The gospel of Jesus Christ can be seen and heard in the remotest places of the world, even in countries that make evangelism difficult or impossible. What a curse digital media is! Child pornography flies around the globe and feeds a sick addiction that's very hard to regulate or control. Violent people out to make a revenge statement know that the internet will spread the story of their deeds far and wide.

Is the world more violent, or are we just more and more aware of how violent the world has always been? Jesus himself cautioned his disciples that the love of most would grow cold as the centuries rolled on. Do the stories of mass shootings and bombings fill you with dread? **"Look, the wicked bend their bows; they set their arrows against the strings to shoot from the shadows at the upright in heart. When the foundations are being destroyed, what can the righteous do?"** (Psalm 11:2,3).

Where do you go with your fears? How about to your Father? He has been sheltering and protecting believers since sin's beginning. His eyes never slumber nor sleep in his care of us. His army of angels carries out heroic defense against the forces of hell.

Believers can't lose. Even if their earthly lives are taken, they get a far better one in heaven.

Entitlement sickness
Pastor Mark Jeske

In our country the consumer is king. Or queen. Businesses fall over each other trying to give consumers what they want, or the herd will move to their competitors. Is that bad or good? Well, it's good in that it pushes businesses to provide excellence in service and products. It can be bad, though, in fostering a me-first mentality in their customers. People today love to hear advertising messages like this: "You deserve it." "Pamper yourself." "You have a right to . . ." "You deserve some 'me' time." "Give yourself a break."

Do you suppose that "entitlement" mentality carries over into people's relationship with God? Do you think that God owes you things? Like a steady income stream or a beautiful home or solutions to all your problems or a place in heaven? You know, if we got what we deserved from God, we would all be heading for hell. We are all prodigal sons and daughters, self-centered and careless.

The only thing we *deserve* from God is condemnation. The appropriate posture before him is penitence on our knees, just like the prodigal son in Jesus' parable: **"The son said to him, 'Father, I have sinned against heaven and against you. I am no longer worthy to be called your son'"** (Luke 15:21). Our great hope is in God's *grace*—that he chooses to love and forgive us for Jesus' sake.

Enjoy his gift—undeserved, unmerited, unconditional.

Lord, give me patience with my healing
Pastor Mark Jeske

One of the great mysteries of life as a Christian is our lack of understanding of God's divine timetable. Why does he do what he does? Why doesn't he do what we need, what we've been asking for, what obviously would make our lives better? Satan massages our doubts about our Father's wisdom, capability, and love. If we are struggling with need, pain, or disease, and nothing is happening, then *logically* God must be unloving or unwise or powerless or maybe all three.

One of the greatest outbursts of divine compassion took place at a spring-fed public pool in Jerusalem near the Sheep Gate. **"Here a great number of disabled people used to lie—the blind, the lame, the paralyzed. One who was there had been an invalid for thirty-eight years"** (John 5:3,5). Jesus asked that man if he wanted to be well. Duh!? Do you suppose he would have preferred another 38 years of immobility? **"Get up! Pick up your mat and walk,"** said the Savior (verse 8). And he did. In fact, he probably *ran*.

That dear man had waited 38 years for his miracle. Truth be told, many hundreds of thousands of people will spend their whole lives on earth with a disability and will die with it. We can glorify God both ways—through our struggles and through our healing. I am convinced that our joy and delight in heaven will be in direct proportion to our sufferings on this earth.

I can't wait to meet that man in heaven.

Fame is fleeting
Jason Nelson

I had some time, so I made a list of famous people I've met. When I say "met," I am using the term loosely. These are celebrities I saw unexpectedly. Some of them I shook hands with and talked to. I had a couple autographs but don't know where they are now. I had a brush with Hubert Humphrey, Don Majkowski, Dennis Farina, Robin Yount, Walter Cronkite, Muhammad Ali, Stan Musial, Mickey Mouse, and Ronald McDonald. I thought about including Pastor Jeske and my town chairman, Terry, but I had to draw the line somewhere.

You may not know some of these people. Their celebrity has faded. Napoleon Bonaparte said, "Glory is fleeting, but obscurity is forever." He added that he preferred obscurity. He would know. He was sent into exile twice because he became a little too famous in Europe for his own good.

Not long into human history people developed reputations (see Genesis 4). Some early people became known for the good work they did because they started doing something positive others could emulate. Other people became known for immoral behavior. Lamech killed a man and a boy and made up a song about it. He wanted to be even more notorious than Cain.

Some people say that any publicity is good publicity. I don't think so. Wouldn't you rather fade into obscurity than be remembered for doing the wrong thing?

"All people are like grass, and all their glory is like the flowers of the field; the grass withers and the flowers fall" (1 Peter 1:24).

Where's home for you?

Diana Kerr

My husband and I recently went to a neighborhood meeting to hear about what's going on in our community. We went with pure intentions, but I let my sin take over.

When some community members got riled up, I joined right in, shaking my head vigorously at some of the elected official's remarks, adding a loud "Yeah!" to the conversation when people asked angry questions, and thinking a couple times in my head, "This is unbelievable. I can't believe I live here."

I'm more comfortable throwing myself under the bus than assuming things about you, but I bet you sometimes feel this way too. I bet you get angry occasionally about what's going on in your city, country, etc. And I know what part of our problem is.

When we place too much identity or interest in earthly things, we're going to feel upset, offended, and dissatisfied. When earthly life, particularly government officials, don't meet our too-high expectations, there's only one thing we can truly do. (Hint: It does not involve getting upset at neighborhood meetings.)

We have to remember that this place is not home.

Friend, we are **"foreigners and exiles"** (1 Peter 2:11). Paul acknowledged to the Philippians that there were destructive people in the world (*Hmm*, so that didn't just start recently?) but reminded them **"our citizenship is in heaven"** (Philippians 3:20). That means you're **"Christ's ambassador"** (2 Corinthians 5:20), and that's a game changer when it comes to how we live in this temporary home on earth.

I love you because Jesus loves you

Pastor Daron Lindemann

A classic *Peanuts* cartoon shows Lucy convincing Linus that he can't be a doctor because he doesn't love mankind. He clarifies by exclaiming, "I love mankind. It's people I can't stand."

We pray for world peace, cheer for our kids' sports teams, strive for harmony in our families, and support our churches but then . . . condemn church leaders who don't consider our opinions to be the best, get irritated at family members whose plans conflict with ours, blame the coaches who don't play our kids as much as the others, and generally decide to be loving toward some people but unloving toward the ones whose viewpoints differ from ours.

Here's something to remember today. Jesus loves everybody.

"For Christ's love compels us, because we are convinced that one died for all, and therefore all died. And he died for all, that those who live should no longer live for themselves but for him who died for them and was raised again" (2 Corinthians 5:14,15).

Jesus loves the person who drives slowly in the left lane. Jesus loves the contractor who messed up your house. Jesus loves your dad who wasn't there for you. Jesus loves your ex who blames you for everything. Jesus loves your friend who let you down. Jesus loves the hacker who stole your identity. Jesus died for them too.

The next time (it'll happen soon, believe me) you have difficulty loving a person, just remember these words: "Jesus loves everybody. Even me."

Humbly self-aware
Pastor Mark Jeske

Satan just cannot abide Christians walking peacefully and happily along the middle of the road of our lives. He will either try to shove us or shame us or intimidate us into sliding off into the ditch of insecurity, despair, and depression on one side. Or he will lure and flatter and entice us into the other ditch where smugness, arrogance, and pride rule. He loves it when we attempt to make ourselves look bigger by making other people look smaller.

"Gnôthi sautón," said the ancient Greeks. "Know yourself." Easy to say; hard to do. How can we cut through the fog of Satan's lies and the fever dreams of our sick culture and our own strong tendency to self-deception and actually accurately assess ourselves? **"By the grace given me I say to every one of you: Do not think of yourself more highly than you ought, but rather think of yourself with sober judgment, in accordance with the faith God has distributed to each of you"** (Romans 12:3).

God has given us several important gifts in self-understanding. One is his Word and the faith in our hearts that listens to and trusts that Word. The Bible is a corrective word when we are wrong and weak and a commending word when we are aligned with God's ways. Another is our family. Who better has the confidence to tell us when we're out of line?

You generally can't go wrong when you make other people feel important.

may

Blessed is the one . . . whose delight is in the law of
the Lord, and who meditates on his law day and night.
That person is like a tree planted by streams of water,
which yields its fruit in season and whose leaf does
not wither—whatever they do prospers.

Psalm 1:1,3

Hope du jour

Jason Nelson

The Bible shows us that our spiritual capacities are not one dimensional. The assets born in us when the Holy Spirit engages with our spirits come in a variety of flavors so we can pair them with whatever challenges are on our plates. Jesus could see *great faith* in the people he healed, and the skeptics had *little faith*. The psalm writers celebrated God's *unfailing love*. Peter urges us to **"love one another deeply, from the heart"** (1 Peter 1:22) because it is possible to love people not so deeply. And there are all different kinds of hope.

The New Testament epistles are filled with recommendations to have a hope appropriate for our circumstances. They all relate to the life and work of Jesus that the gospels tell us about. There is sure hope, firm hope, living hope, blessed hope, good hope, better hope. They warn us against the limitations of human hopes alone and the despair that comes from having no hope at all.

The reformer Martin Luther wrote about his *"battling hope"* becoming vigorous and conquering the devil when his faith was attacked. Martin Luther King, Jr. said, "We must accept finite disappointment, but never lose *infinite hope.*"

What's on your plate today, this week, and as far as the eye can see? Some of it may look appealing and some of it unappealing. Some of it you ordered, and some of it you didn't. All of it will be tough to swallow without the right kind of hope.

Lord, give me patience with my kids
Pastor Mark Jeske

My children are grown now, and I often indulge in a fuzzy and hazy sentimental nostalgia for the days when they were all little and at home. I look at the old pictures, and the emotions just wash over me. How I miss those days! If only I could have them back.

God gave me a gift the other day. He allowed me to spend half a day with a family with four little kids that age. It all came back to me—the burden of keeping them alive, endless repeating of the same life lessons, scoldings, dirt, mess, selfishness, chaos, diapers, injuries, disobedience, stress, fatigue. I forgot how parents of young children essentially are their slaves for years. The children's needs trump their own.

May I ask you to join me today in praying for the parents of young children? They are doing critically important work for our extended families, our churches, and our communities. God says, **"Love is patient"** (1 Corinthians 13:4). It is indeed. Let's pray for parent patience because discipling children is exhausting work. You can assume that any mother of three young ones is teetering on the edge of insanity. Will you lend a helping hand?

If you are one of these noble warriors, please know how much we appreciate you. And so does God. Hang on! These days will soon pass, and then you too will nostalgically wish for them back.

Prayer changes me

Pastor Daron Lindemann

Where in your life has prayer made the biggest difference? Yes, prayer changes things. But God holds interest beyond things. He has his eye—and his heart—on you.

Jacob (whose name means "tripper-upper" or "trickster") deceived his brother, Esau. Years later he thought he masterminded a safe reunion with Esau, who had threatened to kill him.

The night before he was to meet Esau, a mysterious man confronted Jacob and wrestled him. They tussled until morning. Neither gave up. **"Then the man said, 'Let me go, for it is daybreak.' But Jacob replied, 'I will not let you go unless you bless me'"** (Genesis 32:26).

This wrestling changed Jacob, like wrestling in prayer changes you. Jacob realized he was wrestling with God. Instead of trickery, Jacob clung to God's promise and blessing. Anxiety about Esau's anger gave way to confidence in the Lord's gracious help. He limped away from that wrestling match with a handicap in his hip, but in this defeat he found the victory of denying himself and depending on God.

Pray for God to help our nation, but be ready for God to change you, call you to more active citizenship, and challenge you to contribute in new ways. Answers to prayer are often found not outside of us, but in us. Through persistent wrestling with God declare, "I will not let you go." And he'll promise, "I won't let you go either."

All in your head?

Diana Kerr

Years ago a guy told me he had recently switched churches because at his previous church, "People knew a lot about the Bible, but their knowledge rarely left their heads." Knowledge of God, his Word, and the gospel should not just hang out in our minds but change our hearts and our actions as well, he said.

Bob Goff, an injustice fighter, philanthropist, and author has an interesting idea about applying God's Word to your life: Don't just participate in Bible studies but in Bible *"doings."*

I love that concept, but not because I'm advocating to stop studying God's Word. What I'm saying is *don't stop there.*

God encourages us over and over to not just read his Word and know what it says but to put it into practice. **"Do not merely listen to the word, and so deceive yourselves. Do what it says"** (James 1:22). This means obeying God, living out our faith, and sharing the gospel.

Jesus' story of the wise and foolish builders in Matthew chapter 7 is interesting because he doesn't just say *knowing* God's Word is like building your life on a rock. What he says is, **"Everyone who hears these words of mine *and puts them into practice* is like a wise man who built his house on the rock"** (verse 24).

Let's be real: We're sinners who can't do this perfectly. We'll often fail at living out God's Word. Thank goodness his love doesn't depend on our actions and that his grace covers us in forgiveness, motivating us to continue on.

Recognition blues
Pastor Mark Jeske

It's nice when your efforts are noticed, isn't it? It's nice to be appreciated, nice to be thanked, nice to be recognized publicly. One of my pastor jobs is to pay attention to the volunteers in our ministries and acknowledge them every chance I get. I like it when people see that I have worked hard on something and done a good job. Sometimes just a smile is enough to keep me going.

But what about when nobody notices your efforts, or people notice and say nothing? Does that send you into an emotional tailspin? Or when you see others thanked, does it drip bitterness into your soul? Does it make you not want to volunteer for another thing or give another dime? Slow down, my friend. Deep breaths. Listen to the words of your Savior: **"So you also, when you have done everything you were told to do, should say, 'We are unworthy servants; we have only done our duty'"** (Luke 17:10).

Remember for whom you are working and giving. In which direction is the worship supposed to be going? Toward you? Of course not. Toward your Savior! You can find immense satisfaction in giving him the gift of yourself. Know that whenever you imitate his spirit of self-sacrifice, you put a smile on his face. Take humble satisfaction also in knowing that you have made someone else's life better.

Recognition is frosting.

Last word

Pastor Mark Jeske

You and I live in a world of dual causality, i.e., things happen both by human agency and by God's direct working. Did you pass a tough exam because you prepared so thoroughly or because God blessed you? Answer: Yes. Did your business have a good year because you worked so hard or because God blessed you? Answer: Yes. Did you date carefully and thoughtfully and come up with a good spouse, or did God give him or her to you? Answer: Yes.

God encourages our initiatives, wants us to feel personally responsible for our lives, entrusts us with his resources, and gives us a lot of leeway in how we manage things. But—he always reserves for himself the last word: **"In their hearts humans plan their course, but the Lord establishes their steps"** (Proverbs 16:9). Does that sound a little confusing? Maybe. But it's also really cool.

God's great ambition for you is not to control you or act as the grand puppeteer of your life. He has created you with the intent that you should become a miniature version of himself—with a value system aligned with his, a passion for his mission and agenda, a love for people, and the ability to make right choices on your own. But he also loves you enough to reserve the right to intervene here and there to guide events to the conclusion he wants.

Perfect. We win both ways.

God loves big cities
Pastor Mark Jeske

Perhaps it's my imagination, but among my circle of friends, those planning for retirement seem to have a fondness for country living. When I talk to my peers about their retirement dreams, they say things like "mountain view," "deer passing through," "quiet," and "stream." The only thing I never hear mentioned in their scenarios is people. Maybe they're just so stressed out that they need to get away for a while. I have never heard anybody tell me that his or her retirement dream is to move downtown in a big city.

God loves nature. It was he, after all, who made it so beautiful, including the mountains, streams, and deer. But he's crazy in love with cities too. Why? Because that's where all the people are. The centerpiece of God's agenda is not admiring the fabulous world he created but rescuing lost sinful people through the proclamation of the Word. The church today really needs an urban strategy for that very reason.

God once expended a huge amount of energy getting his prophet Jonah where he wanted him—out of his comfort zone in Israel and into Nineveh, the huge capital city of the Assyrian Empire. **"Should I not have concern for the great city of Nineveh, in which there are more than a hundred and twenty thousand people who cannot tell their right hand from their left—and also many animals?"** (Jonah 4:11).

Apparently he likes cows too.

may 8

A little respect for teachers

Jason Nelson

Here's a shout-out to the women and men of my chosen profession. They generally don't sing their own praises. Society takes them for granted or throws them under the bus when schools underperform. Some hear from former students later in life, but most just fade into the chalk dust. I think I know something about teachers. I had some. I was one. I worked alongside both private and public school teachers, and I taught college students who were preparing to be teachers. I can state for a fact that teachers don't operate from an air of their own superiority. The teachers I have known had one thing on their hearts. To do what is best for kids.

According to a National Center for Education Statistics study, the majority of teachers in American public and private schools happen to be Christian women. They are more likely to pray during the day then the population at large. They attend church in higher percentages than the population at large.

Teaching is a favorite vocation for many Christians. It gets as close as anything to doing what Jesus did. "Teacher" is what others regularly called Jesus, and it is how he at times referred to himself.

The reward of teaching becomes tangible in only one way: **"It is enough for students to be like their teachers"** (Matthew 10:25). That would be more than enough for me. If I have a headstone, I want one anonymous line on it: "He was a teacher."

What am I doing here?
Pastor Mark Jeske

In every board game I've ever played, it is absolutely vital that everyone starts out even. In the game of life, however, we all start out lost and confused, not knowing our Maker, ignorant of Christ our Savior, and without the Spirit. Sin is an equal opportunity disease—it has infected absolutely everybody. The Father's grand scheme of creating a huge and loving family of children on earth went terribly awry.

He originally made us to enjoy our world, enjoy each other, and most of all to enjoy him. Paul told a curious gathering of pagans in Athens: **"From one man he made all the nations, that they should inhabit the whole earth; and he marked out their appointed times in history and the boundaries of their lands. God did this so that they would seek him and perhaps reach out for him and find him, though he is not far from any one of us. 'For in him we live and move and have our being'"** (Acts 17:26-28).

The restoration of our relationship with our God is the key to everything. The Word which makes that connection is near you. A loving Father is reaching out his hand to you—it is his desire that all who seek him will find him.

He would also like you to be his smile, kindly voice, and outstretched hand to the lost, agnostics, atheists, pagans, and fallen-away former Christians in your life.

Save room for steak

Diana Kerr

This is going to sound weird considering what you're doing right now, but I want to caution you just a little about reading devotions.

Now, it should go without saying that I think devotions are a great resource. I love the convenience of reading devotions on my phone. I love learning about applications of my faith in today's world. I love how a devotion can enrich my understanding of a verse or give me a new perspective on a story I've heard a million times.

BUT. There is no substitute for the real thing—God's Word. I get so excited about the great resources available that I have to remind myself of this, so I'm encouraging you too. Don't spend so much time consuming *other people's* words about God that you fail to consume the inspired words of God *himself*. Take advantage of trustworthy resources out there to help grow your faith—devotions, podcasts, YouTube videos, books, etc.—but don't fill up so much on spiritual veggies that you're too full to enjoy the steak. (Vegetarians, I'm sorry for the metaphor, but you can't deny that God's Word is meaty and juicy.)

So what's so great about God's Word anyway? Nothing compares with it! **"Every word of God is flawless"** (Proverbs 30:5), God's law refreshes our souls (Psalm 19:7), **"the word of God is alive and active"** (Hebrews 4:12), it's a lamp for our feet and a light on our path (Psalm 119:105), it makes us **"wise for salvation"** (2 Timothy 3:15), and it endures forever (Isaiah 40:8).

Where do I go with my anxiety?

Pastor Mark Jeske

Are you a planner? Planning is good. It is good to think ahead, to imagine the problems and challenges of tomorrow, to take inventory of your resources, and to evaluate risks. It is good to have a Plan B if your first efforts don't pan out.

But sometimes planning becomes worry. Over-thinking tomorrow's problems can leave you tossing and turning on your pillow, unable to relax and sleep. Too much contingency planning can leave you incapable of enjoying the life that's right in front of you right now. Too much living in the future leaves you anxious and restless because you can't do anything about problems that haven't happened yet.

Where do you go with your anxiety? Where else but to your Father: **"Do not worry, saying, 'What shall we eat?' or 'What shall we drink?' or 'What shall we wear?' For the pagans run after all these things, and your heavenly Father knows that you need them. But seek first his kingdom and his righteousness, and all these things will be given to you as well"** (Matthew 6:31-33).

Remember that you are not facing your challenges alone—when you wear the yoke of Jesus, he is pulling the load right next to you. Do your job to the best of your ability. Ask God for forgiveness for your failings and for strength for your weaknesses. Thank people who help you and trust them. Put God first in your life, not your troubles. Give him your worship and trust.

And then close your eyes and let go.

Don't get too attached

Pastor Mark Jeske

The cities of Sodom and Gomorrah have become legendary as benchmarks for violent depravity and the drastic punishment brought upon them by God. Though at one time they occupied some of the most fertile land anywhere in the Middle East, after God was done with them the plain that they inhabited became a smoking ruin. Burning sulfur rained down from heaven. The region south of the Dead Sea is still desolate and bone-dry today, four millennia later.

A remarkable side story is added for our wonder and learning. Angels of God visited Abraham's nephew Lot and his wife in Sodom a short time before the fury descended and ordered them to *get out. Immediately!* They did leave, but Lot's wife was sick at heart about all the wonderful things she was going to have to leave behind: **"Thus** [God] **overthrew those cities and the entire plain, destroying all those living in the cities—and also the vegetation in the land. But Lot's wife looked back, and she became a pillar of salt"** (Genesis 19:25,26).

Let's not be too hard on the woman. Her sacrifice was considerable, and the fact that she lost her life does not mean that she lost her salvation. Perhaps we'll see her in heaven and can hear her incredible story firsthand. But God's warning is crystal clear—this earth is not our real home. It is corrupt beyond saving and will be destroyed. Don't get too attached or addicted.

Travel light. Heaven is your real home.

I have many fears, Lord

Pastor Mark Jeske

Everybody lives with fears. Even tough guys have fears. Which are yours?

Are you afraid of being laid off at work? personal bankruptcy? family breakup? being alone in your senior years? Are your children defiant and rebellious? Is your home in a high-crime neighborhood? Do you fear for your personal safety? Is your spouse violent?

Fear is a destructive emotion. It is good to think ahead, to be alert, to assess risks and dangers in your life. But fear means that you are already experiencing defeat. Fear doesn't energize people—it paralyzes them and drains their energy. In his wilderness years, David, the future king, learned to master his fears through his faith and trust in the Lord: **"When I am afraid, I put my trust in you. In God, whose word I praise—in God I trust and am not afraid. What can mere mortals do to me?"** (Psalm 56:3,4).

Dump your fears in a bushel basket right now and carry them to God's throne in prayer in the name of Jesus Christ. Give them to him. Don't let Satan torment you even one day longer. Take three really deep breaths, and then celebrate the fact that Satan himself cannot take away Christ's love, Christ's forgiveness, Christ's favor, and Christ's gift of immortality. You are precious to the Father, and he will send his angels to help you at just the right time. You are already a winner; what remains are just details.

What can mere mortals do to you?

Patience

Jason Nelson

My pastor said in a sermon, "Patience is going at someone else's speed." Wow! That is profound. I never heard that before. I was glad I was paying attention. I wish I would have heard it a long time ago. I thought patience was what I needed to exercise because people weren't going at my speed. You mean all those times I was pushing others along, they were really being patient with me?

I guess it all depends on our internal clocks. Mine is a stopwatch. I always hear the sound of time running out. *Tick. Tick. Tick. Tick*. I think my wife's internal clock is an hourglass. Maybe that's why she regularly asks me, "What's the hurry?" And God's internal clock is eternity. It's rush proof. We are more likely to lose patience with God than he is to lose patience with us. We get tired of waiting around for him to do something.

"But do not forget this one thing, dear friends: With the Lord a day is like a thousand years, and a thousand years are like a day. The Lord is not slow in keeping his promise, as some understand slowness. Instead he is patient with you, not wanting anyone to perish, but everyone to come to repentance" (2 Peter 3:8,9).

God has been patient with us for thousands of years. I think he will continue to be patient with us until he sees it is no longer in our best interest.

Fear God in the fire

Pastor Daron Lindemann

Fire means serious business! Firearms aren't toys. Getting fired changes things. **"These are the commandments the LORD proclaimed in a loud voice . . . there on the mountain from out of the fire"** (Deuteronomy 5:22). God delivered the Ten Commandments "from out of the fire." They are not personal options like settings on your phone. They are serious business!

How serious are you about God? Hearts burning with passion in the first months of being a believer or by becoming part of a mission project often smolder into ashen embers. Busyness of life deceptively dampens any deep communion with God found in the constant, quiet moments of Scripture and prayer. Awe for God grows cold and "same old."

How can we reignite it?

"Be careful not to forget the covenant of the LORD your God that he made with you. . . . For the LORD your God is a consuming fire, a jealous God" (Deuteronomy 4:23,24). There is only one sure way to rekindle a burning awe for God. It's not in our resolve but in God's burning passion to love and forgive and save us.

You are the object of his fierce loyalty, his jealous grace. When you don't burn with passion for God, by grace he burns with passion for you. His jealous grace wants you, wants everything there is about you (even your sinful mistakes and messes), and wants your reignited loyalty and love.

Like the three men in the fiery furnace (Daniel 3), find your awe for God in his jealous grace.

Choose your friends wisely

Pastor Mark Jeske

How did you end up with the friends you have? Did they choose to hang out with you? Did life (work, school, leisure activity) throw you together and you just hit it off? Or did you consciously choose to pursue a relationship because you admired them or enjoyed their company or wanted to be in their circle?

Parents of teenagers are nervous about their kids' friends. They know that their own influence is diminishing and that of their kids' friends is increasing. They know what happens to impressionable young people when they "fall in with the wrong crowd." How does that happen? Do "wrong crowds" kidnap teens and force them to study their philosophy? No. Kids who should know better make the wrong choices because they valued inclusion and the approval of a certain group more than the approval of their parents. Or of their God.

Some educators think that young people absorb as much from their friends as they do from their instructors. Choose your friends wisely. As best as you can, teach your children to choose their friends wisely. **"Stay away from a fool, for you will not find knowledge on their lips"** (Proverbs 14:7). In Old Testament wisdom literature like the book of Proverbs, the concept of "folly" is not just doing dumb things like 40 mph donuts on an icy parking lot but choosing a life philosophy that will cause you to lose your faith.

Which will cause you to lose your place in heaven.

The Lord will fight for you

Linda Buxa

The player on the bench couldn't believe the ref's call. In the universal gesture of "Are you kidding me?" he raised both arms and looked absolutely surprised.

After the game, his dad pulled him aside and told him, "Don't show your frustration. If it's worth fighting about, your coach will fight for you."

That's the same advice Moses gave to the Israelites. Just after they had *finally* been delivered from Egyptian slavery, they found themselves pinned between the advancing army and the Red Sea. As the people were complaining about their situation, Moses told them, **"Do not be afraid. Stand firm and you will see the deliverance the Lord will bring you today. The Egyptians you see today you will never see again. The Lord will fight for you; you need only to be still"** (Exodus 14:13,14).

We often think the world is pinning us down, leaving us with no options. We grumble and complain because we don't see exactly how a tough situation is going to work out. It's as if we forget that we worship a God who is able to part the sea—both literally and proverbially. We worship the God who promises that he will find a way to make the battle you are facing work for your good, for our good, or God's glory.

Be still. He'll fight for you.

Jesus was obedient to our authorities

Pastor Daron Lindemann

"D'oh!" Homer Simpson's catchphrase has helped make the *Simpsons* TV series famous. It tells the story of parents who are bumbling idiots trying to raise a family. To add to the incompetence of authority on the show, Reverend Timothy Lovejoy just doesn't care. And the corrupt Mayor Quimby is a slick embezzler. No wonder the preteen Bart behaves badly!

Do you ever consider your parents, church, or government just as inept? Before you think that gives you the right to rebel like Bart, I have some news. Jesus loves the Fourth Commandment.

Jesus is not surprised how incompetent God's authorities on earth can be. Jesus knows what it takes to obey them. And Jesus forgives and equips us with his grace to honor, respect, and obey the authorities that God has placed over us: parents, church, and government.

Luke 2:41-52 shares some interaction in Jesus' preteen years between him and his parents, Joseph and Mary. It involves the church and government as well. Two truths stand out. First, these authorities are far from perfect. Joseph and Mary fumble around trying to figure things out. The church and the government in Jerusalem will later condemn Jesus and crucify him. Second, Jesus obeys them perfectly. Even though his parents don't understand, he understands. Even though the church and government will dishonor and kill him, he honors and obeys them. Even to death.

By his obedience, Jesus blesses these authorities, then and today. And blesses us when we honor them too.

Plan and pray
Pastor Mark Jeske

So—when you want to accomplish something significant, is it important to plan or pray? The answer, once again, is Yes. It's another of the paradoxes of the Christian life, because there are two streams of causality that simultaneously are making things happen—you and God. Planning and prayer are like your right arm and left arm—you need and want them both: **"Commit to the Lord whatever you do, and he will establish your plans"** (Proverbs 16:3).

Planning is good. You need to decide on a clear objective, count the cost, build your team, anticipate problems, get advice, work out the supply chain, communicate, accumulate resources, and set a realistic schedule. Now obviously you don't need to be religious to do all these things. But here are the advantages of bringing God into your planning: You honor him by consulting him and his Word. You have a chance in advance to see whether your project and your operating style are in harmony with his agenda. You can check your motives to see whether you just want to make a lot of money or whether you actually want to help people.

Asking for God's help also puts the resources of the universe on your side. When God speaks the word, anything can happen. When God speaks the word, you get twice as strong and your challenges are only half as large.

Oh, by the way—when you are successful, remember to say thank-you.

I'm alive because of the Spirit

Pastor Mark Jeske

It's not too hard to envision God the Father. In your mind you can see the Ancient of Days on his sapphire throne, timeless, all-powerful, attended by legions of angels, and serene. It's really easy to imagine Jesus Christ, his Son, for he took human flesh and walked our dusty streets. But the Spirit—he has no shape or easy visibility. When he acted in human history, he was manifested in fire and wind that did not destroy and as a dove. *Hmm.* Hard to pray to a bird.

Since it's so hard to imagine the Spirit, Christians tend to pray directly to him less. But his unique work within the Trinity is absolutely vital to us, our families, and the church. It is the Spirit who takes Christ's work of redemption for the world and brings it to us *personally.* It is he who encoded the Word of God into writing by inspiring the Holy Scriptures, which are able to make you wise for salvation.

Through the power of the Word he *converted* you, made you to be *born again.* It is his power in Baptism and the Lord's Supper that builds saving faith in our hearts and minds. **"No one can say, 'Jesus is Lord,' except by the Holy Spirit"** (1 Corinthians 12:3). What a magnificent gift! Thank the Spirit for his wonderful work within you. Even more important, let him continue to build your faith through Word and Supper.

The Spirit who powered Pentecost once is still at work today.

No leftovers, please

Pastor Daron Lindemann

When God asked the Israelites in the Old Testament to bring him offerings, they brought him sick sheep, deformed goats, and blind bulls. "After all," they might have thought, "God owns everything, so why should it matter? We can keep the good ones."

God rebuked them, **"I have no need of a bull from your stall or of goats from your pens, for every animal of the forest is mine, and the cattle on a thousand hills. 'Sacrifice thank offerings to God, fulfill your vows to the Most High, and call upon me in the day of trouble; I will deliver you, and you will honor me'"** (Psalm 50:9,10,14,15).

God gave quality sheep and bulls to the Israelites. More than that, he gave the priceless sacrifice of his Son who would come as their Savior. And ours. God doesn't hold back his best.

God asks us for good offerings, not leftovers. God wants our love and our faithful obedience to his saving name expressed in the quality of our gifts. He gives us so much that we have every opportunity to give back what is good.

We want to give God our love, our joyful generosity, yes, ourselves. Our best. Not leftovers. You can't out give God. So when he asks for your first and best instead of your leftovers, don't worry. Give it to him. He can give you more. Perhaps even what is better.

Not lost in translation

Jason Nelson

I consulted with a group of Christians in the former East Germany shortly after the Berlin Wall came down. Democracy was beginning to take hold, but Soviet gray was still the color palette of the buildings and mood of the people. There were indications that the new government might tolerate Christian schools. I was there to help them determine if starting one was feasible.

I don't speak German, but I had a good translator. Through him I was trying to communicate like I did with groups in the U.S. But something was off. The people weren't responding. I pulled out all the stops, but my energy wasn't coming across. My jokes were falling flat. Finally, a brave lady said to my translator, "Tell the American we just came out of Communism and we are not comfortable speaking in public." I hung my head and used the universal gesture of cluelessness. I smacked my forehead with the heel of my hand. They understood that. I looked at the lady and said, *"Danke schön."* Then I sat down and let my translator tell me what I needed to know.

That was a Pentecost moment for me (see Acts 2). A light came on. It hit me how nuanced communication is. So many things can interfere with understanding one another. Words alone don't do justice to the fullness of the gospel. Yet people around the world believe it because the Holy Spirit enables them to grasp it. God speaks every language in the love of Jesus.

Speak up for those who can't

Pastor Mark Jeske

Life is full of inequalities, isn't it? People have vastly different incomes; vastly different net worth; different levels of education, access to professional services, physical health, and personal networks. Jesus noticed all that at his time two thousand years ago, predicting to his disciples that there would always be poor people and victims of catastrophic circumstances like war, the neglect and cruelty of others, or of their own poor choices.

But that is no excuse for casual exploitation or shunning. On the contrary, it brings delight to God when people whom he has blessed with a surplus in some area choose to share with those who struggle. The church is at its best when it matches the vigor of its preaching with the vigor of its ministries of caring. Sharing food and clothing come to mind. Working to bridge the education gap in low-income communities is another.

A mysterious king named Lemuel was given a page of Scripture for his life proverbs, and he offers yet another way for the strong to help the weak: **"Speak up for those who cannot speak for themselves"** (Proverbs 31:8). Our world is blessed by all the people who have chosen to invest time, energy, and passion into advocacy for people with disabilities. Or those who defend the right of unborn children to be born and not be aborted.

In heaven the sufferings and struggles will be over. For now, they are opportunities for love in action.

Mission impossible

Pastor Mark Jeske

If I were Jonah, I would have run away from God's call too. But for the opposite reason. I would have fled because the job was so stupendously impossible. Why should mighty Assyria, on top of the world, its ruthless armies trashing all the smaller kingdoms of the Middle East, pay the slightest bit of attention to a foreign prophet telling them that their religious ideas were all wrong?

Jonah fled from God because he was terrified that his mission would be successful. Though he had some terrible weaknesses, Jonah is a hero of mine because he believed so strongly in the power of God's Word to convert people, even heathen Assyrians. And he was right! Even though his method of gathering hearers and converts seems peculiar to our ears, it had a phenomenal impact on the entire city of Nineveh. People in the city repented of their sins and turned to Israel's God for mercy. And mercy they received: **"When God saw what they did and how they turned from their evil ways, he relented and did not bring on them the destruction he had threatened"** (Jonah 3:10).

Jonah's story shows that there are windows of opportunity in the lives of people and even cities when hearts are ready for the truth, for God, for reconciliation, for faith, for their Savior. God's Word can cut through all excuses, dodges, evasions, idols, and philosophies.

If the gospel could reach Assyrians, perhaps you and I should not give up on the crazy, godless world of today.

There is no grace fatigue
Jason Nelson

Sometimes consuming religious material is like eating a bowl of wheat flakes. You know it's good for you, but there is no snap, crackle, or pop. You know how it's going to taste before eating the first spoonful.

Overexposure to things, even if they are good for us, can leave us weary of them. The almighty God got tired of his own people going through the motions of their religion because their hearts and minds weren't in it. He said, **"They have become a burden to me; I am weary of bearing them"** (Isaiah 1:14). That's a danger with our religious habits too. Familiarity with churchy stuff may not breed contempt, but it can lead to apathy. We reduce power to our attention span because we know how it's going to go down. The formula is predictable. *Sinner repent. Turn to Jesus. Have a nice day.* Then we all sing another slow song.

Wheat flakes have become a victim of their bland consistency. I stopped buying them. So have a lot of other people. I don't want that to happen in my spiritual life or yours. My life isn't predictable. I need to mull things over. I crave some contemporaneous coaching on how to be a Christian adult. And every day I love hearing how much God loves me. That never gets old. There is no grace fatigue in my life. **"No! We believe it is through the grace of our Lord Jesus that we are saved"** (Acts 15:11).

Good medicine

Pastor Mark Jeske

You are probably aware that the United States leads the world in consumption of antidepressant drugs—one in five adults gets prescription medication of one kind or another for mental health reasons. In the decade from 2000 to 2010, usage leaped 29 percent. Wow! Abuse of prescription opiates has also skyrocketed.

Although some people have serious mental health issues that require antidepressant medication, for the rest of us God has another way to get dopamine into our heads, and it does not involve drugs. It is the daily attitude you choose: **"A cheerful heart is good medicine, but a crushed spirit dries up the bones"** (Proverbs 17:22). You can't control what comes at you each day, but you can indeed take control of your attitude.

It's easy to complain, feel cheated, feel bitter, feel helpless and hopeless. That mental negativity, however, just shrivels up the human spirit. Here's the path to a cheerful heart: Reflect on the great love the Father has for you, great enough to sacrifice his Son on the cross for you. Take inventory of the wonderful people in your life. Remember things people have said or done that build you up. Choose to remember your achievements, and refuse to dwell on your failures. Reread Scripture passages that promise God's attention, protection, and providing, and call to mind the times you know you received help from above.

And remember that you are immortal. Heaven awaits.

The triune God makes real news

Pastor Daron Lindemann

Identifying fake news isn't easy. Do I like or share a social media post or picture? Or is it fake? One reason Christians celebrate the triune nature of our God is what it means for truth in the world.

In John chapter 16 Jesus taught this to his disciples, describing the work of the three-in-one God: **"All that belongs to the Father is mine. That is why I said the Spirit will receive from me what he will make known to you"** (verse 15).

God the Father makes truth exist. Zebras have stripes. Every morning the sun rises in the east. Baptism creates saving faith. God loves all sinners. These realities "belong to" the Father. That's real news!

God the Son makes truth work. He takes what the Father gives him and uses it to save sinners with his works of redemption—his living and dying, his rising and ascending, his clothing believers with righteousness and coming at the Last Day. That's real news!

God the Holy Spirit makes truth known. **"He will guide you into all the truth. He will not speak on his own; he will speak only what he hears . . . because it is from me that he will receive what he will make known to you"** (John 16:13,14). He calls us to faith through the Word of God. He enlightens us to new understanding and appreciation. He draws us closer to Jesus. That's real news!

Like and share that news.

Our heroes inspire me

Diana Kerr

About this time every year, we set aside a day to honor American heroes who gave up their lives with bravery and selflessness. I don't ever want to take for granted that the life I lead here in America might not be this way if they hadn't defended our freedoms. They believed in a cause and didn't back down.

Servicemen and women aren't the only heroes to whom I owe a huge debt of gratitude. Hebrews chapter 11 always leaves me feeling inspired and humbled at the sacrifices early Christians made as they stood up for the faith.

"There were others who were tortured. . . . Some faced jeers and flogging, and even chains and imprisonment. They were put to death by stoning; they were sawed in two; they were killed by the sword. They went about in sheepskins and goatskins, destitute, persecuted and mistreated—the world was not worthy of them. They wandered in deserts and mountains, living in caves and in holes in the ground" (Hebrews 11:35-38).

Wow. I wonder what this world would be like today if they'd caved and given up the faith. I know those details are gruesome to read, but we can't avoid honoring people's sacrifices just because it's uncomfortable. Let's thank God for the heroes who gave their lives for our faith or our country (including Jesus' ultimate sacrifice of his life for our salvation). The next time I'm scared to defend what matters most, I'm going to remember their bravery and their unwavering dedication to their cause.

What's your purpose?

Linda Buxa

In 1799, 12-year-old Conrad Reed was fishing on his parents' property in North Carolina when he found a shiny yellow rock. He showed the 17-pound item to his dad, and they used it as a doorstop. Three years later, they learned it was gold. (That's a lot of gold.) What was once considered mundane became incredibly valuable once it was refined and used for its real purpose.

Same with you. Same with me. Too often we don't realize our true value. We live distracted by the world and act as if our relationships, reputation, work, or appearance determine our value and purpose. That makes us about as useful for God's kingdom as a doorstop.

"You are the light of the world. A town built on a hill cannot be hidden. Neither do people light a lamp and put it under a bowl. Instead they put it on its stand, and it gives light to everyone in the house. In the same way, let your light shine before others, that they may see your good deeds and glorify your Father in heaven" (Matthew 5:14-16).

Our God poured all his wrath on his only Son so that we could be called his children. Now, as he refines us through trials and joys, we are used for our real purpose: to do the good deeds he has prepared for us, all to bring him glory.

Where do I go with my doubts?

Pastor Mark Jeske

Can you actually admit it when you have doubts about your faith, or are you too ashamed? Do you have to keep quiet so your perfect Christian friends and family won't think you're a loser? Are you afraid that Satan has his hooks in you, but there are just some things about the Christian belief system that you honestly can't accept?

Don't beat yourself up. John the Baptist had been gifted and appointed Jesus Christ's personal representative on earth. He had a phenomenal 18 months of ministry, and he probably thought he would have a great 40-year career. But then he was arrested and held without trial in one of King Herod's prisons.

As he sat there day after day, his confidence might have started to ebb—either that, or he was afraid that his teaching companions were losing theirs: **"When John, who was in prison, heard about the deeds of the Messiah, he sent his disciples to ask him, 'Are you the one who is to come, or should we expect someone else?' Jesus replied, 'Go back and report to John what you hear and see: The blind receive sight, the lame walk, those who have leprosy are cleansed, the deaf hear, the dead are raised, and the good news is proclaimed to the poor'"** (Matthew 11:2-5).

When doubts trouble your heart, just let the gospels tell you of Jesus' words and deeds. Marvel at his power. Learn from his wisdom. Bask in his love.

God can't be bought off

Pastor Mark Jeske

In the movie the *Godfather Part III*, mob boss Michael Corleone is wracked with guilt about all the murders he has ordered, especially that of his brother Fredo. He gives some immense financial gifts to the church to try to atone for what he has done. You know, people really get that idea. When you hear the word *atone* in day-to-day conversation or read it in essays or articles, it usually refers to people's personal efforts to make up for their evil deeds.

But God can't be bought by human gifts. There isn't enough money in the world to pay him off. There aren't enough animals in the world to be sacrificed for our sins even if all their blood was shed. There aren't enough noble deeds a person could do, not a far enough pilgrimage, not enough devotional prayers, not enough candles to light for people to atone for their own misdeeds.

The Lord can't be bought off: **"The LORD detests the sacrifice of the wicked, but the prayer of the upright pleases him"** (Proverbs 15:8). Get this—what you cannot do for yourself, Jesus Christ did for you. Since wicked people cannot sacrifice their way into God's favor, Jesus sacrificed himself and gave us God's favor. Those who believe it have it, and their status with God now reads "Upright." "Righteous." "Just." "Forgiven." "Holy." "Saint."

Your good works can't buy God's love. But they can express your love for him.

june

When you pass through the waters, I will be with you;
and when you pass through the rivers, they will not
sweep over you. When you walk through the fire, you
will not be burned; the flames will not set you ablaze.

Isaiah 43:2

Facebook envy

Pastor Mark Jeske

Are you a big social media user? Do you subscribe to Twitter feeds, Facebook, Snapchat, Instagram, Pinterest, and YouTube channels? Do you enjoy reading about other people's lives? seeing their children's antics? pics of the big birthday bash? the new clothes and accessories? the restaurant where they ate last night? the dessert that she is about to eat *right now*?

It's great fun to read news about friends. But be honest with me. Do you ever feel envy gnawing at you when you see other people's fabulous parties? new furniture? major sporting event seats? giant new flat screen? trophy perfect children? expensive vacations? Is it hard to see a big group of people having fun when you are alone and blue?

Digital media has been around only for a few years, but envy has been tormenting people since sin began. It is deadly. Shakespeare called it a green-eyed monster. God said, **"A heart at peace gives life to the body, but envy rots the bones"** (Proverbs 14:30). If you've caught yourself with jealous thoughts, what can you do?

1) Take inventory of the blessings in your life, both human and material. Write the list down so you can look at it and then refer to it tomorrow. 2) Take inventory of all the spiritual blessings in your life. 3) Give thanks to God for each of them. 4) Decide to clap and cheer for your friends' good fortune and be genuinely happy for them.

A perfectly good faith

Jason Nelson

"To the faithful you show yourself faithful" (Psalm 18:25).

When I was counseling Christian teenagers, some troubling concerns brought them to my office. Concerns like, "My boyfriend (or girlfriend) is dumping me" or "I'm afraid I'm losing my faith." Young hearts are easily broken. So I handled the first concern with tender-loving care. But I was direct about the second. I told them, "The fact you are concerned about losing your faith is a pretty good indication you are not." People lose faith when it slips away unnoticed.

Maybe you've felt like these students did. They were taught so thoroughly about a strong faith, and theirs didn't measure up. They wondered if theirs was good enough. They did things they were ashamed of, sometimes with their boyfriend or girlfriend. They let God down.

Simple as it sounds, I would talk to them about "monkey" faith and "cat" faith. I told them sometimes we are like baby monkeys. God gives us determination to wrap our arms around Jesus. We are aware we are hanging on to him. We hold on tight so we won't fall. We feel God's strength in our firm grasp of him. But sometimes we are like baby cats. We don't feel secure about much. But God grabs us by the scruff of the neck and hangs on to us even while we flail away in uncertainty. We trust he won't let go. And that is a perfectly good faith.

Loving God
Diana Kerr

For too many years I was content with an inconsistent relationship with God. His commitment to *me* never faltered, but my commitment to him was lackluster. I went to church every week and occasionally read my Bible, but I rarely hungered after him.

I didn't know what I was missing. Thank goodness my sinful, distracted heart eventually turned a little more toward him.

Now I appreciate the value of his words in Deuteronomy 6:5. I see how he loves me and seeks what's best for me even as he gives this command: **"Love the Lord your God with all your heart and with all your soul and with all your strength."**

Jesus referenced this verse when asked about the greatest commandment, so it's clearly an important one. I doubt his motive was merely seeking more love and adoration for himself. See, God knows that loving him above all else, even though it's often challenging, is really, really good for us.

We'll never love him perfectly, but thanks to Jesus, he'll never stop forgiving us. And he doesn't leave us hanging—he gives us ideas to keep our lives focused on him: **"These commandments that I give you today are to be on your hearts. Impress them on your children. Talk about them when you sit at home and when you walk along the road, when you lie down and when you get up. Tie them as symbols on your hands and bind them on your foreheads. Write them on the doorframes of your houses and on your gates"** (Deuteronomy 6:6-9).

Trust the catcher

Pastor Daron Lindemann

Circus performers describe a very special relationship between trapeze artists. One of the performers releases from his trapeze, leaving it behind. He twists up into the air, and at the peak of the arc, when he isn't launching up into the sky any longer, he must stop and remain as still as possible (that performer is called "the flier").

At the same time a partner is swinging on a different trapeze from his knees. At just the right moment, he swoops in like an eagle and grabs the flier with precision timing and strength (that performer is called "the catcher"). It takes years to train for this, with one of the most important rules being that the flier must never try to catch the catcher but must wait in absolute trust. Even in that split second when he thinks he is plummeting to his death.

God asked Abraham to release, to leave things behind: **"Go from your country, your people and your father's household to the land I will show you"** (Genesis 12:1). He'd have nothing to hold on to anymore. But what he had been holding on to wasn't enough. Not for God's big plans and promises.

God has big plans and promises for you too. Oftentimes, however, our heads, hands, and hearts are already full of stuff. Stuff we think is important. But it's just not as important as God's blessings. So let go. Fly into the air and freeze. You won't fall. He'll catch you—and bless you bigger than you can imagine.

It's okay to build wealth

Pastor Mark Jeske

The economic stress of the last decade or two has taken a toll on us all. Everyone suffered losses in the last ten years. As the gap widens between rich and poor, resentment and anger mount toward those with money.

That resentment in the Christian world draws on Jesus' intense imagery as he warned against materialism and greed. How does his metaphor of a camel squeezing through the eye of a needle (Mark 10:25) not stick in your mind? It really is hard for the super wealthy to make it into the kingdom of heaven. The upshot is that there seems to be a dark moral cloud over businesses that try to make a profit or over people who seek to build their family's assets.

Greed and materialism do indeed corrode people's insides. But it is still very possible for Christians to honor God as they seek to make money and not spend it all (a.k.a. building wealth). The book of Proverbs gives God's blessing on hard work, thrift, discipline, and a servant spirit. When God is in the middle of our asset-building labors, the process stays healthy and he blesses it: **"Humility is the fear of the LORD; its wages are riches and honor and life"** (Proverbs 22:4).

Other verses of Scripture reveal how tenderly God cares for the poor. But that does not make poverty a desirable destination. It is better to accumulate a surplus so that you can help other people and honor the Giver with your generous gifts.

What's it like to be right all the time?

Pastor Daron Lindemann

I don't know about you, but I'm right all the time. If you and I have a difference of opinion, there's just no question that I'm smarter.

Toddlers think this. Teenagers think this. And adults think this too. Now think about Jesus who is 100 percent right 100 percent of the time. Sometimes, since we're always right, we disagree with him.

So how does Jesus handle people like us who think we are right and he's not? He hangs in there patiently. He gladly suffers injustice instead of us, as if he's wrong even though he's not. **"From that time on Jesus began to explain to his disciples that he must go to Jerusalem and suffer many things at the hands of the elders, the chief priests and the teachers of the law, and that he must be killed and on the third day be raised to life"** (Matthew 26:21).

Jesus is saying to us, "I need to respond to their lack of faith and their love of self by selflessly taking on injustice and suffering as if I'm the one who is wrong."

Can you follow this Jesus when he is guiding you away from selfishness? Can you be more patient with others and pray for extra understanding of their perspective?

Yes, because Jesus is always right. And his righteousness is not a rule for you but a gift for you. Just the right gift, of course.

Topics or issues
Jason Nelson

We can spend lots of time going back and forth on hot button topics but avoid talking about the underlying issues that heat up the buttons to begin with. We carry on with parallel and sometimes juvenile verbal transactions. We lob innuendos back and forth on the surface of a controversy. "I know you are, but what am I?" Wrangling back and forth is self-sustaining until someone finally musters the courage to cross a long-standing divide. "Why are we still talking about this? There must be more to it."

Drilling down is necessary, scary, and has consequences. Talking about real issues could change the routine of our marriages, the agendas for our meetings, and the dynamic of our friendships. So, we hesitate. Do we really want to go there? Dealing with the real issues could break someone's heart, get someone fired, or expose someone's insecurities. Dealing with real issues got Jesus crucified.

His own disciples brought up a tired, old topic with Jesus: **"Who, then, is the greatest in the kingdom of heaven?"** (Matthew 18:1). "Which of us is better than the others? Who among us is God's favorite?" Jesus cut right through it. He presented them with a child because a child would never ask such a stupid question. He confronted the issue lurking beneath the topic they wanted to discuss and gave them an answer they weren't prepared to hear. Those who don't care whose greatest are the greatest.

Divine paradox

Pastor Mark Jeske

The literature on corporate leadership says that one of the most important characteristics of an executive is the ability to be comfortable in ambiguity. Does that make sense to you? The point is that picking a business path in an uncertain world often involves balancing competing and seemingly contradictory influences but which both have value.

I'd like to suggest that being a wise and knowledgeable biblical Christian means you sometimes have to embrace two seemingly contradictory ideas *but both of which are true.* For instance, we need to live and work and build the church as though it will have to last ten thousand years, but we also live as though judgment day could come today.

The greatest of all the scriptural paradoxes is law and gospel. The seventh century B.C. prophet Nahum offers this insight about the very nature of God: **"The LORD is slow to anger but great in power; the LORD will not leave the guilty unpunished"** (Nahum 1:3). So which is it? Is God a severe judge who will let no sinner slide? Or is he kind and gracious and forgiving? The answer is Yes. They are both true.

The *only* place where these two parallel railroad tracks come together is at the cross of Christ and through the work of the Spirit to help you believe. On the cross God punished all sin by punishing his Son. From the cross God had mercy on the whole human race.

Those who believe it have it.

Resting is a work of faith
Pastor Daron Lindemann

Give a one-year-old a toy drum and that child will keep banging. Nonstop. Until Mom or Dad can't take it anymore and attempt to pull the drum away. "WHAAAAAAA!" the little one screams. That child can't handle the idea of losing the new noisemaker. It gives such pleasure to hear the noise. Instant gratification. Some things never change. Even adults struggle with silence. Being alone with myself can feel scary. There's nothing to distract me from facing the real me. My real fears. My real feelings.

So I cover it all up by binging on Facebook or getting lost in working so much that my head spins. It becomes an addictive pleasure to hear the noise I create, like a little one-year-old with a drum.

In the Third Commandment, God calls us to rest. "I want you to give me the drum, the Facebook login, the overtime schedule, the noise. Give them to me." **"In repentance and rest is your salvation, in quietness and trust is your strength"** (Isaiah 30:15).

God has so many promises, if we could only hear them without all the noise. So repent and press the mute button. Don't be afraid of rest. Your to-do list doesn't surprise or scare God. He can handle it, but first he wants you to pause for his reassuring Word.

Sometimes God takes the drum away so that we stop making noise and start listening to his promises.

Believers bring blessings

Pastor Mark Jeske

I wonder if Potiphar had any idea that his sudden burst of prosperity was due to the Israelite slave that he had brought into his household. He had bought the young man from traveling Ishmaelites at an Egyptian slave market—what a great move! The kid was bright, honest, reliable, and hardworking. **"From the time he put him in charge of his household and of all that he owned, the LORD blessed the household of the Egyptian because of Joseph"** (Genesis 39:5).

Potiphar was experiencing the "believer boost." The favor of God follows his children around—they bring it with them even when they work for heathen employers or governments (like Daniel). Potiphar hadn't seen the half of it. God had plans to bless the entire nation by elevating Joseph one day to the rank of vice pharaoh.

The prophet Jeremiah had told the few remaining Jews in Judah to yield to the Babylonian captivity, to settle down in the East, work hard, and to pray for the cities to which they had been relocated. If those cities then prospered, so would the Jews (and vice versa).

If I were running a business, even if I weren't a believer, I would prefer to hire Christians. Of all the workers in the labor pool, they are more likely to bring value to my business because of their greater integrity, work ethic, and the way in which they treat my customers.

Plus they bring the believer boost.

Under his wings

Linda Buxa

"Surely he will save you from the fowler's snare and from the deadly pestilence. He will cover you with his feathers, and under his wings you will find refuge; his faithfulness will be your shield and rampart" (Psalm 91:3,4).

In September 2017, Hurricane Irma began pummeling Florida with torrential rain and 107 mph winds. That's when another Irma—a Muscovy Duck named after the storm—gained international fame. (She even got her own Facebook page.) While many animals sought shelter, Irma sat unmoving on her nest of 13 eggs. She endured the first round of storms, remained on the nest even through the calm of the eye of the hurricane, and then weathered the second round. The next morning she was alive and uninjured, covered in broken branches and Spanish moss, but with all her eggs intact. It took another 24 hours before she willingly stood up to walk a bit. She protected her nest because that's what mama ducks do.

Because Jesus refused to abandon the cross and took the blows of God's wrath, he protected you with his blood and made you a child of God. Thanks to him, you have a Father who will never abandon you. As you weather the storms of this life—temptation, hurt, loneliness, accidents, divorce, financial struggles—God refuses to leave you. He promises that whatever you are going through, he is your shelter, your peace, your protection. Even after the storms have passed, he stays with you to watch over you.

Because that's what your Father does.

The memo from Jesus

Jason Nelson

Did you get the memo from Jesus? **"God opposes the proud but shows favor to the humble"** (James 4:6). Read any stretch of the gospels where Jesus is telling stories or making observations about his kingdom and you will get the message. "This is how it's going to be from now on. Arrogant is out. Humble is in."

The people around Jesus were typically in three categories: some kind of broken mess, the career fault-finders, and his on-looking students. Jesus sent the memo by ministering to outcasts no one else would go near. He was always showing favor to the humble. The faultfinders just found more fault with Jesus. And his disciples kept scratching their heads, trying to understand what it meant.

Jesus died making his point (see Luke 23). The Humble-Almighty was crucified between the defiant and the repentant. Curious people came to watch the spectacle. Leaders who should have behaved with somber dignity under the circumstances sneered at Jesus. Soldiers who only understood power mocked him: **"Some king you turned out to be."** A man who wouldn't admit he deserved to be on a cross taunted Jesus, **"Save yourself and us!"** (verse 39). A humble man accepted his cross and could see there was only one reason for the innocent man to be on his. He asked for mercy: **"Jesus, remember me"** (verse 42). Jesus showed favor to the humble and told him, **"Today you will be with me in paradise"** (verse 43).

I'm confident in this

Diana Kerr

I'm not an overly confident person. I'm not the type to assume that everything will go well or according to plan. I'm not confident that every person I elect into office will do what they say they will. I'm not confident my plane will always take off on time. I'm not confident I'll have the opportunity to live to see grandchildren someday. I'm not confident everyone I love will die peacefully and avoid the tragedy of illness or violence. I'm not confident I'll never run out of money. I'm not even confident I'll always fit in the same jeans I'm wearing now.

There's a lot I'm unsure of—big stuff and little stuff. You too? If you think about it, almost nothing is a sure thing. I'm really not trying to depress you; I've just learned I can't put my hope in anything on earth with full confidence. But I'm confident in this: 1) I'm a sinner who needs Jesus. 2) Jesus washes me clean. I have faith in those truths.

"Let us draw near to God with a sincere heart and with the full assurance that faith brings, having our hearts sprinkled to cleanse us from a guilty conscience and having our bodies washed with pure water. Let us hold unswervingly to the hope we profess, for he who promised is faithful" (Hebrews 10:22,23).

Don't lean on false hope in people or earthly stuff. On the other hand, hold *unswervingly* to the hope you have in your faithful God who makes you forgiven, clean, and pure.

Naaman's servant girl

Pastor Mark Jeske

You know, the Bible's main characters are almost all adults. Almost. But there are some amazing children in the narrative of God's plan of salvation. One of them is a little Israelite girl (name, alas, unknown) who had been taken captive by raiders from Aram (Syria). What of her parents? Were they killed? captives also? safe back home grieving over their lost daughter? We are not told.

What kind of mind-set would you expect the girl to have? Brooding over the injustice of her forced servitude? Seeking to sabotage operations in a military household? Crafting plans for an escape as soon as the opportunity presented itself? Plotting to assassinate the Syrian general as an act of patriotism? None of the above. Hearing that her master was plagued with leprosy, she offered information to *help* him: **"Now bands of raiders from Aram had gone out and had taken captive a young girl from Israel, and she served Naaman's wife. She said to her mistress, 'If only my master would see the prophet who is in Samaria! He would cure him of his leprosy'"** (2 Kings 5:2,3).

It could not have gone better for General Naaman the Leper. He met the great Israelite prophet Elisha, who put him in touch with Israel's God. He was healed completely, and in gratitude he exclaimed, **"Now I know that there is no God in all the world except in Israel"** (verse 15).

Amazing! Never say, "Only a child."

Satisfied and singing for joy

Pastor Daron Lindemann

Good employers believe that job satisfaction is not the responsibility of the worker but of the company. That company takes the initiative to create satisfied employees *before* it tries to satisfy customers. Southwest Airlines and Disney are two examples of such companies.

God wants believers who are satisfied. Content. So he took the initiative, satisfying the just punishment for our sins in the sacrifice of his Son, Jesus. God makes satisfied believers.

Can you agree that fulfillment in life depends not on abundance but attitude? To put that spiritually, contentment and peace are already yours by faith in God—not by achieving the perfect career, not from better health, not from finding the home of your dreams, not from more investments, not from a friend or spouse who meets every one of your needs.

"Satisfy us in the morning with your unfailing love, that we may sing for joy and be glad all our days" (Psalm 90:14). If you're not finding satisfaction in this life, it's because you can't. Nobody can. By looking for satisfaction in this life, people are setting their hopes in the wrong thing. It cannot deliver.

Put your hope, your dreams, your desire for full satisfaction in God and his love. He will satisfy you. He will never let you down. He is totally committed to your soul's satisfaction. That is where you'll find your joy. All. Your. Days.

Family feud

Pastor Mark Jeske

People have been using money to buy their way out of problems for centuries. No, millennia. Money can buy good attorneys, silence accusers and whistle-blowers, bribe officials, demand preferential treatment, hire "fixers," and pay off rivals.

Mothers and fathers might choose to define being good providers in their home as bringing in enough money. But a family has needs greater than great food and comfortable lodging: **"Better a dry crust with peace and quiet than a house full of feasting, with strife"** (Proverbs 17:1). A bitter spirit in your home can destroy all the joy. You know, you may have to work harder at family relationships than at your job.

Satan hates families because they represent everything that he will never have—trust, love, and security. All he knows is hatred, envy, fear, and grudges, and he will plant those evil seeds wherever he can. On a scale of 1 to 10, what is the strife level in your home right now? What is your plan to lower it?

Here are four steps: 1) Decide to be a servant leader and go first in taking responsibility for things you've said or done wrong. Apologize *without rationalizations.* Dare to model personal accountability especially in front of your children. 2) Ask questions and listen, rather than giving sermons justifying yourself. 3) Work your brain and come up with three things you appreciate about each family member and say them out loud in front of an audience.

4) Hold hands and pray together.

Josiah, the boy king
Pastor Mark Jeske

Was there ever a child champion like Josiah, who became king of Judah as a second grader? His father, an evil man, was assassinated after a short two-year reign, and suddenly Josiah's little head had to bear the weight of a big crown: **"Josiah was eight years old when he became king, and he reigned in Jerusalem thirty-one years"** (2 Chronicles 34:1).

This little guy had no normal childhood. He had to grow up terribly fast. And though he obviously had advisors and personal tutors, his youth did not hold him back from a reign of enormous and positive impact on God's people. At the age of high school sophomores, he began a serious quest to learn about the God of Israel. At an age when American college students are drinking a lot of beer, Josiah led a huge spiritual reformation in the country, tearing down the shrines and altars of Baal and Asherah that had been corrupting the Israelites for centuries. And at age 26 he led a capital campaign to rebuild the temple of the Lord, which had fallen into sad disrepair.

King Josiah's personal leadership, authority, and example brought about spiritual renewal throughout Israel, brought God's protection and blessings, and undoubtedly extended the time of Israel's independence. He was the last good king; the evil of his four short-lived successors brought about Israel's collapse.

Keep your eyes peeled for the talent that God has loaded into his child champions in your world.

Awareness test

Diana Kerr

Have you seen that "awareness test" on YouTube with millions of views? Two teams of basketball players shuffle around amongst each other in a small area, each team passing a basketball around. The two basketballs crisscross all over the screen as the teams, one dressed in white and the other in black, pass their team's ball to their teammates. The "awareness test" is to count the number of times the *white team* passes the ball, and only the white team.

It's a trick, though. As you intently focus on the white team's passes, you miss something shockingly obvious. Someone in a bear costume moonwalks right through the crowd of players. You don't notice until you watch it a second time.

We're more easily fooled than we like to admit. Satan knows this. He wants to keep your awareness off of what really counts. (I'm referring to Jesus, of course, not the moonwalking bear.) I was reminded of how Satan works as I read Exodus 5:9. Pharaoh mimicked Satan's strategy of distraction when he wanted to keep the Israelites from focusing on their desire to worship. **"Make the work harder for the people,"** Pharaoh said, **"so that they keep working and pay no attention to lies."**

Sometimes Satan's tricks aren't blatant temptation but cleverly hidden distraction. Let's pray for proper awareness. Lord, help us **"throw off everything that hinders and the sin that so easily entangles. And let us run with perseverance the race marked out for us, fixing our eyes on Jesus"** (Hebrews 12:1,2). Amen.

Respect is better than money

Pastor Mark Jeske

It is interesting to hear King Solomon talk about money. On the one hand, you'd think he was in no position to talk about how money isn't all that big a deal. He had an immense pile of it, more silver and gold than he could spend in his lifetime. First Kings chapter 10 says that in Jerusalem silver was as common as stones. You might wish that God would lay that kind of wealth on you; perhaps you think you could handle it.

Solomon's money did not bring him happiness. If you read what he wrote in Ecclesiastes, you will hear the sad voice of a man who had everything money could buy but no joy. So when he says that honor is better than money, you should listen. **"A kindhearted woman gains honor, but ruthless men gain only wealth"** (Proverbs 11:16). Honor and a good name are more powerful than money. If you lose your money, you can get more later. If you lose your reputation, you will probably never get it back.

Your money has to stay on earth when you die. There is no financial instrument available to humankind to enable us to take any wealth into heaven. It's temporary. But being a friend to people, helping people, showing kindness to people will bring you honor and friends that can last for all eternity.

Respect is more important than money. Friends are more important than money.

Revelation origination

Pastor Mark Jeske

Think how much of human life is a struggle for control. Investors struggle for control of a business . . . husbands and wives struggle over money, sex, and time . . . parents and children over the children's behaviors and attitudes . . . elected officials over legislation and campaign money.

People want to control their religious beliefs as well. It goes against the grain of the old sinner in us simply to accept and obey what has been handed down to us in the Bible. Our postmodern age despises absolute authority and is convinced that truth, morality, and ethics are relative. The only truth that matters is my truth. The only arbiter of my behavior is how I feel.

God is outraged when his clear messages to the people of the world he created are shunted aside in favor of beliefs that are more "comfortable" and "reasonable." **"How long will this continue in the hearts of these lying prophets, who prophesy the delusions of their own minds? They think the dreams they tell one another will make my people forget my name, just as their ancestors forgot my name through Baal worship"** (Jeremiah 23:26,27).

God punishes disobedience. Realize the great peril of consciously rejecting something you know to be true from the Bible. Let its timeless and universal truth be your truth. Let its words establish your value system, shape your attitude, and guide your behaviors. Let its magnificent love letter from God to you warm and inspire your heart to listen for his voice.

Words mean something
Pastor Daron Lindemann

Is there such a thing as a meaningless word? Words like *emergency* or *winner* command attention more than words like *asparagus*. But the word *asparagus* could answer the question, "Which of the items on this plate is laced with rat poison?" That gives it meaning.

Every word can, and does, have weight and effect. Words make a difference. Words do something. Words often sinfully hurt others. Sarcasm. Harsh criticism. Gossip. Angry arguing. And we don't have the power to take our words back. As a matter of fact, we don't even have the power on our own to change how we speak. We need healing.

First Peter 2:23,24 talks about the enemies of Jesus: **"When they hurled their insults at him, he did not retaliate; when he suffered, he made no threats. Instead, he entrusted himself to him who judges justly. 'He himself bore our sins' in his body on the cross, so that we might die to sins and live for righteousness; 'by his wounds you have been healed.'"**

Because Jesus bore your words of sin, you are healed. You know God's language. Like Texans can detect a Wisconsin accent that gives away a person's identity, people will be able to tell that your identity is found in Jesus. You love him and his words.

With a heart filled by the very words of God himself, your Jesus-like words are going to make a difference. They will change hearts. As much as Jesus has changed yours.

Truth will triumph

Jason Nelson

What happens in Vegas might stay in Vegas, but everywhere else I think the truth will come out. It is a lesson of history. God raises up people who make sure truth is ultimately told. When the truth is revealed, even under the most difficult circumstances, an attribute of God is revealed. Jesus said, **"I am . . . the truth"** (John 14:6). There is truth because there is a God.

Sometimes the truth hurts, but we can handle it. I learned that lesson from my father. He took a love and logic approach to parenting long before Foster Cline and Jim Fay made it popular. Discipline in our house always revolved around a long painful discussion. My dad said, "I won't punish you if you tell me the truth." He meant it and generally kept his promise. But there were always consequences for lying to him. He had a great nose for sniffing out a lie and getting at the truth. I am very grateful he took time to notch the power of truth into my conscience.

The thing that troubles me most about our public discourse is blatant disregard for truth. People aren't allowed to operate with "alternative facts." People aren't allowed to manipulate information to distort reality. People aren't allowed to lie. Didn't they have dads who taught them that? My dad taught me that truth will triumph and that we have every right to expect to hear it because there is a God.

Divine dithering
Pastor Mark Jeske

The Kingdom of Judah had finally collapsed, collapsed in every way—economically, militarily, socially, politically. The few surviving army officers and inhabitants of Jerusalem took flight and begged the prophet Jeremiah for God's guidance: **"'Pray that the Lord your God will tell us where we should go and what we should do.' 'I have heard you,' replied Jeremiah the prophet. 'I will certainly pray to the Lord your God as you have requested.' . . . Ten days later the word of the Lord came to Jeremiah"** (Jeremiah 42:3,4,7).

Those may have been the longest ten days of their lives. They were terrified that the Babylonians would find and destroy them. What on earth took God so long to give an answer? What could explain his dithering? Does God get confused? Is he that indecisive? Was he unaware of the vulnerability of that little flock of believers?

Have you ever had to wait for an answer to urgent prayer? Ten days? A month? A year? Ten years? Of course God hears his children. Of course he cares. Of course he has a plan, and that plan may need some time to unfold. His agenda for our personal development matters more to him than making our lives more comfortable. God told the Israelites not to fear the king of Babylon. Why? **"For I am with you and will save you"** (Jeremiah 42:11).

When he waits to act and answer, it's because he's waiting for the perfect moment.

Because God said so

Diana Kerr

"Because I said so." Were you ever on the receiving end of that statement as a kid? Your dad asked you to do something, you responded with "But *why*?," and he replied, "Because I said so." Boom. End of discussion.

It's such an unsatisfactory answer, isn't it? We all want to understand the reasoning behind something. "Because I said so" requires us to blindly obey without an explanation.

The widow in 1 Kings inspires me with her unquestioning obedience to her heavenly Father. The quick synopsis is that Elijah asked her for food, which God had directed her to supply him, but she only had enough food left for one meal. She and her son were literally starving to death. However, Elijah assured her they wouldn't run out of food.

What would you do in this situation? I'd probably wonder, "Why me? Why not choose someone else who has the resources available? How will I not run out of food?" But her obedience was incredible. **"She went away and did as Elijah had told her"** (1 Kings 17:15).

She trusted God with the details. She placed obedience above fear of uncertainty.

God was good on his word. **"So there was food every day for Elijah and for the woman and her family. For the jar of flour was not used up and the jug of oil did not run dry, in keeping with the word of the LORD spoken by Elijah"** (verses 15,16).

Where the separation ends

Jason Nelson

In the Bible, God told us government and the church are both his agents. They are the only institutions he ordained to exist. He permits us to have outlet malls and nice restaurants, but he didn't ordain them. He gave church and state distinct purposes. Jesus honored that distinction when he said, **"Therefore render to Caesar the things that are Caesar's, and to God the things that are God's"** (Matthew 22:21 ESV). Thomas Jefferson said the "establishment clause" in the First Amendment was there to "erect a wall of separation between church and state." The Supreme Court has consistently upheld that principle. We are twice blessed in America.

But church and state have the same constituencies—us. And when they get all up in each other's business, both tend to suffer. It is disrespectful to God when Christian people bash government as an inherently bad thing. It is disrespectful to God if government makes being a Christian more difficult than it already is.

The place for church and state to merge is in the conscience of a citizen. In good conscience, we can speak with a strong voice and vigorously influence the actions of government so they align with Christian morality. And in good conscience, we can recognize that government must pursue order that is good for all citizens. In good conscience, we may have to live with policies necessary for society that might make us a little uncomfortable as Christians.

Super seniors: Abraham
Pastor Mark Jeske

The older I get, the more "senior moments" I have. You know what those are, don't you? Where you try to pull up a name or place from your memory but there's nothing in your head? At first you get angry with yourself, but as time goes on you just think less of yourself. Everybody knows that the older you get, the more wrinkly and saggy your skin gets, your hair thins out, your eyesight dims, and your hearing fades. In other words, seniors should just be quiet and get out of the way. Right?

Wrong! God strenuously disagrees. He used some super seniors to advance his kingdom in some significant ways. When he saw how spiritually bankrupt and rebellious the generations after the great flood had become, he decided to build a nation of believers out of one couple. But the job was too important for young people. He needed seniors. **"The Lord had said to Abram, 'Go from your country, your people and your father's household to the land I will show you'"** (Genesis 12:1).

Abraham was 75 and Sarah 65 when they were directed to leave their comfortable home and way of life and head to Canaan hundreds of miles away. Age 75! Abraham had been getting AARP mailings for 25 years already, and God had him and Sarah start over in life. God's choice was perfect. They accomplished their mission. Abraham finally became a father at age 99.

We call him the father of believers.

Super seniors: Anna

Pastor Mark Jeske

You know, don't you, which adjective is used most often with *old lady*? Yep—*little*, as in *little old lady.* Somehow small size seems to imply small importance, especially among the elderly. Anna might have been in her mid-80s, but she was chosen for a huge role.

Mary and Joseph had brought the baby Jesus to the temple to fulfill the Old Testament law of Presentation to the Lord. God decided at that moment that he needed a prophet to explain the significance of the God-man, the world's Savior. In fact, he knew he needed one of his best people.

He needed a super senior, and she was right there at her post. **"There was also a prophet, Anna, the daughter of Penuel, of the tribe of Asher. She was very old; she had lived with her husband seven years after her marriage, and then was a widow until she was eighty-four. She never left the temple but worshiped night and day, fasting and praying. Coming up to them at that very moment, she gave thanks to God and spoke about the child to all who were looking forward to the redemption of Jerusalem"** (Luke 2:36-38).

Being a widow had not turned Anna bitter and reclusive. She was a spiritual warrior for God's people, worshiping, praying, and fasting. She was given the gift of seeing *and recognizing* the Messiah in person.

And then this super senior gave others the gift she had received.

june 28

Super seniors: Daniel
Pastor Mark Jeske

When I was a young man, I heard a pastor in his 60s speaking longingly of retirement. I chided him for even thinking about getting out of the game. He just smiled at me and said, "You'll understand."

Somebody forgot to tell the statesman and prophet Daniel that he could have moved to Florida in his 60s. God had decided that he needed a super senior working for him at the top levels of government to look out for the interests of the Israelite people in captivity. Daniel was still working for the Babylonian, and then Persian, governments as an imperial administrator, overseeing one-third of the territorial governors, *in his mid-80s!*

A crisis erupted. Envious Persian governors who chafed at being accountable to Daniel flattered the Persian king into demanding divine worship for himself and pronouncing the death penalty on dissenters. Daniel was busted. **"So the king gave the order, and they brought Daniel and threw him into the lions' den. The king said to Daniel, 'May your God, whom you serve continually, rescue you!'"** (Daniel 6:16).

Can you imagine an 85-year-old man spending the night in a pit with starving lions? God shut the lions' mouths and spared this amazing senior for even more significant work.

Seniors, be ready for God's opportunities. God probably doesn't need any more lion pit heroes, but your age is absolutely no hindrance for God's ability to use your witness.

Super seniors: John
Pastor Mark Jeske

You'd think most 90-year-olds would envision a pleasant and secure life in a retirement community, doing a little gardening, talking with friends, reading some favorite books, and enjoying visits from the grandchildren. What does not sound like fun is being forced to live in exile on an island from which you cannot escape.

When God needed a witness to a series of visions of what lay ahead for the believers, he selected one of his super seniors, the aged, 90+-year-old apostle John. **"I, John, your brother and companion in the suffering and kingdom and patient endurance that are ours in Jesus, was on the island of Patmos because of the word of God and the testimony of Jesus"** (Revelation 1:9). Numerous times John was given looks into the future. What he saw was terrifying—assaults on the believers by Satan and his demons from hell, assisted by willing human helpers on earth. He saw terrible suffering and God's angry judgments and punishments.

But he saw also the triumphant Christ, the Lamb of God who had taken away the sin of the world. He saw also the hosts of angels who protect the saints. And he was able to see the endgame—all the believers of all ages gathered around the throne of God in worship. All was serenity, beauty, and perfect peace.

John's gift to you is the record of his revelations. Why don't you have a look and see what's in there?

june 30

Super seniors: Moses

Pastor Mark Jeske

When God intervenes in human history and wants to show that things are not happening by accident, he chooses the number 40. He gave Moses 40 years of education and leadership training in Egypt's royal courts, and then God gave him 40 years of humility therapy tending sheep for his father-in-law in the wilderness. The last 40 show one of God's super seniors at work. Most people dream of leisurely retirement activities in those senior years. Moses was governor of the entire Israelite nation for those extremely stressful four decades. **"Moses was a hundred and twenty years old when he died, yet his eyes were not weak nor his strength gone"** (Deuteronomy 34:7).

Moses' maturity and people sense made him a great leader. Listening and following God's advice made him even better. Though he had grown up in Pharaoh's palace, his last four decades were spent in a tent.

But he held the nation together, occasionally assisted by divine miracles. And it was during those years that the oral transmission of the Word of God was set down on paper (probably papyrus) for the first time. Moses authored the matchless first five books of the Bible. What a debt we owe him! What a great example of senior service he provides. Inspired by his work, how can we not answer God's call to work even if it comes near the end of our lives?

Now if only God would give us physical strength and clear eyesight till we're 120 . . .

july

Let everyone be subject to the governing authorities, for there is no authority except that which God has established. The authorities that exist have been established by God.

Romans 13:1

By faith, not by sight

Pastor Mark Jeske

We all have to navigate our way through life, trying to avoid the rocks and reefs that would cause us to shipwreck. Of all the fears that dog us, however, the big one behind them all is the fear of dying and death. We talk to *mourners* at funerals about their *loss* and say how *sorry* we are.

The resurrection of Jesus turns that narrative inside out. Only Jesus can change dread to joyful anticipation, turn weeping into smiling, and turn grief into hope. Only Jesus can help us look past the certain signs of defeat—the cold, still body; casket; vault; headstone—and see victory.

The apostle Paul loved his life and spent himself trying to tell everyone he met about the Savior. He loved the congregations he founded and exhausted himself in his travels trying to visit them all. But he knew that his real life was still coming, and he was anxious with anticipation of the glory to come: **"Therefore we are always confident and know that as long as we are at home in the body we are away from the Lord. For we live by faith, not by sight"** (2 Corinthians 5:6,7).

Faith in Christ sustains us in all our times of loss and suffering. As we age, things are taken away from us—friends who pass away, our youth, energy, strength, our mobility, memory, hair, hearing, and clarity of eyesight—but those losses only mark the approaching reunion with our Creator and Redeemer.

The best is yet to come.

Look back

Pastor Mike Novotny

When my eldest daughter popped into this world, everything was different. Marriage was different. Work was different. Sleep was WAY different. Life was different.

Different can be hard and not just for parents of newborns. It's hard when Dad takes a new job and you move to a new school. It's hard when you divorce and start dating again in your 40s. It's hard when your company is transitioning to a new team with a new vision and a new market. And different is tough for our routine-loving hearts.

I wonder how Joshua felt. The book named after him begins, **"After the death of Moses the servant of the Lord, the Lord said to Joshua . . ."** (1:1). After over 40 years of being Joshua's mentor, Moses was dead. After spending decades in the wilderness following Moses, God's people were about to follow Joshua into the Promised Land.

So what did Joshua do? He looked back. He looked back at God's saving love during the exodus. He looked back at God's promises kept in the wilderness. Joshua couldn't look ahead to the future, but he could look back to the past.

Maybe that's what you need to do too. Look back and fix your eyes on Jesus. See his love and power at the cross. Hear his triumphant cry that your sin is finished. Let his departing words echo in your ears: **"Surely I will be with you always"** (Matthew 28:20). Because when life is different, our hearts need the One who is the same—yesterday, today, and forever. Once you look back, you'll be ready to look forward to the different days you are facing.

One perfect place
Sarah Habben

At the end of August 2017, my family moved from Canada to the Caribbean. Near and dear ones (and our packing company) looked on with barely concealed envy.

We're a few months in now, and it is apparent that this earthly paradise has its share of annoyances. Potholes instead of black ice. Mildew instead of snow. Bites to scratch instead of windshields to scrape. Long hours of queuing in place of frenzied multitasking.

No matter what destination is stamped on your ticket, you will never find paradise on earth. When Eve and Adam chose sin over obedience, perfection grew potholes. Sin's mildew spread through God's creation, through our bodies, and our attitudes. It is cause for dismay, for sorrow—but not for hopelessness. In faith, by the Spirit, we repent. We fix our eyes on Jesus, who paid the price of our sin. We loosen our grip on the world. We join the queue of ancient believers who **"did not receive the things promised; they only saw them and welcomed them from a distance, admitting that they were foreigners and strangers on earth. . . . They were longing for a better country—a heavenly one. Therefore God is not ashamed to be called their God, for he has prepared a city for them"** (Hebrews 11:13,16).

Today will disappoint. But rather than complain, Lord, help me confess: I am but a stranger here; heaven is my home.

And what a perfect place it is.

Dependence day

Pastor Mark Jeske

In the United States, the Fourth of July is a national holiday. It commemorates the date on which the Continental Congress adopted Mr. Jefferson's draft of a declaration of independence from England. On that date, arguably more than any other, the 13 English colonies ceased to be colonies. And yet the new nation owed an enormous debt to the motherland. Its language, culture, education models, business enterprises, and widespread Christian faith had been planted in the New World by the English.

The New Testament talks a lot about our freedom in Christ. Indeed we are free—free from the curse and condemnation of our sin, free from its lingering guilt, free from Satan's hammerlock on our souls, free from the fear of death and hell, free to follow Christ. But paradoxically we are not independent beings.

We are still totally *dependent* on our Creator, Savior, and Sanctifier: **"In him we live and move and have our being"** (Acts 17:28), said St. Paul to the curious and learned Greeks on Mars Hill in Athens. Jesus told his disciples only hours before he died that he was like a vine and they the branches. Cut off from him, they would be dead and dry branches, fit only for firewood. Our physical universe, our divine salvation, and our eternal destiny are still *completely* in God's hands.

May I suggest to you today, as you think and talk about freedom and independence, that you give a little thought to how dependent we are on our God?

Be with him

Jason Nelson

There is nothing more important in relationships than spending time together. Too much time apart eventually dissolves closeness because relationships aren't frozen at the peak of perfection. They can get stale after too much time apart. People don't just pick up where they left off. That's a myth. People always pick up right where they are.

Perhaps you feel distant from God. Maybe you were close once but not anymore. Maybe you never were that close. But if you miss him in your life, you can pick up right where you are. There's no need to try to make up for lost time because he has kept in touch with you. You don't have to fill him in or catch him up. You don't need to fear awkward moments of becoming reacquainted. The lapses are in your time spent with him, not in his time spent with you. He did what he promised: **"I am with you always, to the very end of the age"** (Matthew 28:20).

So go ahead and be with him. Be with him and find a great fellowship of Christians to be a part of. You don't owe anyone any explanations about where you've been. Be with him and listen to him speak to you in the Bible. Be with him and believe his Son, Jesus, laid down his life for you. You are forgiven. You can be with him like you never were apart because he has always been with you.

Pray for leaders
Pastor Mark Jeske

You know the old saying about what drives the value of real estate, right? Location, location, location. Do you know what drives the growth of congregations and parachurch ministries? Leadership, leadership, leadership. Only God and his mighty Word can turn an unbeliever into a believer. But God is determined to wait for us to gather a crowd, proclaim that powerful Word, and shepherd the flock.

It pained Jesus to see what happened to the flock when the spiritual leadership was poor or nonexistent: **"When he saw the crowds, he had compassion on them, because they were harassed and helpless, like sheep without a shepherd. Then he said to his disciples, 'The harvest is plentiful but the workers are few. Ask the Lord of the harvest, therefore, to send out workers into his harvest field'"** (Matthew 9:36-38). Jesus did his part—he recruited and trained a dozen men, 11 of whom graduated from his training course and led the mission to bring the gospel to the world.

Leadership is more desperately needed today than ever. The church needs leaders who are articulate, passionate, loving, fearless, creative, engaging, and biblically grounded. Pray for leaders!

But don't just pray. Act! Recruit young people to consider full-time ministry careers. Give generously to schools and seminaries to train them. Speak highly of church leaders whenever you can in order to make their position something a young person might aspire to.

And then pray some more.

Outrageous gospel

Pastor Mark Jeske

If you want your financial situation improved, waiting around for someone else to give you a ton of money just isn't a very good strategy. Ain't likely. It's up to *you* to do something. You have to *make* things happen—get a promotion, get a job that pays more, take a second job, or sell some possessions for the cash.

The DIY mind-set pervades the religious world too. Every man-made religious philosophy is based on rewards promised to people who either perform well according to the religion's rules, who observe the religion's rituals, or who buy the deity's favor with their contributions and gifts.

The Christian faith is unique in that it reveals the portrait of a God who dares to give it away. **"Now to the one who works, wages are not credited as a gift but as an obligation. However, to the one who does not work but trusts God who justifies the ungodly, their faith is credited as righteousness"** (Romans 4:4,5). Did your jaw drop at that outrageous concept? God *justifies the ungodly*! That does not mean that God rewards disobedience to his will. What he does mean is that he loves people so much that he sent his Son to a bloody cross in order to *give* people the righteousness they could never earn.

This means that you can live your life out of gratitude to God instead of nervously trying to earn his favor. This means that the central message of your congregation must always be grace, not the demands of the law.

Big ideas

Jason Nelson

Good teachers motivate students with big ideas. They take Bloom's Taxonomy and its learning domains to heart and usher their students to higher-order thinking as quickly as possible. They trust their students will gather basic knowledge on the journey. Boring teachers lose students by always mucking around in low-level recall of facts and terms. But today, the details and definitions are one click away. Even a highly technical skill like writing computer code is only meaningful if it serves a big idea like helping people learn. Students show they have learned by coming up with big ideas of their own.

This was the constant rub between Rabbi Jesus and the boring rabbis. The boring rabbis always wanted to engage Jesus in an intellectual duel at the lowest levels. "Is it legal for your students to shuck corn on the Sabbath?" Jesus responded with a big idea: **"'I desire mercy, not sacrifice.' . . . For the Son of Man is Lord of the Sabbath"** (Matthew 12:7,8). Jesus is as big as it gets. He is the Lord of everything and the embodiment of God's love for people who will never fully grasp it. But every thought we have that is captive to that idea will be better for it.

After I gave an assignment to a college class, a modest young man asked me, "When we write for you, do we have to use lots of big words?" I told him, "I don't care about the size of your words. I care about the size of your ideas." Thank you, Jesus.

Different parts

Pastor Mike Novotny

If some wonderful, elderly Mexican women ever offer you a tamale, make sure you remove the corn husk before your first bite. One day, years ago, I chomped into an unchewable husk, and the ladies from my English class roared with laughter. In my defense, I was a gringo from Wisconsin who was uninformed about the details of Mexican cuisine.

Being uninformed can be dangerous. It's true with Mexican tamales. And it's true with Christians. That's what Paul wrote to the Corinthians—**"Now about the gifts of the Spirit, brothers and sisters, I do not want you to be uninformed"** (1 Corinthians 12:1). Paul wanted to inform his friends about the unique ways that the Holy Spirit wires and equips us to glorify God. Without Paul's help, they would fall into that obsessive comparison trap where some smugly felt superior and others felt completely unnecessary.

God doesn't want you to be uninformed either. When you meet Christians who are different in impressive ways (like natural evangelists) and those who are different in frustrating ways (like the never-stops-talking woman at Bible study), you need to be informed. You need to remember that different gifts and different personalities come from God. We are one body in Christ, but we are, by divine design, different parts.

After all, the Father who made you made them. The Son who saved you saved them. The Spirit who guides you guides them. There. Now you're ready for church. Just make sure to unwrap any potluck tamales.

Bitter setbacks
Pastor Mark Jeske

History when written by amateurs can always be made to look inevitable. Earnest college essays often include phrases like "the North was destined to triumph," when in fact nothing of the sort is true. People's choices do matter. Our heroes and champions didn't just sweep through their agendas as all opposition melted before them. In shock after the rebels' crushing victory at Fredericksburg, President Lincoln groaned, "If there is a place worse than hell, I am in it."

Even the great apostles and evangelists of the biblical era experienced faith-shaking, bitter setbacks: **"Alexander the metalworker did me a great deal of harm. The Lord will repay him for what he has done. You too should be on your guard against him, because he strongly opposed our message"** (2 Timothy 4:14,15). Intriguingly enough, God didn't think we needed to know about that episode and didn't include it in the book of Acts. It was enough to know that even the great St. Paul was allowed to be pushed backward at times.

Does that terrify you or bring you some degree of comfort? Have you had stretches of your life when you felt as though you were just treading water? making absolutely no headway? desperate just to survive? Those miserable times are no proof of God's neglect. In his masterful strategic plans, you arriving in heaven is *always* the outcome.

God allows bitter setbacks only to keep us close to him, depending on his power and Word, and hungry for heaven.

The Spirit gives spiritual life

Pastor Mark Jeske

You probably have some stressful memories of being dumped somewhere and left to fend for yourself. Maybe your parents pushed you into some kind of new and unknown activity and "abandoned" you to die of fear and embarrassment. Maybe your boss gave you a job for which you didn't have either skills, experience, or interest. But do you ever feel all alone to struggle with the pressures and threats in your *spiritual* life?

When you became a believer, God immediately began to make some changes in your capabilities and resources. You do not have to strain to win his approval all by yourself, confused and dispirited. You do not have to wrestle with Satan alone: **"If the Spirit of him who raised Jesus from the dead is living in you, he who raised Christ from the dead will also give life to your mortal bodies because of his Spirit who lives in you"** (Romans 8:11).

You came to faith because the Spirit of the Lord, working through Word and Baptism, came to live in your mind and heart. Imagine that! You are actually a walking church; your God dwells inside you. The living Spirit makes you spiritually alive, gives you confidence of your forgiveness, and guarantees your immortality. You will rise from the dead just like Jesus, your Savior.

The Spirit will help you find answers for your dilemmas in his Word, give you strength for your wobbly backbone, and shed light on your path. Rejoice!

God makes our sufferings work for us

Pastor Mark Jeske

Nobody escapes suffering. We are all hurting to some degree right now . . . some of us are in terrible pain. But do you know what's even worse? It's suspecting that all this hardship is *in vain,* that it serves no good purpose.

You may be dragging a load of student debt, but at least you have a degree. You may hate your job, but at least you're bringing in a paycheck. You may be bedridden, convalescing from surgery, but at least you got it done and hope to improve. But what if the pain is just pain?

St. Paul knew a lot more about suffering than I ever will, and he celebrated the amazing promise of God that *none of his life pain was wasted*: **"We do not want you to be uninformed, brothers and sisters, about the troubles we experienced in the province of Asia. We were under great pressure, far beyond our ability to endure, so that we despaired of life itself. Indeed, we felt we had received the sentence of death. But this happened that we might not rely on ourselves but on God, who raises the dead"** (2 Corinthians 1:8,9).

Maybe God uses our suffering to make positive changes in us. That's a win. Maybe our sufferings give us a platform from which to connect somebody else with Jesus. That's a win. Maybe our pain helps us prepare to let go of this broken and tired world and lift up our eyes to heaven.

That's a win.

Live like redwoods

Linda Buxa

When we lived in California, we visited the redwoods. What astonished us is that some of these trees started growing possibly when Jesus walked the earth. With good reason, the enormous ones get all the attention—and everyone takes photos.

However, what impressed me more are the groves of newer trees. These tiny saplings often grow so close together that their bases merge, and eventually they grow into one tree. If the saplings are a little farther away, they may not be absorbed into one, but they still become interconnected. Though the roots are only a few feet deep, they extend up to 100 feet from the trunk, intertwining and giving each other the strength to withstand high winds and strong storms.

The apostle Paul prayed for believers to be like the redwoods. As the Word is planted in you and you grow up in your faith, you become connected by that faith to the people around you. You fuse together. Then, when storms come, you are so interconnected that you can withstand them because others are lending you their strength.

"We will grow to become in every respect the mature body of him who is the head, that is, Christ. From him the whole body, joined and held together by every supporting ligament, grows and builds itself up in love, as each part does its work" (Ephesians 4:15,16).

A very great reward

Sarah Habben

Once I made the short list in a nationwide writing competition (Canada is a relatively small nation). I won $1,000 and was interviewed by my local paper and radio station. The money got invested. The interviews were awkward. A handful of years later, I'm the only one who remembers what I wrote.

What's your biggest reward? A race medal? A work bonus? How long did the glow of your reward last?

God told Abraham in a vision: **"Do not be afraid, Abram. I am . . . your very great reward"** (Genesis 15:1). I love that phrase. God didn't just say he was Abraham's reward. He didn't even say that he was his *great* reward. He said that he was Abraham's *very* great reward.

God doesn't deal in minimums. It wasn't enough for God to send Jesus to forgive our sins. He also sent Jesus to give us an eternal life of happiness. To be clear, we didn't *earn* this very great reward. No hours spent laboring, sweating, or practicing *could* earn this reward, because sin disqualifies us. (Even the kind word I offered this week was partly prompted because it made me feel good about *me*.)

God's reward is a reward of *grace*, offered to a world of losers and haters. It's a reward won by Jesus and presented to us, his brothers and sisters, through Baptism. It's a reward that never gets passé.

Are you feeling underappreciated today? overlooked? ignored? Stop dealing in minimums. Let your actions be motivated by this gleaming truth: God himself is your very great reward.

A singular gift

Jason Nelson

God's gifts come in multiples. Even though one particular star is really important to us, a clear night reveals God made too many to count. Who really knows what's orbiting the other ones? A good tree doesn't produce just one piece of fruit. It produces many. And Jesus said if it doesn't produce much fruit, it should be cut down and thrown into the fire. I challenge you to go on a holy scavenger hunt and come up with something God made that is just one of a kind. Even things like people and potatoes that are unique in some way are not singular.

Except Jesus. He was the only begotten. He had to be. There couldn't be multiple saviors. There couldn't be variations of God's redemptive theme. God only conceived of one way to save all the different kinds of people he dearly loves. There is only one truth and one life. **"This is how God showed his love among us: He sent his one and only Son into the world that we might live through him"** (1 John 4:9).

Here is another challenge for you. Read through the gospel of John and the epistles of John. Get a marker out and underline every passage that refers to the "onlyness" of Jesus. Then pay very close attention to what that singular gift means for you and me. Because Jesus was the only begotten, we are the many sons and daughters of the living God.

Still at risk
Pastor Mark Jeske

How different Israelite society was 3,400 years ago! The conquest of Canaan had just begun; most of the people had a subsistence lifestyle and owned no property or home.

How different and yet how much the same. There will always be people whose well-being and lives are at risk, people who need the help of others to survive. **"At the end of every three years, bring all the tithes of that year's produce and store it in your towns, so that the Levites (who have no allotment or inheritance of their own) and the foreigners, the fatherless and the widows who live in your towns may come and eat and be satisfied, and so that the Lord your God may bless you in all the work of your hands"** (Deuteronomy 14:28,29).

Moses' words still resonate. Like the Levites, church workers today have a certain vulnerability. They don't unionize, never go on strike, and don't argue much over salary. Foreigners, whether documented or not, are always taken advantage of by earlier arrivals. Widows have more protections today but deserve special consideration by their churches. And how is fatherlessness any less a curse today than it ever was? It is an epidemic and getting worse. A congregation can be a rich source of role models, coaches, and mentors to help boys and girls without dads in their lives.

God loves it when people help people. It makes him want to turn on the resources faucet for the helpers.

Not a coincidence

Pastor Mark Jeske

God is subtle, isn't he? He's so quiet that some people can go through their entire lives and not notice his work at all. They attribute all their wealth and successes and fame and possessions to their own ability, initiative, and hard work. And maybe some luck and coincidence.

The indwelling of the Holy Spirit in our minds helps us begin to notice God's cause and effect. God is *engaged* in our lives, and he works to make them better: **"He lifted me out of the slimy pit, out of the mud and mire; he set my feet on a rock and gave me a firm place to stand. He put a new song in my mouth, a hymn of praise to our God. Many will see and fear the** Lord **and put their trust in him"** (Psalm 40:2,3).

The Bible calls these divine interventions "blessings." A blessing is a gift that God gives because he loves us, not wages we've worked for. And notice the two important outcomes: Number one is the new song coming from our mouths. Every time we become aware of God's work, we can send up some praise, and it's *new* because it's praise for a new thing. Number two is the impact that our words and prayers of thanks and new songs have on other people.

People who are truly grateful for blessings usually make some noise, and their friends and family who are not in God's immediate family may decide that they want what you have—an engaged heavenly Father.

No excuses

Pastor Mark Jeske

Children don't have to be coached to know how to attempt to weasel out of responsibility for their misdeeds. They figure out denial ("Not me"), blaming ("It was her!"), playing dumb ("Huh?"), and pleading ignorance ("I dunno").

Parents see right through those dodges. And so does God. On the day of judgment, he will get a lot of arguing, but his decisions will all be final. Nobody will be able to shout at him that he or she didn't know: **"The wrath of God is being revealed from heaven against all the godlessness and wickedness of people, who suppress the truth by their wickedness, since what may be known about God is plain to them, because God has made it plain to them. For since the creation of the world God's invisible qualities—his eternal power and divine nature—have been clearly seen, being understood from what has been made, so that people are without excuse"** (Romans 1:18-20).

Even people who have refused to go to church and refused to crack a Bible know that they are in someone else's world. The brilliance of the design and execution of the universe, its stunning billions of galaxies of stars, wild array of vegetation, astoundingly diverse animal world, and complex miracles of human beings tell anyone with an open mind that there is a Creator. The consciences that exist in every human being also give testimony to our *accountability* to that Creator.

"I didn't know" isn't going to work on judgment day.

Where are you, Lord?

Pastor Mark Jeske

How you can you live with the disconnect?

You know what I mean—the gap between what God's Word promises you and what you see in your world. You hear that God always takes care of his children, that the angels surround the believers to prevent harm, that there will be divine justice, and that evildoers will not get away with their crimes. That's what you hear. But what you *see* is that believers suffer some terrible disasters.

What you see also is that skeptics and scoffers seem to be doing even better than believers because they are not "handicapped" by God's rules of love, fairness, integrity, and personal morality. The prophet Jeremiah ground his teeth at the disconnect: **"You are always righteous, Lord, when I bring a case before you. Yet I would speak with you about your justice: Why does the way of the wicked prosper? Why do all the faithless live at ease?"** (Jeremiah 12:1).

Why do swindlers seem to get to enjoy their millions? Why do so many Christians live in poverty? You know, many of the psalms and prophecies in Scripture do not end with a tidy solution where God simply fixes everything. Sometimes the dilemma is left hanging. In our broken world, there still is much injustice as we wait for Jesus Christ's return.

In desperation Jeremiah cried out to God for relief. You know, maybe that's exactly the response God wanted.

Living with loss: Your wealth
Pastor Mark Jeske

Nobody is immune from financial disaster. It can happen in so many ways—expensive health catastrophe, protracted loss of income to the family breadwinner, bad investments, war, uninsured natural catastrophe like flooding or fire, or collapse of the family business. Sometimes everybody in the whole country suffers financial loss through recession and depression.

The Lord never promised wealth and ease to all his children, but he did promise daily bread. People who are struggling financially really mean it when they pray the Lord's Prayer. They should also not torment themselves that they are being punished by God. An Old Testament saint named Job suffered terrible losses of family, wealth, and health, and his unhelpful friends constantly tried to find the cause in some hidden evils in Job's life: **"Should not your piety be your confidence and your blameless ways your hope?"** (Job 4:6).

No, our hope is not in our blameless ways. Our hope is in the mercy, kindness, power, and love of our God. Our hope is in the blameless ways of Christ our Savior. Forgiven of our sins, we no longer tremble in fear over the coming judgment, and we do not have to interpret our hardships as proofs of God's anger.

In our times of severe financial stress, we will count on God's providing. We will work very hard to rebuild, take our needs to him in prayer, and open our eyes to watch for his help.

All the wondering isn't done

Jason Nelson

I wonder what ethical challenges or unintended consequences may come from artificial intelligence and machines that learn. They are behind innovations like driverless cars, Alexa and Watson, better product distribution, and more efficient capital markets. If past is prologue, we will be okay. There will be some fussing and fuming. Some old guy will say something like, "If God intended men to fly, he would have given us wings." And then we will see that the blessings outweigh the risks. The fact is that machines can do some things better than people.

Except wonder. So far that is a distinctively human capacity. Modern marvels exist because people wondered about them. The Christian community has a contribution to make. We can amaze the human spirit with the accomplishments of God and merits of Jesus in a world we have never seen before. All the moral guidance people need hasn't been given, all the uplifting hymns haven't been written, and all the breathtaking art isn't already in cathedrals.

We have seen God's wonders in the making. The Bible tells us more are to come. **"Many, LORD my God, are the wonders you have done, the things you planned for us. None can compare with you"** (Psalm 40:5). God is incomparable. What more can we do to help other people believe he is wonderful too?

Comm-union
Pastor Mike Novotny

Would you think I was creepy if I told you that I like to watch people during Communion? Okay, I know that sounds slightly stalkerish, but I do. And I have no plans to stop.

Because the people who come forward during Communion are so different. Tall and short. Black and white. Male and female. Young and old. Introverts and extroverts. Musicians and accountants. The cautious and the risk-takers. The routine lovers and the free spirits. The big, confident personalities and the big, compassionate hearts.

Yet they all come to Communion for the same reason: **"For all have sinned and fall short of the glory of God"** (Romans 3:23). And they all come to Communion eager for the same gift: **"This is my blood of the covenant, which is poured out for many for the forgiveness of sins"** (Matthew 26:28). They all leave with the same Spirit on the same mission for the same purpose. Same bread, same wine, same body, same blood, same God, same grace.

There they stand side by side, these radically different people. And I watch them. I marvel at the artistry of our Creator, who loves different shapes and sizes and colors. As they return to their seats, I cannot help but smile. Because I realize why they call it Comm-union.

Complaining talk

Pastor Mark Jeske

We all know the saying, "I'd complain, but nobody wants to hear it." We all nod. We agree in theory. Who wants to hear somebody else's boring litany of frustrations and failures? Gack! Conversational buzzkill. So why do we keep doing it?

I know why I complain. It helps me blame other things or other people for the breakdowns in my life (of course they aren't my fault). Complaining makes me look like a victim instead of a perp. Complaining lets me off the hook for responsibility for failure. Complaining helps me explain away my shortcomings because there must be a conspiracy to keep me down.

Complaining is trash talk. Our God spoils us with gifts and opportunities. Here's a better way to respond to that generosity: **"Since we are receiving a kingdom that cannot be shaken, let us be thankful, and so worship God acceptably with reverence and awe, for our 'God is a consuming fire'"** (Hebrews 12:28,29).

A thankful heart and thankful talk are learned behaviors. They need to be cultivated. If you are ready for some gratitude therapy, here is your assignment: Get a notebook. Keep it where you sit when you're on the phone at home or going through your social media sites. Each day for two weeks write down good things that God sent into your life that day and thank him out loud specifically and from the heart for each one.

It will change your life.

Divine urgency
Pastor Mark Jeske

I see it clearly now. In my youth I had the mind-set that unlimited time stretched before me. If I wanted to learn to play a musical instrument, I could master it because I had plenty of time. If I wanted to learn another language, afford a really cool car, have a great house, accumulate some dough, travel abroad, get a postgraduate degree or two, no problem. Unlimited time lay ahead.

That optimism about unlimited time was an illusion, though I didn't know it back then. Time, in fact, flies. Life happens. Opportunities start to recede into the sunset. The limitless array of choices to the young shrink steadily.

Our window of opportunity to bring the gospel to a lost, corrupt, and broken world is also closing steadily. So also is the chance for people who are dithering and procrastinating with serious thought about the Word of the Lord. Like the younger me, they may think that they have endless time.

God feels a divine urgency to connect people with his Word. Only those who acknowledge their sinfulness will repent. Only those who believe and are baptized will be saved. Only those who trust in Christ are forgiven. Only those who are forgiven will skate through the fearful trial of the last judgment and enter heaven.

"'In the time of my favor I heard you, and in the day of salvation I helped you.' I tell you, *now* is the time of God's favor, *now* is the day of salvation" (2 Corinthians 6:2).

Running a marathon

Linda Buxa

I never really wanted to do it. It wasn't a lifelong dream. Yet I did it—and I'm not doing it again. Why? Because it absolutely hurts to run 26.2 miles.

If I had the body, speed, or mental fortitude of a Kenyan, I might have enjoyed it more. Still, I ran, because at the time it was my only opportunity for exercise. As I ran, I also used that as my devotion time. On one three-hour run, I listened to six sermons in a row. As a mom with young kids, it was nearly miraculous to hear one sermon, let alone six!

Those runs are when I started to think more about the passages that referred to exercise: **"Have nothing to do with godless myths and old wives' tales; rather, train yourself to be godly. For physical training is of some value, but godliness has value for all things, holding promise for both the present life and the life to come"** (1 Timothy 4:7).

My running was of some value. My heart got strong, and so did my legs. I was training myself to run long distances. But the training in godliness was even better. I left for most runs a little tired and a little discouraged, with the heaviness of this world on my heart. After being filled with God's Word and having some time to pray, I came home refreshed—a better wife, a better mother, closer to my God.

I knew I was never going to get the prize in my earthly marathon, but my training in godliness reminded me that I have a heavenly medal—an inheritance stored up for me in heaven that can never perish, spoil, or fade.

How's your training going?

His ways are best

Sarah Habben

Living overseas can challenge a person's North American sensibilities. In my current home on the island of Antigua, I don't always understand what's going on. Will the electricity be back in time for supper? Why did that work crew leave a pile of wet cement to harden in the middle of the lane? Why can't my husband pick up mail addressed to me without my written permission?

My ways aren't Antiguan ways. I am sometimes judgmental, as if my ways aren't just different, but better.

Do we ever feel the same about God's ways? We confess that Jesus died for the whole world but inwardly feel that so-and-so is such a jerk he or she doesn't deserve God's mercy (or at least not *ours*). We pray, "Thy will be done" and then tell God exactly what his will should be. We chafe under God's timing and testing.

God reminds us that his ways aren't just different; they're better. Not just better, but best. **"'For my thoughts are not your thoughts, neither are your ways my ways,' declares the Lord. 'As the heavens are higher than the earth, so are my ways higher than your ways and my thoughts than your thoughts'"** (Isaiah 55:8,9).

In nothing is this more apparent than in God's plan to save us. We are wicked. We don't deserve his love. An eternal death sentence would be fair and right. Instead, with a love higher than we can conceive, God sent a Savior bearing mercy and pardon. Whether I take blessing or hardship from his hand, I know . . . his ways are best.

I know just how you feel

Pastor Mark Jeske

People mean so well. They really do. They want to show that they care, that they know what you are going through, that their hearts are with you. So they say, "I know just how you feel." You want to snap back, "You have absolutely no idea how I feel right now."

When you attend a funeral wake, use your time well as you are waiting in the long line behind the casket. Think! Think what you are going to say. Don't pretend that you are on Pain Island with the bereaved. Your own experiences with death and dying might have been very different: **"Each heart knows its own bitterness, and no one else can share its joy"** (Proverbs 14:10).

Just be with people. Just show up. Hug them and say, "I love you." Tell a story of appreciation for God's gift of the deceased in your life. Listen to their words. Look into their eyes. You don't have to pretend that you're a professional grief counselor. You don't have to try to fix them or fix their problem. They don't need a detailed theological rationale. They don't want to hear that this death is just a little thing. Death is often a huge bomb dropped on a family.

It may also be that your most helpful words come not at the funeral but a month later, when the numbness has worn off and the crowds have left. Each heart knows its own bitterness. Let them tell *you* how they feel.

What do you follow?

Linda Buxa

In 2005 sheep were grazing while Turkish shepherds ate breakfast. Suddenly, one sheep jumped off a cliff. To the shepherds' astonishment, one by one nearly 1,500 others leapt from the same spot.

In the end, 450 of them died. (The ones who lived were saved as the ones on the bottom absorbed their fall.) Those sheep belonged to 26 families and were valued at $100,000—a significant amount of money in a country where the average GDP per person is around $10,000 a year.

We can think those sheep were just dumb, but we aren't any better. **"We all, like sheep, have gone astray, each of us has turned to our own way; and the Lord has laid on [Jesus] the iniquity of us all"** (Isaiah 53:6).

Whom are you following? Another dumb sheep? Fifteen hundred dumb sheep? Blindly putting your trust in your career, your income, or unhealthy relationships and behaviors can easily take you off the cliff. We've all done it, focused solely on ourselves and what we think is best.

This is why you need not follow just any shepherd, but the Good Shepherd. First, you want one who doesn't get distracted while you're in this world. More important, though, is that you need the Shepherd who laid down his life for the sheep. Jesus jumped off the cliff and absorbed the Father's wrath for you.

Now God calls you his sheep—and he gently and tenderly leads you.

I'm third

Pastor Mark Jeske

Have you ever seen the "I'm Third" license plate brackets? Only Christians would want to drive around with that message on their ride because it states the unpopular philosophy that in your life God is first, other people come second, and you come in at third priority.

To people's ears today, that sounds like a recipe for being walked on like a doormat. Only the Holy Spirit could persuade a selfish person like me to care about what somebody else needs. When you become a believer, you are adopted into a large family. A very, very large family. When you bond with Jesus Christ, you also become connected with all the other believers: **"In Christ we, though many, form one body, and each member belongs to all the others. . . . Honor one another above yourselves"** (Romans 12:5,10). Seriously! He made himself poor so that he could make me rich. I honor him when I act like him.

Those two statements from Romans have profound implications for the way in which we live. They teach us that the way of Christ is to deny self and find joy in serving other people *to whom we have an obligation.* They teach us to see ourselves as uniquely gifted to bring benefit to the "body" and also to appreciate the gifts that other members of the body bring.

Think about your plans for today—how do you intend to honor other members of the body above yourself?

Personal civil war
Pastor Mark Jeske

Some people kind of enjoy drama and conflict. Not me. I hate it. I don't like the feeling of tension in my gut. I don't like having to look over my shoulder all the time. I flee from discomfort and pain and get no joy in inflicting them on others.

It distresses me that for my entire life on this planet I will be a walking civil war. And like it or not, you, like me, are a walking schizophrenic. There are two minds within us, locked in mortal combat for control. St. Paul calls these two internal adversaries "flesh" (bad) and "Spirit" (good): **"The flesh desires what is contrary to the Spirit, and the Spirit what is contrary to the flesh. They are in conflict with each other, so that you are not to do whatever you want. But if you are led by the Spirit, you are not under the law"** (Galatians 5:17,18).

Every day you and I must wage war. Nothing will come easy. The reborn Christian in us must assert control of our personal value system, must choose to be informed and guided by God's Word, and must daily rebuke and suppress our sinful appetites and lusts. But here is greatly encouraging news: God's mercy triumphs over judgment. His law no longer condemns us.

One day the war will be over. In the meantime, God has sent reinforcements. His Word gives us his Spirit, our greatest ally in our personal civil war.

You might thank him today.

An indispensable sense

Jason Nelson

When babies can sit in high chairs, they start learning about their senses. With a tone that would be patronizing to anyone but a baby, Mom and Dad will ask, "Where are your eyes?" After a little coaching, baby girl will giggle and cover her eyes with her hands. Then they will ask, "Where is your nose?" and she will grab it. Next come the ears, mouth, and maybe the toes. It's how children are trained to appreciate God's gifts of seeing, hearing, smelling, tasting, touching—and laughing. There are adults I would like to wedge back into a high chair and with that same tone ask, "And where is your funny bone?" because it seems like they don't have a sense of humor. Laughter is how we vocalize joy, which is the value God adds to our best experiences. It is released by shaping our lips into something recognized as a smile.

Laughing for real is no joke. It is high praise for our freedom in Christ because we are not captives anymore. **"It seemed like a dream, too good to be true, when God returned Zion's exiles. We laughed, we sang, we couldn't believe our good fortune. We were the talk of the nations—'God was wonderful to them!' God *was* wonderful to us; we are one happy people"** (Psalm 126:1-3 MSG). Happy people send a message to the world. There is something very special going on in our lives.

august

Devote yourselves to prayer,
being watchful and thankful.

Colossians 4:2

It's new, but God is with you

Pastor Mike Novotny

What's new? I don't ask that question to pass the time with small talk. I mean, what are you dealing with that is terrifyingly new? Are you starting a new job or a new school? Are you moving to a new city or considering a new career? Are you at a new stage of life as a first-time dad with bags under his eyes or a first-time widow crying in an old bed that suddenly seems too big?

New is scary. Uncertain. Faith testing. Anxiety inducing. But that's why I love Joshua chapter 1. These words were written when God's people were about to enter a new land (Canaan) under the leadership of a new man (Joshua). As the people looked across the Jordan River to the towering walls of Jericho, you can just imagine the "news" that shook their hearts.

No wonder God repeated himself. **"I will be with you,"** he promised Joshua. **"I will never leave you nor forsake you,"** God said a sentence later (verse 5). One paragraph after that, God promised, **"The Lord your God will be with you"** (verse 9). Before the end of the chapter, we read it again, **"The Lord your God be with you"** (verse 17).

The repetition is God's reminder that what we need when things are new is something old. Rather, Someone old. Ancient. Eternal. Trustworthy. Reliable. The God who, in olden times, made plans to be in total control of what seems so new to us. So when your "news" shakes you, run to the God who is eternal. Thankfully, you don't have to run far. He is with you always.

Eternal life insurance

Pastor Mark Jeske

Millions of people have found the security and comfort of investing in a risk pool (aka insurance). Modest regular payments guarantee that in the event of death the individual's survivors will be compensated for the loss of the breadwinner. All of the major parts of our lives can be protected in this way—lives, homes, furnishings, health, and automobiles. Financial contracts like those allow us to live securely, without fear of financial disaster.

The Holy Spirit is your broker of eternal life insurance, and Jesus Christ has paid the premiums for you! Although you live in a broken world as a broken individual, although you are mortal and know that your time here is fleeting, although you are a sinner and are owed nothing by God, the Spirit brings you the unconditional love of your Savior Jesus.

"You also were included in Christ when you heard the message of truth, the gospel of your salvation. When you believed, you were marked in him with a seal, the promised Holy Spirit, who is a deposit guaranteeing our inheritance until the redemption of those who are God's possession—to the praise of his glory" (Ephesians 1:13,14). Your baptism initiated a new relationship with God. Through Christ he has forgiven all your sins and claimed you as his child. He has obligated himself to care for you and has made you an heir of heaven.

Your baptism is a deposit, a down payment. Soon, soon you will cash in that policy for the real thing.

Church rules

Pastor Mark Jeske

I have counseled many, many troubled people over the years, but never once has anybody ever admitted being a Pharisee.

Although the Pharisees as a particular Jewish "sect" died out long ago, their spirit is alive and well. Insecure and controlling church leaders over the centuries have never been able to resist the temptation to make rules and laws that go beyond Scripture's. Perhaps they mean well, trying to use the law to "improve" people, or perhaps they just enjoy exercising power over others.

Jesus considered Pharisaism a plague that he wanted his disciples to avoid: **"Jesus said to the crowds and to his disciples: 'The teachers of the law and the Pharisees sit in Moses' seat. So you must be careful to do everything they tell you. But do not do what they do, for they do not practice what they preach. They tie up heavy, cumbersome loads and put them on other people's shoulders, but they themselves are not willing to lift a finger to move them'"** (Matthew 23:1-4).

Legalists make rules and neglect love. They keep people feeling guilty as a form of mass control. They quote denominational decrees and the writings of past heroes when they should be quoting Scripture. They chafe when God's Word has ambiguity or silence and rush to fill the gaps with pronouncements on worship styles, dress, and diet.

When you are speaking for God, say no less than Scripture does. But say no more, either.

Before all else fails
Jason Nelson

I don't know why this is so hard. But we struggle to build sturdy bridges from our lonely little islands to the lonely little islands of people around us. Sure, we like our privacy, but God also put affinity for other island dwellers in our souls. The old English poet John Donne said, "No man is an island entire of itself; every man is a piece of the continent, a part of the main."

Humanity is not a frictionless network. There needs to be contact. From Donne's time to the present, we have experimented with things like handshakes, hugs, and Instagram to relate to others because we can't survive in isolation from one another. Donne continued, "Any man's death diminishes me, because I am involved in mankind. And therefore never send to know for whom the bell tolls; it tolls for thee." We are in this life together until we are no longer in it at all. So **"above all, love each other deeply, because love covers over a multitude of sins"** (1 Peter 4:8). It takes faith and it takes hope not to be an island. And it takes love because love never fails.

God sent Jesus to be part of the main. He was God incarnate, which is also love incarnate. That is how God reconnected with us and showed us how he wants us to connect with others. The distance between us and others isn't a moat. It is a place for a bridge, and the bridge is love.

Who is your real enemy?

Linda Buxa

In the book *Catching Fire,* Katniss, a tribute, is about to enter the arena for the second time when her mentor, Haymitch, offers some final advice: "You just remember who the enemy is." Katniss doesn't understand at first but eventually realizes she isn't fighting against the other tributes. The real enemy is the Capitol, the masterminds of the Hunger Games—events where tributes fight to the death.

How often do we go into the world—our personal Hunger Games arena—thinking other people are the enemy? Maybe those whose political beliefs or social standards are different or who do anything differently from us. Maybe those in other churches or even in our own churches. Sometimes it's even our own family members.

Our God, our ultimate mentor, has a different idea: **"Our struggle is not against flesh and blood, but against the rulers, against the authorities, against the powers of this dark world and against the spiritual forces of evil in the heavenly realms"** (Ephesians 6:12).

We minimize Satan's existence. We aren't comfortable talking about evil spirits, so we pretend they don't exist. We blame our earthly struggles on the people around us or politicians or media or culture. We forget the devil is the mastermind, the enemy.

Today is another battle in the arena, but remember who your real enemy is. You are no longer a tribute, but a *victor.* Not because of what you've done, but because Jesus **"disarmed the powers and authorities, he made a public spectacle of them, triumphing over them by the cross"** (Colossians 2:15).

Wonderfully made
Pastor Mike Novotny

Have you ever heard of the StrengthsFinder personality test? After a brief exam, it reveals your top strengths out of a list of 34 categories. If you're up for a good time, take the test, pass out copies to your closest friends and family, and listen as they laugh, "That is *so* you!"

What I love about the test is that the odds of another person having your top six strengths in order are one in seven billion. That's right—seven billion! In other words, you are statistically the only human alive who is just like you. Rank your other 28 categories and sprinkle in your personal experiences, and you will realize how uniquely made you are.

It reminds me of David's words: **"I praise you** [God] **because I am fearfully and wonderfully made"** (Psalm 139:14). David wasn't bragging. He was praising. Praising the God who forgave and saved and knit David together in his mother's womb. He is the same God who knit you too.

So who are you? How did God make you wonderful? Whether you choose the StrengthsFinder test or some other way, I would encourage you to discover who you are. Unearth the compelling reasons that God did not decide to clone the person you envy most in this world. Instead, he decided to handcraft you. That is "wonderful" enough to give God a shout of praise!

Capital punishment

Pastor Mark Jeske

The practice of capital punishment has a long and intense debate over it that has lasted for centuries. There are powerful arguments both for it and against it. Nineteen states do not allow it, and thirty-one states do, as well as the federal government and military. Because of the finality of this procedure, that intense debate will continue forever.

Christians of good will can make a good case for either retaining or outlawing the procedure, and neither is right or wrong. It is a judgment call as to whether you think capital punishment is appropriate for heinous crimes like mass murder, as well as a necessary deterrent, or whether you think any kind of judicial execution is murder, especially because it has been proven that juries are sometimes wrong.

You cannot say that capital punishment is against God's will. St. Paul wrote on how God entrusts governments with keeping order in a chaotic and violent world. In his view sometimes violence is needed to suppress and restrain violence: **"The one in authority is God's servant for your good. But if you do wrong, be afraid, for rulers do not bear the sword for no reason. They are God's servants, agents of wrath to bring punishment on the wrongdoer"** (Romans 13:4). Here are two things of which you can be sure: the debate over punishment appropriate for the worst of crimes will continue indefinitely. So will extremely violent crime.

Only in heaven will that argument cease.

Be still

Sarah Habben

As Pharaoh's gleaming chariots approached, fear struck the Israelites. Voices clanged like alarm bells: "Why?" "What have you done?" "Didn't we say . . . ?" "It would have been better if . . . !" Moses spoke over their panic: **"Do not be afraid. Stand firm. . . . The Lord will fight for you; you need only to be still"** (Exodus 14:13,14).

This week, my Caribbean neighborhood is under a wind advisory. Bathers and small-craft fishermen are urged to stay ashore to avoid the 10-14 foot waves. The wind blusters and gusts and whips the palm branches, hurling dust through the windows and debris across the yard. Blow. Blow. BLOW. I wish I could holler, "Be still!" and force the fretful wind to cower like a chastened dog.

My worry is a lot like that wind. It buffets and blows and sweeps away patience. Those around me get sucked into the tempest. My children snipe and stomp and argue. I know it's because I started it.

God should pin me down and thunder, "BE STILL!" Silence my foolish fears with an almighty "Shadd*aaaap*!"

But that's not how God deals with our doubts—not in ancient times nor today. Isn't God's love mysterious? It defies logic: giving up a beloved Son in order to adopt a surly family. It defies limits: never stretching to a snapping point like old elastic. God's mighty love fights for us, silencing Satan and sin and death. God's gentle love forgives.

When the winds of worry rise, I can shelter in that love—and be still.

Wiping away our tears

Linda Buxa

In the movie *Inside Out*, when Riley's family moves from Minnesota to San Francisco, Riley is miserable. The whole point of the movie is exploring her emotions—and ultimately she learns that her memories are rarely all positive or all negative.

Adults understand that. The joy of a graduation is tinged with the sadness of goodbyes. The birth of a new baby brings sleep deprivation and worry. The deep love of close friendships means goodbyes cut deeply. The excitement of a wedding is tinged with sadness because Grandma isn't there.

You know what gets us through? (It's pretty much a standard Sunday school answer, so it's hard to get it wrong.) Jesus.

We know that one of Jesus' promises is this: **"In *this* world you will have trouble,"** so no matter how great our happiest moments are in this world, sin and its effects always leave us yearning for more. Thankfully Jesus ended that statement with, **"but take heart! I have overcome the world"** (John 16:33).

That's why we look forward to heaven. Because Jesus suffered the Father's wrath for us, we are now called children of God. Because we are his kids, we now have a place where our Father **"will wipe every tear from their eyes. There will be no more death or mourning or crying or pain, for the old order of things has passed away"** (Revelation 21:4).

And then, finally, *all* will be well with our souls.

The water always wins
Jason Nelson

I would like to revisit an expression I heard when I was watching coverage of hurricanes Harvey and Irma: "The water always wins." Meteorologists used it to sound a warning. When it comes to catastrophic weather events like hurricanes, don't think you can take on the water and win. It always seeks its own level and will rise as high as it wants to go. It can force its way through a hairline crack in a wall and wash everything away. Water can kill you. Most people who die in hurricanes lose their lives in the surge of water. The water always wins because God made so much of it. Over 70 percent of the earth's surface is water now, and there could be more in the future if glaciers and ice caps continue to thaw.

Let's flip this idea. With the power of ordinary H_2O in mind, think about what Jesus is saying about himself here: **"Everyone who drinks this water will be thirsty again, but whoever drinks the water I give them will never thirst. Indeed, the water I give them will become in them a spring of water welling up to eternal life"** (John 4:13,14). Jesus takes water to a divine level. He is the risen tide of our spiritual survival and eternal salvation. He won. **"It is done. I am the Alpha and the Omega, the Beginning and the End. To the thirsty I will give water without cost from the spring of the water of life"** (Revelation 21:6).

Living with loss: A spouse

Pastor Mark Jeske

Do you have the idea that your life as a Christian is just going to get better and better? That one by one your problems will disappear? That because God always answers prayer, God knows your dreams, and so yours will all come true one by one?

Sometimes those things happen. But so does the opposite. Death, war, financial disaster, and destruction visit all homes, those of believers and unbelievers alike. God's people sometimes have to swallow bitter pills and suffer terrible losses.

Like the loss of a spouse. A godly woman named Naomi suffered the catastrophic loss of her husband (and two sons), made all the worse in that they had been living as lonely exiles in the land of the Moabites. Naomi's outlook was bleak: **"'Don't call me Naomi'** [i.e., "pleasant"]**, she told them. 'Call me Mara** [i.e., "bitter"]**, because the Almighty has made my life very bitter. I went away full, but the Lᴏʀᴅ has brought me back empty. Why call me Naomi? The Lᴏʀᴅ has afflicted me; the Almighty has brought misfortune upon me'"** (Ruth 1:20,21).

Compounding her pain was the fear that her suffering was a punishment from God. But the Lord's steady blessings in her life gave her new confidence and hope. Her daughter-in-law Ruth remarried and gave Naomi a home, and her life was crowned with the unexpected pleasure of holding a grandchild on her lap.

We can help hurting people who are obsessing over their losses by reminding them to be mindful of the direct blessings God is still sending.

Just the crickets

Jason Nelson

Before summer is over, I hope you can go someplace where all you can hear are the crickets. I'm not talking about crawling around in your bedroom closet to exterminate the one cricket that's keeping you awake. I'm talking about going far enough away where engines aren't revving, no sirens force you to face hard realities, and no gunfire pierces the heart of your personal safety. I'm talking about going to a wide-open space at dusk when the crickets collaborate to make the sound of peace and quiet. Take a companion with you and say, "*Shh*, do you hear that?" And when your companion says, "I don't hear anything," you say, "Exactly."

All of the noise in our lives, all of the sonic disturbances around us, are reminders that we're not there yet. We are not in that place Jesus is preparing for us. We don't yet have our room in our Father's mansion, but we are on our way. Someday we will enjoy the full-throated righteousness Jesus won for us when he could barely whisper from the cross, "It is finished." Let the crickets give you a hint that it will be amazing because of what you no longer hear once you are there. **"The fruit of that righteousness will be peace; its effect will be quietness and confidence forever. My people will live in peaceful dwelling places, in secure homes, in undisturbed places of rest"** (Isaiah 32:17,18).

Teach your children

Pastor Mark Jeske

Why is it that children learn everything bad all by themselves? Lying, laziness, blaming, evading responsibility, cheating, stealing, and disobedience just sprout like weeds. That's what makes parenting so exhausting— all the good qualities we desire to see in our kids as they become adults must be taught, encouraged, modeled, and retaught.

The most important of all characteristics we need to pass on to our children is our faith. Just like all the other good attributes, faith in Christ is not present in a human being at birth. It must be given to the child by the power of Word and sacrament.

It must also be encouraged, tended, and strengthened just like every other virtue. Parents have the awesome privilege and responsibility of making sure their children know that they are created, redeemed, and cared for by a loving God who literally moved heaven and earth to make it possible for them to enjoy eternity with him: **"We will not hide them from their descendants; we will tell the next generation the praiseworthy deeds of the Lord, his power, and the wonders he has done"** (Psalm 78:4). You can't believe for them. What you can do is share the Word in your home devotions, prayers, and story time and let the Holy Spirit loose in their hearts.

Did you have a Christian upbringing as a child? Today would be a good day to thank the Lord for the gift of Christian parents, and also to resolve to keep teaching your children and grandchildren the praiseworthy deeds of the Lord.

Two little prayers
Jason Nelson

"If God is for us, who can be against us? He who did not spare his own Son, but gave him up for us all— how will he not also, along with him, graciously give us all things?" (Romans 8:31,32).

When we feel defeated, Lord, give us a victory. When we are overwhelmed by evil around us, Lord, make us strong. When we doubt ourselves and others, Lord, give us confidence. You refused to accept our defeat. You sent Jesus to love us and give his life for us. He overcame death and every problem we face in life. In him we win. Lift us up with promises from your Word. Help us believe we are what you say we are—more than conquerors. Amen.

"Seek the Lord while he may be found; call on him while he is near. Let the wicked forsake their ways and the unrighteous their thoughts" (Isaiah 55:6,7).

Like heaven is above the earth, your ways are above our ways. Lord, you see what we miss and do what we can't imagine. Like rain and snow water the earth, your Word revives our weary souls. Every time we seek you, we find you. Every time we call on your name, you draw near. Every time we ask for your mercy, you pardon us. Help us forsake our wicked ways and evil thoughts. Put your blessing on us so we can go out in joy and into the world at peace. Amen.

Schadenfreude not allowed

Pastor Mark Jeske

Laughing at and enjoying other people's misfortunes is in our DNA. Renaissance-era puppeteers invented the "Punch and Judy" routines where one puppet with a stick beats another on the head. People always laughed, and then they told their friends to catch the next show. The audience was back for more the next year. Slapstick comedians know why people laugh when they put a banana peel on the ground near where their victim will walk.

The Germans call this *Schadenfreude*, that is, "delight in (others') troubles." The Bible calls it sin. One of the mandatory hallmarks of ideal Christian behavior is kindness toward all, even your enemies, *especially* your enemies. **"Do not gloat when your enemy falls; when he stumbles, do not let your heart rejoice, or the Lord will see and disapprove"** (Proverbs 24:17,18). It takes no special Christian grace to be glad when a friend of yours succeeds. It's much harder, and better, to offer help to an enemy.

If you catch yourself smirking when someone you don't like is getting chewed out by the boss, give yourself a kick. If someone in your class you really can't stand just got a bad grade, take no pleasure.

Remember that the Bible tells us that Christ died for us while we were still awful sinners.

Mercy melts hearts, you know.

Is ambition good or bad?

Pastor Mark Jeske

I guess it depends on whom you ask. If you check in with parents whose teenage kids spent countless hours in the basement playing video games, they would dearly love to see them more ambitious about building careers. Managers whose employees do only the minimum and show no creativity or spark would love to see some ambition.

Even in the church, growth of congregations and planting of new missions must wait for leaders' initiative. St. Paul described it like this: **"It has always been my *ambition* to preach the gospel where Christ was not known, so that I would not be building on someone else's foundation"** (Romans 15:20).

When the agenda is not God's, however, when people's ambition is just selfish, to aggrandize their own reputation, consolidate their control, or stack up their own wealth, it is another pathway to the idolatry of Self: **"Who is wise and understanding among you? Let them show it by their good life, by deeds done in the humility that comes from wisdom. But if you harbor bitter envy and selfish ambition in your hearts, do not boast about it or deny the truth"** (James 3:13,14).

How can you tell if your ambition is the good or bad kind? Will it wound or crush other people? Is the financial risk so high you could be ruined? Do you have to lie or cheat or steal to win?

Above all—does God gain glory?

Flex your thanks muscles
Sarah Habben

True thankfulness is more "flex" than "reflex." Here in my new home of Antigua, reflex-thanks is what happens when I pull the laundry off the line just before a downpour. Phew! Thanks! Reflex-thanks is when the local grocery store has an overstock of expired milk and a gallon sells for $4 USD instead of $8 USD. Awesome! Thanks!

But what about the kind of thanks that Paul talks about in 1 Thessalonians 5:18: **"Give thanks in *all circumstances*; for this is God's will for you in Christ Jesus"**?

All circumstances? Wet laundry and costly groceries? A breaking heart? A failing heart? Well, that requires more flex than reflex. If you hold a weight and flex your arm, after a while your bicep protests. Further flexing takes a deliberate, conscious effort. Likewise, flex-thanks is a deliberate, conscious bending of the heart toward thankfulness, no matter whether it is holding a featherlight joy or a heavy sorrow or an awkward load of annoyance.

I can fight through another set of bicep curls by sheer willpower. But willpower isn't enough to create genuine thankfulness. Flex-thanks is *only* possible through God in Christ Jesus. When hardship nips my heels, my Savior reminds me of my heavenly home. When my reflex is to grumble, my Savior reminds me I am forgiven. Whenever I receive God's grace in Word and sacrament, the Spirit bends my heart toward thankfulness.

Lord, whether I face ease or hardship today, let my reflex be "thank you."

Don't break reeds

Linda Buxa

This status update popped up in my Facebook feed: "Confession: I'm not an overly religious person. I believe in God and go to church, but sometimes I have a hard time buying into the 'rules' that follow certain religions. I just sort of think that if you are generally a good person and you try your hardest to be compassionate, empathetic, caring, loving, and kind, then JC gives you a thumbs-up."

Admittedly, I started to think, "Do you *really* think you can earn God's approval?"

Before I got too far along in my arrogance, the Holy Spirit brought a passage to mind: **"A bruised reed he will not break, and a smoldering wick he will not snuff out"** (Isaiah 42:3).

We are surrounded by bruised reeds and smoldering wicks. Some people had a bad church experience that left them with an incomplete or skewed picture of God, or during a personal crisis they received judgment from church members. Maybe some were taught they had a role to play in saving themselves.

Whatever it is, a whole group of people know just enough about Jesus to believe he has something to say to their lives but don't know just how much he offers. For me—and maybe for you too, and definitely for the church—it's time to be gentle. Lovingly remind them that when Jesus said, "It is finished," it was for them too. Now JC does give them a thumbs-up—not because of what they did, but because of what he did.

Anointed

Pastor Mark Jeske

It's a high compliment to a church worker. "Pastor, you were anointed this morning!" By these kind words the hearer means to say that the message was so unusually interesting and powerful that the Spirit of the Lord must have injected extra energy and wisdom into the delivery. But I doubt that you will ever hear the word *anointed* at the warehouse or office on Monday morning. It's Christian speak.

The word *anoint* referred originally to the special oil put on the heads of high priests, kings, and some prophets to identify them publicly for their leadership roles and to power them up for the big challenges they faced. "Anointed One" is the meaning of Jesus' special names Messiah and Christ, for he was anointed by the Father and the Spirit in the River Jordan.

But it is fitting to use the term also of us, for when we were baptized and brought to faith, the Spirit came to live within us as a sign of God's claim on us: **"Now it is God who makes both us and you stand firm in Christ. He *anointed* us, set his seal of ownership on us, and put his Spirit in our hearts as a deposit, guaranteeing what is to come"** (2 Corinthians 1:21,22). Let your anointing thrill your heart, for it means that God cared enough about you to pursue you, find you, change your heart, and declare you his child and kingdom agent.

Meditation time

Pastor Mike Novotny

My daughter acts like a Buddhist. Whenever I talk about meditating on the Bible, she assumes the lotus position, pinches her index fingers to her thumbs, closes her eyes, and chants, *"Hmm."* Then she peeks one eye open to make sure we are paying attention to her performance.

The Bible talks a lot about meditation. But it's not about clearing your mind. It's about laser-focusing your mind on the Word of God. As God said, **"Keep this Book of the Law always on your lips; meditate on it day and night"** (Joshua 1:8). In Hebrew, the word *meditate* means to enjoy something so thoroughly that your body emits a sound, like a dog instinctively growling as he enjoys a bone. That's God's goal, that we would not just check the Bible-reading box but instead savor his promises like a gourmet feast.

What else can we do but savor when we chew on the gospel and read how committed God is to us, despite our sins? How else could our souls react when we hear that God is with us, even though we have struggled to obey fully?

In our family, we have a saying—Chew first. That's our slang for "meditate on the Bible before everything else." We don't want to skim the surface of the Word that has changed the world. We want to chew on it. We want to enjoy it. We want to meditate upon it.

As a guy who can't touch his toes, I can't assume the lotus position like my little girl. But thankfully I can meditate on the gospel all day long!

Angry talk

Pastor Mark Jeske

There's a lot of negativity coming at you each day over which you have no control. You are going to be criticized today. Disagreeable people will drain energy from you. Someone will let you down. Something positive you hoped for will not happen.

But you can take a lot of trash out of your life by reducing the trash talk. And since you have complete control over your own mouth, that means you have the power right away to eliminate 50 percent of it: **"My dear brothers and sisters, take note of this: Everyone should be quick to listen, slow to speak and slow to become angry, because human anger does not produce the righteousness that God desires"** (James 1:19,20).

You bet it doesn't. Venting your anger on someone else briefly feels good, because you think you gave somebody a piece of your mind, but now you're worse off because the other person is plotting a nasty comeback and is going to hit you harder.

You will truly feel better inside if you don't go off on other people. Have the self-awareness to know if your desire to retaliate is coming from your own insecurity or shame. Realize that some people's trash talk is an attempt by a person who feels small trying to make himself or herself bigger. Jesus is your hero. He was an anger heat sink, absorbing injustice instead of seeking revenge.

You get more points from God for ending an argument than for trying to crush an opponent.

Higher ground
Jason Nelson

Ralph Waldo Emerson said, "If you would lift me up, you must be on higher ground." He uses a physical fact to conjure up an ultimate reality. We know from history that noble statesmen and women, reformers, and humanitarians have stood on higher ground and pulled the trajectory of events in a positive direction. It can be done. We don't have to settle for what we are currently getting. We can insist that our leaders go to higher ground so we can follow them there.

If we as Christians don't insist on it, who will? We regularly meditate on the major events of Jesus' redemptive work that really did occur on higher ground. Mount Calvary comes to mind. Every example he set for us shows us what taking the high road looks like, especially when others want to take us down. Every admonition from his lips encourages us to follow him to higher ground in the way we live. The hard climb to higher ground is in our spiritual DNA as Christians.

It is so disappointing when public figures wrap themselves in a cloak of Christianity to appeal to a constituency or raise money and then wrestle in the mud like everyone else. That gives Jesus a bad name and makes people cynical about Christianity and the gospel that saves. Higher ground isn't pie in the sky. Higher ground isn't unattainable even in a sinful world. Higher ground is where Christian character is most at home.

Joy and sorrow intertwined

Pastor Mark Jeske

Have you ever noticed how closely joy and sorrow are intertwined in our lives? You just can't separate them, though you may wish you could and though you try pretty hard. The Christmas gathering was fun, but you missed Grandpa, who won't be coming to holiday gatherings anymore. Your kid graduated from high school (hurray!) but did not get accepted to the college she wanted (arrgh!). You got the promotion (yay!), but it did not come with a pay raise (sigh).

It's not just you who's cursed with this phenomenon—it is universal: **"Even in laughter the heart may ache, and rejoicing may end in grief"** (Proverbs 14:13). Since with this insightful Scripture passage God pulled back the curtain a little on the absurdities of human life, you can be a little more prepared and not sink into such disappointment when it seems as though there's a fly in every bowl of soup you are served in life.

We all so badly want heaven on earth, but alas, heaven will come only in heaven. For now, so many things are broken on earth that we should anticipate disappointments and not let our spirits be crushed. The trick is to let your mind dwell on the blessings God is giving you and not obsess over what you don't have or what went wrong.

And when you are enjoying the friends God sends you, your griefs will seem only half as heavy and your joys twice as great.

One of us
Sarah Habben

A 1995 chart-topper asked the question, "What if God was one of us?" It went on to speculate about God being a stranger on a bus, a slob like the rest of us on earth. Do you know that song?

The author of those lyrics was probably just going for shock value, but he came pretty close to the truth.

God *did* become one of us. The second person of the Trinity took a human name—Jesus. He took on a body and face that would attract no attention from *Vogue*. And far more shocking than becoming a slob, Jesus became *sin*.

"God made him who had no sin to be sin for us, so that in him we might become the righteousness of God" (2 Corinthians 5:21).

It's shocking. On the cross, sinless Jesus chose to become what we are. Lazy Student. Sassy Brat. Adulterer. Abuser. Grudge Holder. Gossiper. Worrywart. Whiner. As Jesus hung on the cross, his Father stripped his faultless identity and gave him all our ugliness. God made his Son to be sin. And then he shut the door to heaven and abandoned him.

It's shocking. That cross was rightly ours. That heavenly door should have been slammed in our faces. Jesus' blood should condemn us as murderers. Instead—the opposite. He died for us. His blood erases our sinful identity—we are righteous in God's eyes. His grace adopts us—we are no longer strangers but heirs. His resurrection proves that his payment was good. We don't have to try to find our way home.

Jesus *is* our way home.

Living with loss: Your reputation

Pastor Mark Jeske

The past cannot be changed. What a heavy burden on all fools and sinners! Our misdeeds, our failings, our thefts and lies and moral collapses and cheating and acts of cruelty are all frozen in time, untouchable and unchangeable. We have to live with our memories, see the faces of the people we've hurt, and live with painful consequences, including loss of reputation.

That's worse than losing money, because it's so much harder to rebuild. Trust takes a long time to build but can be squandered in five minutes. The disciple Peter had heard Jesus' prediction that he would deny him three times. He loudly protested that he would never be ashamed of his Lord. That boastful claim did not even survive its first test. As predicted, he failed three times: **"'Man, I don't know what you're talking about!' Just as he was speaking, the rooster crowed. The Lord turned and looked straight at Peter. Then Peter remembered the word the Lord had spoken to him: 'Before the rooster crows today, you will disown me three times.' And he went outside and wept bitterly"** (Luke 22:60-62).

For the rest of his life, painful memories of that failure would have kept Peter humble. But the fact that the past can't be changed is also a great thing. Jesus' bloody payment for your sins is permanent. Jesus' resurrection can't be altered. Your baptism's washing can't be stolen from you.

Since your past cannot condemn you, you are freed to create a new narrative today.

You belong

Pastor Mike Novotny

If this pastor thing doesn't work out, I could never make it as a foot model. After a freak Zamboni accident years ago (not kidding), I permanently lost part of my big toenail. Combine that with some random tufts of standard-issue male foot hair and you'll realize why shoes always beat sandals in my wardrobe selection.

Feet have it pretty bad. Compared to the hands, they do so little. Hands shake, wave, and greet. Feet have no such marketable skills. No wonder Paul wrote, **"Now if the foot should say, 'Because I am not a hand, I do not belong to the body,' it would not for that reason stop being part of the body"** (1 Corinthians 12:15). Feet might wonder if they even belong.

Some people are the same. Maybe you don't have the "big and flashy" talents like public speaking or natural musical ability. Maybe other people get the attention, the praise, the compliments. Maybe you wonder if your family or your church even needs you.

If so, God would like a word with you. Because he created you to be a vital part of your church community. Your volunteer work might not make the church newsletter. Your compassion for a first-time guest at church might be forgotten before the first song. But your Father in heaven knows. He sees what you do to thank him for the forgiveness of your sins.

You might not be an impressive hand. But you are an essential part of the body of Christ.

Bad apples: Rahab

Pastor Mark Jeske

You have probably heard the old saying about the risk of having even one bad apple in the apple barrel—just one rotten apple can rot the rest. That saying is based on scientific fact—a rotting piece of fruit releases, among other things, the gas ethylene, which is a ripening accelerator. Any mold in the rotting apple will also seek to jump to another host site and multiply.

You might think that God would want his children to have nothing to do with people who are society's "bad apples." The Pharisees would certainly agree. And yet, God's grace is rationed out not only to the good boys and girls. His Fatherly heart wants to win back the bad ones too: **"Joshua son of Nun secretly sent two spies from Shittim. 'Go, look over the land,' he said, 'especially Jericho.' So they went and entered the house of a prostitute named Rahab and stayed there"** (Joshua 2:1).

We must assume that Joshua's scouts did not go to Rahab's house to rent her services. Rahab learned of their identity, protected them, and decided to join the Israelite nation. The fresh start and her own talent and character inspired Salmon, the head of the tribe of Judah, to marry her. Both the book of Hebrews and the apostle James list Rahab in the catalog of heroes of faith. She and Salmon became great-great-grandparents of King David.

That makes this one-time bad girl also an ancestor of our Savior, Jesus Christ.

Bad apples: King Manasseh
Pastor Mark Jeske

King Manasseh was one of the baddest apples ever to disgrace the Israelite barrel. He practiced things like sorcery, divination, witchcraft, consulted mediums, and even ritually slaughtered some of his own children to appease the gods whose approval he wanted. **"Manasseh led Judah and the people of Jerusalem astray, so that they did more evil than the nations the Lord had destroyed before the Israelites. The Lord spoke to Manasseh and his people, but they paid no attention"** (2 Chronicles 33:9,10).

But get this—God didn't give up on him. I would have, but God didn't. He kept reaching out to him, finally resorting to the "divine two-by-four"—he allowed Manasseh to be taken captive and hauled to Babylon in chains. There he repented and humbled himself before the Lord. In his captivity he finally had time to reflect and pray. He was allowed to return as king, and he launched a spiritual reformation of purging away Baal worship and bringing back the Word of the Lord.

This is a big deal. People who have made a string of rebellious mistakes in their lives may imagine that it is too late for them, that God could never forgive their past, that there is no hope. God's restoration of a bad boy like Manasseh shows that it is never too late, that God's mercy triumphs over judgment, and that the time is now to humble yourself and repent.

Is there a bad apple in your family who could stand to hear of God's mercy one more time?

Bad apples: Judah and Tamar

Pastor Mark Jeske

Judah, Abraham's great-grandson, was a prince in the growing Israelite community. Fourth son of the patriarch Jacob, he had wealth and standing. But his wife had passed away, as had two of his three sons. His widowed Canaanite daughter-in-law Tamar was terrified that she would have no spouse or children.

She cooked up a plan to masquerade as a prostitute and seduce her father-in-law! Their one hookup miraculously generated the pregnancy she was so desperately hoping for. Then, **"about three months later Judah was told, 'Your daughter-in-law Tamar is guilty of prostitution, and as a result she is now pregnant.' Judah said, 'Bring her out and have her burned to death!'"** (Genesis 38:24). What an egregious example of the male double standard! Judah actually intended to compound his adultery with judicial murder.

Thankfully Tamar was allowed to testify: **"As she was being brought out, she sent a message to her father-in-law. 'I am pregnant by the man who owns these,' she said. And she added, 'See if you recognize whose seal and cord and staff these are'"** (verse 25).

The royal line of the Israelite kings would run through Judah and his "illegitimate" son, Perez, and thus so would the bloodline of Jesus Christ. Judah gave his name to tribal land, a kingdom, and ultimately to the entire Israelite people (*Jew* is derived from *Judah*). You know, if God could use adulterers like Judah and Tamar in his royal agenda, perhaps he can use you too.

Bad apples: Abraham
Pastor Mark Jeske

Okay, Okay—how on earth does the great patriarch Abraham make a "bad apples" list? He was chosen by God to found a nation of believers. All Israel looked to him as father of the nation; in fact, all believers of all ages are his spiritual children. His life was sprinkled with towering examples of faith, courage, and trust in God. Romans chapter 4 and Hebrews chapter 11 hold him up as a shining example of faith in God's promises.

But this pillar of faith had shameful moments of fear, doubt, and cruelty too. In his impatience to "help" God give him the son he and Sarah were so desperately waiting for, he committed adultery with Sarah's maid Hagar. She conceived a son, Ishmael. But when Sarah finally bore Abraham her own son, Isaac, the two women could not abide each other.

Though a wealthy herdsman with many servants working for him, Abraham basically threw Hagar and his son Ishmael out into the desert with only a bag lunch: **"Early the next morning Abraham took some food and a skin of water and gave them to Hagar. He set them on her shoulders and then sent her off with the boy. She went on her way and wandered in the Desert of Beersheba"** (Genesis 21:14). These painful stories remind us that Abraham's righteousness came from his Savior, not his own perfect life performance.

Note also that God's team is made up of some pretty flawed people. Like you and me.

Bad apples: Solomon

Pastor Mark Jeske

Born to comfort and privilege, Solomon led what we might consider a charmed life. His warlike father, King David, had conquered all of the nations surrounding Israel. Solomon inherited peace, the largest amount of territory Israel would ever hold, and stupendous wealth. It was his privilege to oversee the building of the grand temple in Jerusalem. And then on top of all that, in a shocking personal interview, God gave him the ultimate "genie in the lamp" experience—he allowed Solomon to request a gift from God, whatever he wanted. In a burst of faith and humility, Solomon asked for wisdom, wisdom to govern well. It was granted. He was now the richest and smartest guy on the earth.

But good apples can turn rotten, especially when they're in a barrel with a lot of rotten ones. **"King Solomon, however, loved many foreign women besides Pharaoh's daughter—Moabites, Ammonites, Edomites, Sidonians and Hittites. They were from nations about which the LORD had told the Israelites, 'You must not intermarry with them, because they will surely turn your hearts after their gods.' Nevertheless, Solomon held fast to them in love. He had seven hundred wives of royal birth and three hundred concubines, and his wives led him astray"** (1 Kings 11:1-3).

How did that happen? Pride. Arrogance. Materialism. Wanting the admiration and approval of other kings more than from God. Deafness to the counsel of godly advisors.

It can happen. Now you know. Be warned.

september

See that you do not despise one of these little ones.
For I tell you that their angels in heaven always see
the face of my Father in heaven.

Matthew 18:10

The kid on Jesus' lap

Jason Nelson

You've seen me in pictures, but you don't know my name. I'm one of the most famous people in the Bible, and one of the cutest. I'm the kid on Jesus' lap.

My parents took me to see Jesus. I think it was bring-your-kids-to-Jesus day because there were lots of other kids there too. We just wanted him to bless us. Some scary-looking guys were acting like bodyguards. They pushed us out of the way. I felt sad and scared. Then Jesus spoke up and said, **"Don't push these children away. Don't ever get between them and me. These children are at the very center of life in the kingdom"** (Mark 10:14 MSG). I don't like hearing adults raise their voices to each other. All of a sudden Jesus picked me up and set me on his lap. He hugged me and talked softly to me. I could tell he loved me very much.

Do you ever wonder why we were always there when Jesus needed to make a point or borrow a lunch to feed other people? It's because we were disciples too. We were just little, that's all.

I got big enough that I could lift a palm branch. The day Jesus rode into Jerusalem on a donkey lots of us were there again. I shouted to him, "Hosanna, Jesus!" I think he remembered me because he looked my way and winked. I really love that guy.

Waiting is the hardest part
Linda Buxa

A few years ago, my just-waking-up child walked into the kitchen and asked for scrambled eggs. I said no—because the bacon, apple, and cheddar frittata was in the oven and would be ready in 15 minutes.

After some arguing and begging, he said, "You're not my real mom. If you were, you'd care about me."

I was trying not to laugh while I thought, "I'm making you bacon! What part of *bacon* with the eggs don't you fully grasp?"

Right then the Holy Spirit gave me a gentle, "Does this remind you of anyone?"

At times I think God must not care for me because my plan, which consists of immediate relief, peace, and happiness, doesn't seem to be his plan, which consists of discipline, refining, and waiting. I am often willing to settle—and whine about—a proverbial plate of scrambled eggs, while God has a bacon frittata almost ready for me.

I can always look back and testify how God worked in every situation, but in the middle of it? That is when I forget to trust these words: **"For when you did awesome things that we did not expect, you came down, and the mountains trembled before you. Since ancient times no one has heard, no ear has perceived, no eye has seen any God besides you, who acts on behalf of those who wait for him"** (Isaiah 64:3,4).

God does awesome things, and he acts on my behalf—in his time. I'm still learning. And so are my kids.

I'm anxious all the time

Pastor Mark Jeske

All of us have at least one disability of one kind or another. Sometimes that challenge in our lives proves to be a great energy source: the youngest child who is ignored and patronized in the family becomes an overachiever "to show them I'm somebody." A middle schooler with a stutter is driven to overcome it and become a great speaker. Someone who lives with daily anxiety might compensate by channeling that fear and energy into excellence at work. Or the reverse—the frequent panic attacks make every kind of scholastic test or work evaluation a time of total emotional terror and shutdown.

Daily anxiety is a widespread plague—over 10 percent of American adults take some form of antidepressant medication. Whether you are on a med or not, there is a form of relief available to all believers in Christ: **"Cast all your anxiety on him because he cares for you"** (1 Peter 5:7). Scripture promises us that God is indeed tracking our day-to-day lives, that he cares deeply for us, that his ears are attuned to our prayers, that each prayer receives an appropriate answer at the right time, and that God actually does intervene in human history for the benefit of believers.

He is not merely watching us. He is engaged. That means you're not alone. That means even your hardships can turn into blessings. That means you always win in the end.

Go ahead. Cast your anxiety on him. His shoulders are big enough to take it all.

People notice generosity
Pastor Mark Jeske

All promoters of their particular version of religion are good talkers. They all have a particular value proposition that they are peddling. People who are searching spiritually can hear the talk, and they are interested in the topic, but they are often skeptical. They don't want to be hustled. Long before Sinclair Lewis satirized Christian evangelists with his novel *Elmer Gantry*, people viewed religious talkers as first cousins of carnival barkers.

That will never change. People today are in as desperate need for Christ as they ever were. And they are just as skeptical as ever, perhaps more so because every smartphone gives every listener the chance to fact-check every bit of information instantly. The need for Christian talkers to back up their messages with deeds of love has never been more important than right now. Religious talk is cheap. True love expressed in sacrificial service will always be noticed and respected.

St. Paul not only brought the doctrine of Christ's saving work to the people in Corinth; he recruited them into a compassion project that was painfully important back in Jerusalem. The Corinthians were relatively wealthier than the poor saints in Judea because of an artificially constructed punitive famine there: **"Because of the service by which you have proved yourselves, others will praise God for the obedience that accompanies your confession of the gospel of Christ, and for your generosity in sharing with them and with everyone else"** (2 Corinthians 9:13).

Sacrificial service is a triple play: People are helped. God is worshiped. And seekers notice.

What happened to Bartholomew?

Jason Nelson

I was thinking about all of the times I've mentioned Peter, Paul, John, or even James in one of these devotions. Then I realized I've never mentioned Bartholomew. Why the oversight? What happened to him anyway? I don't remember Jesus ever having a conversation with Bartholomew. I can't write, "As our Lord said to Bartholomew" or "As we learn from the apostle Bartholomew." Commentators suggest his identity may have been mistaken with Nathanael, which doesn't help matters. He may have taken Matthew's gospel to India. He was 1 of the 12 whom Jesus chose personally. He saw Jesus by the lake after the resurrection (John 21:2). He was there with the rest for Jesus' ascension and the bestowing of the Holy Spirit (Acts 1). That's all a pretty big deal, but there's no buzz about him.

I've known other people like that. The Holy Christian church is filled with stealth servants. Maybe you're one of them. They quietly slip in and do God's work, and they slip out without fanfare. What would be noticed is if they stopped doing it. In one of my churches, there was a man who washed the windows every week. No one asked him to do it. But he saw the windows were dirty, so every Saturday he brought his bucket of ammonia water and stack of old newspapers and washed each window until it was squeaky clean. I don't remember his name, but I'll think of him as Bartholomew.

Ego medicine
Pastor Mark Jeske

There are some pretty cool things about being an only child. You certainly don't lack attention, and you have a shot at better resources to pay for a better education. But there are some serious advantages to being a kid in a large family. One of the most profound is that you are not allowed to take yourself very seriously. The peanut gallery will keep you humble.

St. Paul knew that our sinful egos are restless forces that need to be controlled throughout our lives: **"By the grace given me I say to every one of you: Do not think of yourself more highly than you ought, but rather think of yourself with sober judgment"** (Romans 12:3).

How will you know if you are getting a little too full of yourself? Just listen to the people around you. Ask them, and they will tell you. Pay attention to their little suggestions about talking less in a group and listening better. Choose to be more interested in drawing out other people's stories than in telling tales of your own exploits. Decide that making other people feel important doesn't diminish you. You won't have to thump your own chest to get noticed—your works of love will speak for themselves.

It is one of the sweet ironies of the Christian life that the more you serve other people and the more you deny yourself and follow Jesus, the more other people will like and appreciate you.

Refinement by fire

Linda Buxa

I find the concept of trial-by-comfort pretty appealing. It sounds so much better than the whole trial-by-fire thing, which is a concept I'm not particularly keen on.

Yet as I live this life, I realize that trial-by-fire is a large part of the human experience. Grandpa has ALS. Your best friend struggles with loneliness. You are just barely winning the battle against pornography. Your brother buried his child. Work has been brutal. Your teens are trying to navigate high school temptations, relationships, and pressures. You are tired of being told you're ignorant for believing in Jesus.

You know what stops you from being overwhelmed by the weight of it all? Hearing this message from 1 Peter: **"In** [God's] **great mercy he has given us new birth into a living hope through the resurrection of Jesus Christ from the dead, and into an inheritance that can never perish, spoil or fade. . . . In all this you greatly rejoice, though now for a little while you may have had to suffer grief in all kinds of trials. These have come so that the proven genuineness of your faith—of greater worth than gold, which perishes even though refined by fire—may result in praise, glory and honor when Jesus Christ is revealed"** (1:3,4,6,7).

I'm not asking you to wear rose-colored glasses. Death, temptation, illness, and trouble are hard. Yet God is using those to refine us and draw us closer to him in faith—until the day he literally draws us closer to him by taking us home to heaven.

So we greatly rejoice.

I feel lukewarm spiritually

Pastor Mark Jeske

Nothing on this volatile planet ever stays the same, and that includes all of our relationships. We are either growing closer to people or drifting away from them.

That's true of our relationship with God too. It's not that he has moved or lost any interest in us. Scripture says that our God does not change like shifting shadows. He is rock steady. It is we who change. Every day Satan presents us with a variety of attractive idols to put into the center of our hearts and push God out. Every relationship consumes fuel, and if you don't refill the tank, the relationship sags.

If you feel lukewarm spiritually, if the old stories of Creation, Christmas, Good Friday, Easter, and Pentecost no longer thrill your heart, if the Great Commission to make disciples of the world no longer stirs your blood, it may be time to be more intentional about refilling your tank with God's Word. The Word brings reality, power, and clarity of purpose to our lives.

You may be feeling spiritually sluggish because you are far too inwardly focused. You might be just a little too full of yourself. The best medicine for unhealthy self-absorption is to become a servant again: **"A generous person will prosper; whoever refreshes others will be refreshed"** (Proverbs 11:25).

Who needs your help today?

A grandparent's legacy

Sarah Habben

Grandparents. You have a bit of a reputation, you know. You hand out cookies before dinner. You obey the bedtime plea, "Just one more story!" You fork over change for bubblegum machines and Happy Meals. You hug instead of lecture. You cheerfully push swings, occupy bleachers, make muffins, buy pizza, chauffeur, tutor, and send birthday cards.

Thank you, dear grandparents, for your legacy of love.

But thank you infinitely more for your legacy of faith. Biblical grandparents left this legacy too. As death neared, Jacob/Israel made it a priority to pray over his grandsons and ask God to bless them: **"When Israel saw the sons of Joseph, he asked, 'Who are these?' 'They are the sons God has given me here,' Joseph said to his father. Then Israel said, 'Bring them to me so I may bless them'"** (Genesis 48:8,9).

Thank you, grandparents, for all the grandkid prayers that have gone from your hearts to God's ear.

In another Bible account, Paul reminded young Timothy that his faith was a legacy from his grandma: **"I am reminded of your sincere faith, which first lived in your grandmother Lois and in your mother Eunice and, I am persuaded, now lives in you also"** (2 Timothy 1:5).

Thank you, God, for the "sincere faith" that our Christian grandparents have so carefully shared from their laps, over coffee, through the mail, and on the phone . . . so that one day we can share a home with them in heaven.

What a precious, priceless inheritance.

Washed clean
Pastor Mark Jeske

What a break! The brilliant, raging young Pharisee named Saul had been on a tear, using his organization's influence, connections, and money to pursue Christians, have them arrested for their beliefs, fined, imprisoned, property confiscated, and even killed.

And now a wonderful Christian man in Damascus named Ananias had Saul, temporarily blinded and helpless, in his power. Would he do to Saul what Saul had done to other Christians? Whatever revenge fantasies were playing in his mind, what he actually did was love and encourage his "prisoner," even calling him Brother Saul: **"The God of our ancestors has chosen you to know his will and to see the Righteous One and to hear words from his mouth. You will be his witness to all people of what you have seen and heard. And now what are you waiting for? Get up, be baptized and wash your sins away, calling on his name"** (Acts 22:14-16).

How could the soul of a persecutor of God's children ever be washed clean? How could the heart of a stone-cold killer ever be softened? Through the gospel of Christ and the washing of water and the Word, both things happened. Saul was renamed Paul, and the persecutor of Christ now became his most ardent evangelist.

Your baptism has done the same thing for you. Declared clean and pure before God, you are now set free to be filled with his Word and to carry out his agenda for your life.

Lying talk
Pastor Mark Jeske

Why do people tell lies? Well, that's easy. Because lying might enable guilty people to escape responsibility and consequences for their misdeeds. Because lying might preserve the illusion of their innocence. Because lying helps the sinner avoid having to face up to the ugly and soul-polluting reality of the sin.

But here's the problem—when you tell lies, you not only lie to a person; you are also lying to yourself. And if you do that often enough, you will lose your ability to tell the difference between truth and lie. Furthermore, you are lying to God, damaging your relationship with him. Words of truth are his saving lifeline to us—when we trash the truth, we risk the gospel itself. Jesus once called lying Satan's native language, **"for he is a liar and the father of lies"** (John 8:44).

You can't control what other people do with their mouths, but you can control your own: **"Do not lie to each other, since you have taken off your old self with its practices and have put on the new self, which is being renewed in knowledge in the image of its Creator"** (Colossians 3:9,10). Let your love for God be accompanied by a love for truth, for all truth is his. Trust that he will bless you for telling the truth, even when you fear it will cost you. In the long run, your life will be better.

Would God lie to you?

Be strong and courageous

Pastor Mike Novotny

Being a Christian is dangerous. Ask the grandmother who stands up for the first time to the gossips in her circle of churchgoing friends. Or the Caucasian kid who posts pictures of his black and Mexican roommates, knowing what his bigoted parents will mutter under their breath. Or the successful woman who bucks the cultural trend to keep her faith to herself and brings up Jesus with her Buddhist neighbor. Or the pastor who dares to preach the uncomfortable things Jesus said.

Given that historians believe Matthew, Thomas, James, Philip, Peter, Andrew, Bartholomew, James, Simon, and Thaddeus were all murdered for following Jesus (Judas betrayed and John survived being boiled in oil, which makes all 12 apostles), we should probably expect a bit of danger if we follow the sandal tracks of our Savior.

In those moments, when fear threatens to change our minds and make us play it safe, we need the words Joshua heard as he ventured into the Promised Land: **"Be strong and courageous"** (Joshua 1:6,7,9). God encouraged him not once, not twice, but three times in a single chapter.

The danger Joshua faced was as real as yours. But you and Joshua share the same source of strength—God. The Father will be with you. Jesus will forgive your sins and compel you to take the risk. The Spirit will give you wisdom in your time of need. So don't give in to fear. Do what God is calling you to do. Be strong and courageous! God is with you!

We don't earn it
Linda Buxa

When my kids were 18 months, 3, and 4 years old, my husband was trying to get their help on some chores. They weren't excited, so he declared, "I'll give you three Super Helper Points!" The kids raced to pitch in. After all, they were earning Super. Helper. Points.

In the aftermath of that off-the-cuff-no-actual-plan-in-mind remark, we had to scramble to figure out exactly what Super Helper Points were—and what the reward would be. (At that age, the reward was often ice cream.) After that, we started dishing out Super Helper Points like Monopoly money. Charts were made, progress tracked, ice cream purchased.

Sometimes it's easy to think that good things from God work like Super Helper Points. If I follow the rules, God should reward me. If I'm helpful at church, I won't have budget problems. If I work hard, I should get the promotion. Ultimately, if I was a good person, then I should get into heaven.

That is not at all how God works. It's not at all about what we've earned. Instead, **"it is by grace you have been saved, through faith—and this is not from yourselves, it is the gift of God—not by works, so that no one can boast"** (Ephesians 2:8,9).

It's not at all about if we've been a super helper; it's only about how Jesus helped us. By dying on the cross to pay for our sins, he earned heaven for us. It's a gift, and we can't boast.

But I still hope there's ice cream.

Alone at the top
Pastor Mark Jeske

Imagine just for one minute that you can see the world as God does. Imagine that you are he, looking at all the homemade gods that people have designed and worship. How could you not snort in derision that seemingly bright people are giving such honor and glory to things that don't exist. Their gods are vapor. Imaginations. Fantasies. They are nothing.

The world in which we live today esteems tolerance and diversity as its chief values. Every religion is treated as having equal legitimacy. Everyone is encouraged to find his or her own "truth." Here is what God thinks: **"See now that I myself am he! There is no god besides me. I put to death and I bring to life, I have wounded and I will heal, and no one can deliver out of my hand"** (Deuteronomy 32:39).

We show no love to people in our circle of influence if we know they are disconnected from the God of the Bible and we say nothing. That isn't fairness or open-mindedness or sophistication. That is just muteness during suicide. We need to find courage and words that show gentleness and respect to people, but words that nonetheless pass on the truth about the Creator, Savior, and Counselor. We need to stand firm in insisting that there is absolute truth and that every religious philosophy that is not grounded in Scripture is a fantasy.

The God of the Bible is alone at the top.

Come soon, Lord Jesus

Pastor Mark Jeske

There's lots to love in this life. God's creation is so beautiful. Childbirth is such a stunning miracle. Children's voices and laughter are so joyful. Music and poetry and dance and painting and architecture enrich our spirits. Achievements at work can be really satisfying. The love of family and friends gives such warmth.

But the burden gets heavier each year, and sometimes we are just so ready to go home to heaven. We've had enough pain, frustration, and disappointment for a lifetime. Certain of our salvation, grateful for grace, eyes heavenward, cleansed and confident, we can say the Revelation prayer: "*Maranatha.* Come soon, Lord Jesus."

He *is* coming soon. Expect him at any minute (maybe today). **"Look, I am coming soon! Blessed is the one who keeps the words of the prophecy written in this scroll"** (Revelation 22:7). Here's the core of the prophecy you need to keep in your heart: Jesus loves me unconditionally. He has forgiven me everything. I am safe in his arms. Everything is going to be all right.

A gifted English priest named Samuel Stone wrote this amazing and encouraging verse about the embattled Christian church. May it give you hope today:

Though with a scornful wonder
the world sees her oppressed,
By schisms rent asunder, by heresies distressed,
Yet saints their watch are keeping;
their cry goes up, "How long?"
And soon the night of weeping
shall be the morn of song.

A tale of two kids

Pastor Mike Novotny

Walk into my eldest daughter's bedroom and you will marvel at the tidy space. Stop next door at her younger sister's room and you'll wonder if a tornado touched down on a stuffed animal factory. My kids are different. The clean one is quiet and smart like her momma. The messy one is funny and beautifully compassionate. They have different gifts, different personalities, different passions. Same mom, same dad, different kids.

The same thing is true of Christians. Same God, same Bible, different people. Paul writes, **"All these [gifts] are the work of one and the same Spirit, and he distributes them to each one, just as he determines"** (1 Corinthians 12:11). The Holy Spirit determined to give us all different gifts, even if we are part of the same church family or even the same biological family.

So can I encourage you to stop competing and start complementing? You don't have to be like your older sister or your younger brother. You don't have to communicate like your brothers in faith or solve problems like your sisters in Christ. You can be you. You can thank God for gracing you with your gifts, your passions, and your personality. When God made you, he meant it.

If you're a parent, can I offer a similar encouragement? Kids thrive when they can be themselves, without obsessive comparisons to their siblings. So remind them of the Savior who died for their sins and sent his Spirit so they could be unique parts in the body of Christ.

Two more little prayers

Jason Nelson

"My sheep listen to my voice; I know them, and they follow me. I give them eternal life, and they shall never perish; no one will snatch them out of my hand" (John 10:27,28).

Spirit of God, open our hearts. We want to hear your voice today. Sometimes we close our minds to what you say in the Bible because it's not convenient to hear. Obeying you might disrupt some things on our schedules. In the name of Jesus who was obedient to death on a cross, forgive us for ignoring your will. Help us remember you love us. Help us appreciate all the good that comes from righteous living. Help us want those blessings for ourselves and our families. Amen.

"Do not cast me from your presence or take your Holy Spirit from me. Restore to me the joy of your salvation and grant me a willing spirit, to sustain me" (Psalm 51:11,12).

Lord, we let you down. We do things we shouldn't and don't do what we should. And we make lots of excuses. We are sorry. Keep us humble but remove our shame. In the name of Jesus, restore us in your mercy. Embrace us in your grace: not just once, not just twice, but every time we bow our heads and fold our hands to confess our sins. Make us bold to resist temptation. Help us show the world your forgiveness isn't wasted on us. We want to live for you. Amen.

What am I living for?

Pastor Mark Jeske

From the moment our eyes pop open in the morning, we are driven by our appetites, our physical and emotional wants and needs. All of us feel powerful compulsions for food, security, stimulation, communication, power, intimacy, and significance. We are driven to avoid things that cause discomfort, stress, and pain. We strive to manage events to our advantage, always looking for an angle, always interested in what's in it for us.

Until we are converted to Christ, our lives center on ourselves, our own pleasures, comforts, and desires. In the hearts of believers, however, lives the Holy Spirit, and he reorients our life focus.

"I urge you, brothers and sisters, in view of God's mercy, to offer your bodies as a living sacrifice, holy and pleasing to God—this is your true and proper worship" (Romans 12:1). This is a monumental revolution in our life drivers. It literally turns our life focus inside out, down to up. Putting God first in our life agenda is radical.

What does this mean for us? It means adopting God's principles of right and wrong. It means being willing to suffer short-term inconvenience or pain, trusting that doing the right things will benefit us and others in the long term. It means seeking God's approval first, before even that of family and friends. Our hero and model is Christ himself, who put himself through a humble, service-oriented life; terrible suffering; and a criminal's death in order to redeem the human race.

This is true worship.

Judging talk

Pastor Mark Jeske

Being "judgmental" is one of the greatest social sins you can commit today. You can hold any ideas you may care to, but you absolutely may not ever make somebody else feel uncomfortable or "othered" because of his or her lifestyle or beliefs. As Christians we know that God expects us to witness to his Word and hold onto his standards. So what is the difference between faithful witness and judging?

"Judging" is looking down at someone else, imagining yourself to be more worthy of God's mercy, despising others for their weakness, lasering in on others' faults while never looking at your own. St. Paul was once a Pharisee, and he knew the deadly danger of becoming one: **"You, therefore, have no excuse, you who pass judgment on someone else, for at whatever point you judge another, you are condemning yourself, because you who pass judgment do the same things"** (Romans 2:1).

Here are more helpful attitudes to adopt: interpreting the words and actions of others in the kindest possible way instead of the worst . . . keeping your words soft and humble . . . if you must say things that point out someone else's flaws, open *your* life up to correcting by that person . . . looking always to build up other people instead of tearing them down.

Imagine that Jesus is in the room with you and your talk. Would he like what he is hearing? You know, don't you, that he is actually in the room?

God uses people to help people
Pastor Mark Jeske

There's a reason why magicians and illusionists are pretty much permanent features of the entertainment circuit. When David Copperfield and Penn & Teller retire from their Las Vegas theaters, others will take their place.

People love magicians because they want to believe in magic. We all have a driving inner fantasy that the right person with the right powers can just do some abracadabra and "Poof!" Our problems are fixed. The Bible stories of God's instantaneous miracles are popular in every Sunday school. Who can resist the stories of miraculous wine, bread, fish, and healing?

I suspect that's the kind of solution a lot of Christians have in mind when they bring their troubles to the Lord in prayer. Sometimes God does intervene with a physics-defying act of power. But it seems to be his considerable preference to work more quietly than that—sending key people into our lives.

St. Paul's prayers at a desperate time were answered in this way: **"When we came into Macedonia, we had no rest, but we were harassed at every turn—conflicts on the outside, fears within. But God, who comforts the downcast, comforted us by the coming of Titus"** (2 Corinthians 7:5,6). At first Paul may have thought, "What? God, I asked for *you*! This is all you've got?" But he was perceptive enough to see shortly that Titus' unique gifts and capabilities were *exactly* what he needed at that time.

Look around you. Your gaze has probably landed on some of God's answers to your prayers.

Hell week
Linda Buxa

You don't simply get to be called a Navy SEAL. You have to earn that title—through an almost-incomprehensible amount of training and testing. Most notorious is Hell Week. As the defining moment of their training, potential SEALs have to make it through five and a half days of brutal training conditions while getting fewer than four hours of sleep.

All the while, they are told to give up. If they ring a bell that signifies they are quitting, they can get warm and dry and then get some sleep. Only 25 percent make it through—and only those who have suffered themselves get the title.

Jesus didn't simply get to be called Savior. He earned that title—through an almost-incomprehensible amount of testing. He endured the brutal conditions of being tempted in the wilderness for 40 days by Satan, who encouraged him to give up. But he didn't quit.

That prepared him for his other Hell Week, what we now call Holy Week. After having people mock him, spit on him, and whip him, it ended with him thirsty, naked, and hanging on a cross. They encouraged him to "ring the bell" by coming off the cross and saving himself. Even worse, he hung there, separated from the Father, and cried out, **"My God, my God, why have you forsaken me?"** (Matthew 27:46).

But he didn't quit. Instead, he said, **"It is finished"** (John 19:30).

Now we simply get to be called children of God—because Jesus earned the title for us.

Heroes need the Word too
Pastor Mark Jeske

Mental cloudiness is the curse of every human being. Until we get to heaven and finally see, hear, and understand everything clearly, we squint and peer ahead, trying to make sense of a world gone crazy. We're all sinners. Even reborn and sanctified Christians, even (especially) Christian leaders, need to stay tuned into and obedient to God's Word.

Despising and shunning Gentiles had been so deeply ingrained into the Jewish culture in which Simon Peter grew up that he apparently had only partially bought into the Pentecost idea that the doors of faith were really being thrown open to all the world. He backslid into practices of racial and religious segregation. Paul was outraged: **"When Cephas** [i.e., Peter] **came to Antioch, I opposed him to his face, because he stood condemned. For before certain men came from James, he used to eat with the Gentiles. But when they arrived, he began to draw back and separate himself from the Gentiles because he was afraid of those who belonged to the circumcision group. The other Jews joined him in his hypocrisy, so that by their hypocrisy even Barnabas was led astray"** (Galatians 2:11-13).

Our own hypotheses and conclusions and habits and customs may be sincere. They may have been held for a long time and held by many others, maybe even the majority of your congregation or denomination. You too may be afraid of your version of "the circumcision group."

Back to the Word. Always, back to the Word.

Is pride good or bad?

Pastor Mark Jeske

"Pride goes before a fall." Even people who have never had their noses in a Bible know that proverb. It is usually applied to others who are perceived as arrogant and spoken by people who are intimidated and jealous, hoping the jerk will stumble and face-plant.

Pride most certainly is a terrible sin. The more one's ego is inflated, the smaller God becomes in the person's life. Here's a story from one who knows. The sovereign of imperial Babylon had been temporarily cursed by God with insanity. Hair and beard wild and unkempt, he grazed on pasture grass like a wild beast. When he regained his right mind, he acknowledged the God of heaven: **"I, Nebuchadnezzar, praise and exalt and glorify the King of heaven, because everything he does is right and all his ways are just. And those who walk in pride he is able to humble"** (Daniel 4:37).

On the other hand, when God is firmly seated on the throne of your life, it *is* possible to take pride in what has been accomplished through you. Paul was justifiably proud of the progress the Christians in Corinth had made in their lives of faith and deeds: **"I have spoken to you with great frankness; I take great pride in you. I am greatly encouraged; in all our troubles my joy knows no bounds"** (2 Corinthians 7:4).

There is a great satisfaction in using God's gifts with God's people to accomplish God's agenda. Yes, be proud.

Weaponizing faith
Jason Nelson

The Bible uses military language to characterize the good fight of faith. The Holy Spirit issues "swords" and "shields" to us so we can fend off evil with the precepts he teaches us. But if our only view of the world is from up in a mighty fortress, we risk assuming the enemy is everywhere. We isolate ourselves and misread others who are just as scared as we are. We mark them for avoidance, demean them with labels, and keep them outside the walls. At this stage of my service to God, my deepest concern is for weak people who were driven away from Jesus by "strong" Christians who weaponized the faith.

Isaiah knew a thing or two about being a believer in a hostile environment. And he understood Jesus as well as anyone. He foretold how Jesus would deal with damaged people with keen awareness that we are all damaged people. **"He won't brush aside the bruised and the hurt and he won't disregard the small and insignificant, but he'll steadily and firmly set things right"** (Isaiah 42:3 MSG).

Jesus set things right with steady, firm, and vulnerable love. He engaged people from a cross, not in combat. His marching orders to us also resound with words of compassion, patience, forgiveness, and peace. He wants us out of the fortress and in the world with his message of reconciliation. That's a tough battle because the only way we can join it is by letting our guard down.

I feel overwhelmed

Pastor Mark Jeske

Sometimes life is good—you're caught up with all your obligations, bills paid, health good, daily pressures manageable, no crises at work.

But other days you feel overwhelmed. The water level of troubles just keeps rising and is past your chest and up to your chin right now. There are messes in your family, your creditors are leaning on you, you don't feel well, can't sleep, and then the car won't start. You don't know whether to lash out or just slump to the floor and give up. Every day people you know wish they were dead. Last year over one million people in the U.S. acted on suicidal impulses. Twenty-five percent succeeded.

Our Savior Jesus has huge compassion for all his brothers and sisters who are struggling to survive, physically and emotionally. He himself experienced the full measure of human exhaustion, rejection, hunger, thirst, pain, and the torments of the devil.

Jesus' ancestor, the poet and musician King David, gives us a vocabulary for expressing our fear, suffering, anxiety, and longing for relief: **"As for me, I am poor and needy; may the Lord think of me. You are my help and my deliverer; you are my God, do not delay"** (Psalm 40:17). David's miseries were real, but so were God's interventions in his life to rescue him. At just the right time, God answered David's prayer and brought him relief.

Don't give up. Pray to your God. Remind him that he is your Father. Articulate your struggle. Let go. Await his good plan.

Special
Sarah Habben

You might have been picked for recess teams based on your fast feet.

You may have attracted someone with your sense of humor, stunning looks, or skills on the dance floor.

You might have been hired because you're organized and efficient.

But why did *God* choose you? Why did he decide to rescue, protect, and bless you?

A deep-down part of me assumes that God chose me because, well, I'm ME. I'm *nice.* (And you should see me dance.)

Now I sound just like the Israelites. They, too, figured that God had plucked them from slavery and obscurity because they were special. Surely they had sealed their privileged spot in his affection with their expensive sacrifices and careful diet. But Moses was blunt: **"The Lord did not set his affection on you and choose you because you were more numerous than other peoples, for you were the fewest of all peoples.** *But it was because the Lord loved you and kept the oath he swore* **to your ancestors that he brought you out with a mighty hand and redeemed you from the land of slavery"** (Deuteronomy 7:7,8).

Moses said, "You were nobodies. God chose you for two reasons: 1) he loved you 2) he was keeping his promise."

Same here. God didn't rescue us from Satan because we're special. He liberated us with Jesus' blood out of love and loyalty to his word.

God has graced a world of nobodies with his love and promises. That's what makes us special.

Lord, place us in families

Jason Nelson

Lord, even when we are surrounded by people, we can feel so alone. We feel isolated and cut off from others because no one has our problems or is going through what we are going through. We are never alone, but the devil wants us to feel that way. It is easier for him to pick us off and take us down when we think we're all alone.

When King David felt alone and under attack on every side, he said, **"God sets the lonely in families, he leads out the prisoners with singing; but the rebellious live in a sun-scorched land"** (Psalm 68:6). So we ask you, Lord, to place us in as many families as you possibly can.

Make us who live under the same roof a close-knit family. Remove any serious conflict among us and help us stop the silly bickering over unimportant things. Make us a family at work because we are all dedicated to being productive and earning an honest living. Make our country a family of citizens who share the values of life, liberty, and happiness for everyone because we were all created by you. Make our church a close and growing family because we listen to your Word, sing songs, and pray all at the same time.

And when we are by ourselves, help us remember we are never alone. You are always our Father, and we are always your children. Jesus is always our brother and our Savior. Because of him, we are never alone.

People fail

Pastor Mike Novotny

I have a pastoral pet peeve. Can I share it with you? I get annoyed when people give up on church too quickly. I could tell you a dozen stories of people whose spiritual lives were being changed at the church . . . until someone from church failed them. Then they lost their fire. They drifted. They left.

Apparently, I need to do a better job communicating what the church is—a big gathering of failures. A community of people who love Jesus, not because he's nice but because they need him. Maybe being clearer about our own sinfulness will keep people around long enough to hear more about Jesus.

That's exactly what Joshua did. When the people of Israel got ready to enter the Promised Land, they swore, **"Just as we fully obeyed Moses, so we will obey you"** (Joshua 1:17). I imagine Joshua chuckled at that line because he was there when the Israelites shook their fists at Moses and picked up rocks to stone him. Exodus and Numbers should be called the Book of Grumbling, Parts 1 & 2.

But when the people failed him, Joshua did not bail on his calling. He stuck around. He learned perseverance. Perhaps he knew his own failures well enough to expect a few of theirs too.

I guarantee someone will fail you this week. Your secret shared. Their promise broken. His vow unkept. An unneighborly neighbor. When that happens, take a deep breath, remember your own failures, and ask God to help you. Because he is the One who never fails. Ever.

Teaching kids not to be selfish

Pastor Mark Jeske

My wife and I still laugh about our good intentions about discouraging violent play between our children. We gravely pledged that we would not buy them toy guns. We didn't. So they just made their own guns out of Legos to shoot each other. When we took the Legos away, they killed each other each day with their fingers. We sighed and gave up. To this day they have a massive Nerf arsenal.

You might think it will be the same battle trying to teach kids not to be selfish. How can you stop people from looking out for their own interests? Isn't that human nature? Isn't that a critically important survival skill?

Parents, don't shrink from this struggle. Worship of Self is the most basic kind of idolatry: **"Who is wise and understanding among you? Let them show it by their good life, by deeds done in the humility that comes from wisdom. But if you harbor bitter envy and selfish ambition in your hearts, do not boast about it or deny the truth. Such 'wisdom' does not come down from heaven but is earthly, unspiritual, demonic. For where you have envy and selfish ambition, there you find disorder and every evil practice"** (James 3:13-16).

Our Savior loved and served other people above himself. We must teach our kids to do no less . . . to make other people feel important . . . to think ahead of the impact of their actions . . . to notice if anybody around them is struggling and straggling.

Encourage and reward servant hearts in your kids. Eventually they'll get it.

Gold

Sarah Habben

Job, the Old Testament believer, was at a loss. God had stripped him of so much. Worldly goods. Family. Friends. Dignity. Respect. Health. If only Job could plead in person for God to relent! But in his grief, Job could not even find God in prayer.

"If only I knew where to find him; if only I could go to his dwelling! . . . I catch no glimpse of him" (Job 23:3,9).

What has been stripped from your life? Maybe your list of losses rivals Job's. Even one such loss can spiral through a person's life like an over-torqued screw, splitting the fibers of what seemed whole and beautiful, cracking it down the middle.

If only there was a way to make the pain end. If only you knew what to pray. If only you could find God!

Take heart, believer. You can't always know the way that God takes. But like Job you can confess: **"*He* knows the way that *I* take; when he has tested me, I will come forth as gold"** (Job 23:10).

Though you stumble, you follow God's way, led by his goodness and mercy. When you fold your hands and fumble for words, the Holy Spirit groans on your behalf. When you feel an amputee's longing for better, bygone days, God promises your time of testing will end. As you dress your heart's wounds with God's promises . . . *you are loved, you are forgiven, heaven awaits* . . . your good gift of faith is made better.

And you will come forth as gold.

october

In the gospel the righteousness of God is revealed—
a righteousness that is by faith from first to last,
just as it is written: "The righteous will live by faith."

Romans 1:17

Big forgiveness, big love

Pastor Mark Jeske

There are some very bad boys in the Bible. Some bad girls too. One of them had been so convicted and so encouraged by Jesus' teachings that she chose a very unusual way to thank and worship him. She brought a jar of extremely expensive perfume, poured it on his feet, and dried them with her hair (!) as she wept in gratitude.

Have you ever been terrified that you had outraged God so deeply that you were going to hell for sure? Have you known the deep despair of the damned? This woman had. Whatever pleasures and profit she thought she had gained in her sinful life crumbled away, and she thought she was lost forever. Jesus gave her hope of God's favor, and her heart started beating again. It changed her life.

The peanut gallery in the house wanted to criticize her. Jesus shushed them and taught a powerful lesson: **"I tell you, her many sins have been forgiven—as her great love has shown. But whoever** [thinks he] **has been forgiven little loves little"** (Luke 7:47). Those who think they need no Savior, who think they are fine and righteous and moral people on their own, feel no obligation to serve anybody. But the gospel of forgiveness of sins through the blood of Christ is a transformative experience. Those who are grateful for grace show it by their changed lives.

Their worship is intense. Their love is from the heart.

october 2

Happily ever after?

Pastor Mike Novotny

Getting to happily ever after is complicated. No disrespect to Disney, but a good relationship is not that simple. It's not (1) love at first sight, (2) slight misunderstanding that causes tension, (3) defeat the fill-in-the-blank villain, and (4) live happily ever after. Sorry, I've seen too many grinning wedding couples grimace in divorce court to believe that.

That's why I love the Bible. Because the Bible gives us a better script for happily ever after; whether you're married, single, or divorced; a realistic view of finding true love, lasting happiness, and a deep contentment whatever your relationship status. Listen to what Paul, a single follower of Jesus, once wrote: **"I have learned to be content whatever the circumstances. I know what it is to be in need, and I know what it is to have plenty. I have learned the secret of being content in any and every situation, whether well fed or hungry, whether living in plenty or in want. I can do all this through him who gives me strength"** (Philippians 4:11-13). Paul learned the secret to happily ever after. Notice the word *learned*. This isn't something we know by nature. This isn't obvious. It's a secret that must be learned by God revealing it to us.

What's the secret? Jesus. Through Jesus we are always and eternally loved, cherished, pursued, accompanied, forgiven, befriended, and desired. Through Jesus we have someone who cares, who listens, who wants to help us with our problems. That is the truth—in all the complicated ups and downs of singleness, dating, divorce, and marriage—that leads to happily ever after.

A new master
Sarah Habben

In April 2018, Operation Libertad rescued nearly 350 victims of human trafficking in the Caribbean and Latin America. Some victims worked in spaces no bigger than coffins. Some were forced to work as prostitutes near remote gold mines. Others were stripped of their passports and savings and forced into total dependence. Essentially, they were slaves. But tragically, some of those victims wouldn't acknowledge it. Slavery was a price they were willing to pay for the faint hope of a better life.

At one time, we were slaves too. Our taskmaster was Satan. Our work was to roll in sin like pigs in mud. Our severance package was death. Sounds horrible, doesn't it? And yet, left to ourselves, we would never admit or realize we were being exploited. We would choose to stay in Satan's employ, prostituting ourselves to sin with hell as our final destination.

But God wouldn't allow it. He planned a coordinated raid on our hearts. He sent a specialist, Christ, to disarm the devil and break sin's shackles . . . and to give us a new master. **"But now that you have been set free from sin and have become slaves of God, the benefit you reap leads to holiness, and the result is eternal life. For the wages of sin is death, but the gift of God is eternal life in Christ Jesus our Lord"** (Romans 6:22,23).

When we were slaves of Satan, death was our due. As servants of God, we are made holy and given the gift of eternal life.

Who's your master?

Pray for the children

Pastor Mike Novotny

Ever heard of what happens to pastors' daughters? I have. And it freaks me out. The other night I snuck into my daughter's room and knelt at the side of her bed. Her pigtails poked out as her little face snuggled into a sea of stuffed animals. I smiled. And I prayed. Because I know it's coming. With big girl height and big girl teeth come big girl desires. As much as I want to threaten every boy who talks to her with the thickest leather-bound German Bible I can find, I know I can't. That's how pastors' daughters go wild.

So what do I do instead? I pray. I pray for the boy who will one day catch her eye. I pray he knows God. The God who gives. The God who forgives. The God who died so he could live. And I pray for his parents. I pray they show him what happens when Jesus is at the center, when a guy leads by asking, "How can I help?" I pray, and then I go to hold the hand of the woman who worships with me every day. I think of the psalmist's words, **"How good and pleasant it is when God's people** [including husbands and wives] **live together in unity!"** (Psalm 133:1).

Could you start praying today? For your son or daughter? Your niece or your nephew? The little kids you give high fives to at church? Maybe you can help lead them to the only place that truly is happily ever after—the presence of God.

Humility in prayer
Pastor Mark Jeske

I am glad I don't work in the office of my local alderman. People don't call to tell the alderman what a great job he's doing. They call because they're *furious* about all the potholes in their street . . . because the parking regulations on their block are so *stupid* . . . because the nearby tavern spills noisy drunks out onto the street at 2:00 A.M.! For good measure, the callers always remind the alderman that they deserve better service because of the *fortune* in property taxes they are paying.

Do you suppose God gets prayer messages on his "call-in line" that are demanding, petulant, aggrieved, and full of complaints? I'm sure he does. Occasionally I even catch myself feeling a sense of spiritual entitlement, as though I deserve a better stream of divine interventions in my life. You know, there's only one appropriate posture for our body language when we come to God's throne, and that's humility.

Like the Roman military officer who came to Jesus desperate for a medical miracle for a treasured member of his staff: **"That is why I did not even consider myself worthy to come to you. But say the word, and my servant will be healed"** (Luke 7:7). That officer is my hero. He made no demands. He assumed that Jesus already knew his needs. He didn't beg, bully, whine, argue, or offer a bribe. He just humbly presented his aching need and expressed complete confidence in Jesus' wisdom and power.

Just say the word!

The value of volunteering
Pastor Mark Jeske

I wouldn't blame newbies to Christianity for being a little confused at first. So many of the main teachings of the faith are paradoxes, i.e., seeming contradictions. For example: the teaching that God is simultaneously one and three. Another: that on Calvary God punished the plainly innocent and pardoned the obviously guilty. Or this: Jesus said that you have to lose your life to be fully alive.

Paradoxes abound as well in the way God invites us to live our daily lives. You would think it's an obvious truism that the more you give away, the less you will have. Not so, says God. Just the reverse! **"A generous person will prosper; whoever refreshes others will be refreshed"** (Proverbs 11:25).

This is the paradox of generosity: In giving you always end up with more, and it is in serving that your needs are always met. People who encounter this principle for the first time are undoubtedly skeptical. I get that. But just try it out and see what happens. People who volunteer to tutor low-income children; who spend of themselves as coaches and mentors; who work on Habitat builds; who volunteer at thrift stores, clothes banks, and food pantries; who help out frail, elderly, and disabled people in their neighborhood—all end up with more than they started with! Seriously! God's guarantee of refreshment always happens. Generous people always prosper.

Don't believe me? Ask a volunteer.

Jealous. Exclusive.

Pastor Mark Jeske

Generally speaking, jealousy is not considered a particularly desirable trait. Jealousy suggests that you are envious of someone else's blessings and achievements. Or that you are so possessive of your spouse that you will resort to violence if you think he or she is cheating on you.

Does it surprise you to hear God call himself a *jealous* God? He chose that word deliberately, for his passion burns hot for the people he created and redeemed and with whom he has a relationship through faith. A personal relationship with each and every man, woman, and child on earth is the entire reason for which he made the universe in the first place, and he is *intensely* interested in how people treat that relationship.

The Israelite believers in Old Testament times often severely tested God's commitment to them. He poured out his passion for them through prophets like Hosea: **"I have been the Lord your God ever since you came out of Egypt. You shall acknowledge no God but me, no Savior except me"** (Hosea 13:4). God today is just as insistent on an exclusive relationship. He will not share worship with any other gods, calling them worthless idols. He jealously claims first place in our love, trust, and obedience. His Word narrates all of the spectacular things he has done for us, and he will accept nothing less in response than exclusive worship from us.

Do you believe that?

A common text

Jason Nelson

Every year my wife and I try to read the same current book. It's usually nonfiction. Sometimes it's devotional in nature. Sometimes it's historical, biographical, or addresses something going on in our society. This little habit has given us more to talk about with each other and helps us develop a shared point of view. Through the ages many people called the Bible the Good Book for the same reason. Because they had all read it, they could say to each other, "You know what the Good Book says." And they could nod in agreement. A sense of community forms around a common text.

The Bible is a text that reveals its own authority and creates its own power. **"All Scripture is God-breathed and is useful for teaching, rebuking, correcting and training in righteousness, so that the servant of God may be thoroughly equipped for every good work"** (2 Timothy 3:16,17). That's a really good book that can do all that.

I'm pretty sure I've read the entire Bible. But I'll be honest; it wasn't front to back in one big burst of spiritual concentration. I'm too antsy for that. But I've studied every part I was privileged to teach. I've searched it for new ideas to write about. I've turned to favorite portions when I've needed to feel more of God's presence in my life. And I've been able to discuss it with other Christians because we have that text in common.

Deep trouble

Pastor Mark Jeske

What's the worst trouble you've ever been in? Persistent unemployment? Disabling automobile accident? Massive debts? In jail? Caught cheating on your spouse? Multiple DWIs? Terribly prodigal children? Drug addiction?

King Jehoshaphat's worst nightmare was coming right at him: a huge army of bitter enemies was moving in on his land from the south. As he made military preparations, he did the best and wisest possible thing—he prayed passionately and from the heart to his God on behalf of the nation: **"Our God, will you not judge them? For we have no power to face this vast army that is attacking us. We do not know what to do, but our eyes are on you"** (2 Chronicles 20:12). God heard their prayers. He not only gave victory to the Israelites; he confused the minds of the various nations in the attacking coalition so that they attacked and killed off one other. It took the Israelites four days to collect all the plunder.

When you are overwhelmed, when you don't know what to do, when you feel as though you have no power, say King Jehoshaphat's prayer. God has not lost even one kilowatt of power, and his love for you still burns bright. Call out for help in the name of Jesus, and let God know that your eyes are on him.

And then watch and listen for his rescue—in his way, at his time. The right way. The right time.

In God's house

Sarah Habben

"Lᴏʀᴅ, I love the house where you live, the place where your glory dwells" (Psalm 26:8).

David loved God's house. When he was away, his heart yearned to be in the courts of the Lord.

I confess, I don't always love being in God's house. Sometimes I get distracted by the hard wooden bench beneath me or the way my dress sticks to my legs on a Caribbean morning. Amid the clamor of steel pan and drum, my ears miss the plenum of a pipe organ; my heart misses the hymns of my past. I yearn for coffee more than the absolution, because the neighborhood dogs barked all night. I wonder how long the service will last.

I am ashamed of this side of my nature, this one that is not God's hot-blooded enemy, but worse—his lukewarm acquaintance. I tarnish his glory with my indifference. He should open the doors of his house and spit me out.

Then my wandering eyes settle on the cross and baptismal font, those visible reminders of God's glory and grace. Forgiveness was won on the beams of Christ's cross. There Jesus paid for my half-hearted praise. There new, true songs of joy and thanks are born. Grace flows from the font, where my sins were washed away in a flood of mercy.

In this house where believers have gathered in God's name, where God's Word of grace is spoken, God's glory dwells among us.

Lord, give me a heart that yearns to be here and to sing your praise.

Naughty fever! Bad fever!

Pastor Mark Jeske

I have limits to how much stress and trouble I can absorb when reading the news. When I've had enough, I just have to turn away and do something else. I'm afraid I will empathize too much and get too sad.

I cannot imagine how God can monitor the world's activity without burning out. How can he take it all in without getting angry and depressed about the wreckage of his once-perfect world? I might suspect that he has just stopped caring. But then we encounter Jesus in the home of Simon Peter, his most outspoken disciple. Peter's wife's mother was seriously ill. But instead of turning away, Jesus invested himself in the family's stress and fear and showed how much he cares about people: **"Simon's mother-in-law was suffering from a high fever, and they asked Jesus to help her. So he bent over her and rebuked the fever, and it left her. She got up at once and began to wait on them"** (Luke 4:38,39).

Isn't that an amazing statement? Jesus *rebuked* the fever, as though it were a family dog that had just piddled on the living room rug. "Naughty fever! Bad fever!" He scolded the fever for tormenting one of his sisters, and it obeyed him. Instantly Peter's mother-in-law felt well and jumped up to serve her guests.

I can't wait for the day when Jesus rebukes all human ills once and for all.

Part of the puzzle
Linda Buxa

Back when my kids were younger, we had a Star Wars lenticular puzzle. Have you seen those? They have a 3-D holographic thing going on. Each puzzle piece had shades of red, yellow, and black, depending on which way you held it, so they all looked the same. What made it worse was that each piece was the same shape. We finally threw it away.

It's frustrating when everything looks exactly the same.

This is why God created his church with all sorts of unique pieces. My gifts and talents (my colors and shape, if you will) are different from yours. So what if you don't write devotions? I can't build a building to his glory—because it would fall down! I wouldn't do so great as a surgeon or a welder or a math teacher either! And that is the beauty of his design. All of God's children—his puzzle pieces—are colorful and unique on their own—and he put them together exactly how he wanted them to be.

"We have different gifts, according to the grace given to each of us. If your gift is prophesying, then prophesy in accordance with your faith; if it is serving, then serve; if it is teaching, then teach; if it is to encourage, then give encouragement; if it is giving, then give generously; if it is to lead, do it diligently; if it is to show mercy, do it cheerfully" (Romans 12:6-8).

Use your God-given gifts to his glory!

Does virtue always bring rewards?

Pastor Mark Jeske

Parents, teachers, and coaches all stress to their young charges over and over that doing the right thing will always bring you benefits. Wouldn't you agree? Of course you would. You've taught that philosophy many times. Virtue always brings rewards.

Except when it doesn't. Sometimes you do the right thing and lose a friend. Get mocked on social media. Get fired. Joseph, the patriarch Jacob's 11th son, is a hero to all believers in overcoming sexual temptation. The wealthy Egyptian cougar in whose house Joseph was a servant came on to him strongly. When he backed away, she retaliated by accusing him of rape. **"Joseph's master took him and put him in prison, the place where the king's prisoners were confined"** (Genesis 39:20). What did virtue get Joseph? Punishment!

But God's eyes were on him, and his prison cell became the platform for an amazing rise to the very top of Egypt's government. God used Joseph and his special gifts to spare both his family and the Egyptian nation from famine. God also realized that he needed to get Jacob's family out of the corrupting land of Canaan, and Egypt became protective custody for the growing Israelite family/nation.

Virtue does indeed pay off, but sometimes it will cost you in the short run. Is Satan working on you right now to sell out your principles? cheat to get ahead? lie to your spouse? Obedience to God's will is always good all the time.

Ahem. Do you believe that?

Birthday praise

Pastor Mike Novotny

Who was the first crafty kid to hustle his parents into praising him for being born? I'm trying to envision the conversation . . . "Mom, remember when I caused you to vomit with morning sickness? And I stamped on your bladder at 3 A.M. all those nights? And I came out breach so your labor lasted forever? So . . . I was thinking that you should make me a cake! And buy me presents! And sing me songs of praise!" For real? Who were the first parents who agreed to that?

Peter would be baffled by our birthday customs. He wrote, **"Praise be to the God and Father of our Lord Jesus Christ! In his great mercy he has given us new birth"** (1 Peter 1:3). Who deserves the praise, the presents, and the cake for "new birth"? God! The Father who has given us new birth. The heavenly Dad who turned natural-born sinners into his born-again kids.

Think of the miracle that is your faith. Born in sin (Psalm 51:5), hostile to God's authority (Romans 8:7), without the Holy Spirit (1 Corinthians 2), and dead in transgressions (Ephesians 2). Yet the God of grace did not let that stop him. He used his living and enduring Word (1 Peter 1:23) to give us new birth, new life, new hope, all by his great mercy in Jesus Christ.

So the next time you have a birthday, give a word of praise to your parents. And the next time you think about being part of the family of faith, give a shout of praise to our Father.

Husbands: Love!

Pastor Mark Jeske

It's a wedding cliché that the bride and groom say "I do" to each other, as in "I do love you." Well, forgive me for sounding a little grumpy, but that's the wrong question. The real question to the groom is not, "Did you love her in the past?" or "Do you love her right this minute?" but "*Will* you love her till death parts you?" True Christly love is a decision and commitment, not an assessment of your feelings at the moment.

Considering the importance of the subject, it is interesting to see how relatively few passages in the New Testament speak directly to marriage. But when God does utter something, it is profound. He tells all husbands of all time that their prime directive for a happy wife and a happy home is this: **"Each one of you also must love his wife as he loves himself"** (Ephesians 5:33).

Easy to say; hard to do. A husband who wishes to wear the name of Christian needs to choose to love her. And not just in a sexual way, to gratify his own appetites. To love your wife means to give her value, to make her feel precious and beautiful, to provide her a sense of safety and security, and to be willing for a lifetime to spend yourself to make her life better. These are expensive undertakings and will cost the man.

It is valuable to have him state that commitment in the presence of as many people as possible.

Wives: Respect!

Pastor Mark Jeske

It is extremely interesting that God did not give identical instructions to men and women in his prime directive for marriage. Men need to be *told* to love their wives as themselves, and as Christ loved the church, because it doesn't come naturally and because it's hard.

God has wired women for relationships; perhaps that's why he thought he didn't need to tell women to love their husbands. What women need to be encouraged to do is to provide something else for their husbands, something that also doesn't come naturally: **"The wife must respect her husband"** (Ephesians 5:33). The reason is that while men like to be loved, they absolutely *must* have respect. It is oxygen for their souls.

God gave his women an enormous role in sexuality and human reproduction, and he assigned men the role of family leadership. Men can't fulfill that commission if wives refuse to follow. God invites married Christian women to choose to yield some of their independence, not because men are smarter (they aren't) but because in God's opinion families need a leader. This has always been a difficult task for believing women, and it has gotten harder in the superheated gender climate of today. Men have behaved so badly so often that in a sense it is understandable that a lot of women are fearful and disdainful of any marital submission whatsoever.

Sisters, do it anyway. Give your husbands a chance to grow into their roles and fulfill the mission God himself has given them to do.

The feelings of a father
Jason Nelson

America was a mere 50 years old when Andrew Jackson was president. The country was frontier, and the unitedness of the states was a work in progress. There were pockets of resistance to the idea of a federal system, and slavery and taxes were divisive issues. South Carolina was a proxy for what a confederacy of southern states would do later. It declared the authority of Washington D.C. null and void. But Andrew Jackson felt about his young country the way he felt about his family. It was his responsibility to hold it together. He threatened military action to preserve the *United* States. He sent a declaration to the people of South Carolina explaining what he was prepared to do. He said he was writing to them "with the feelings of a father."

Inescapable responsibility is the feeling of a father. Fathers know the buck stops with them. There is no holiday from their duty to be their children's providers and protectors. Jesus referred to fathers as proxies for God: **"Which of you, if your son asks for bread, will give him a stone? Or if he asks for a fish, will give him a snake? If you, then, though you are evil, know how to give good gifts to your children, how much more will your Father in heaven give good gifts to those who ask him!"** (Matthew 7:9-11). We can depend on God because he cares for us with the feelings of a father.

Pray without fear—it's your Father!

Pastor Mark Jeske

I can't help it. I am so aware of my sinful short-comings (good thing) that I feel too embarrassed and unworthy to pray (bad thing . . . very bad thing). I just can't ask for things I need because I don't feel I've earned them. The mental confusion that I have to work very hard to overcome derives from a mixing of a sense of personal responsibility (generally a good thing) with the basis for confidence that I enjoy God's favor (bad thing). My life performance, good or bad, is not the determining factor for God's favor. Everything begins with grace. Everything begins with God.

Jesus knew one day that he was speaking to a group of people who shared my prayer dysfunction. They felt too dirty to approach the royal throne of heaven, and so they didn't. Jesus used the comforting and familiar situation of a child asking for help from a parent. Even naughty children know that relationship trumps performance: **"If you then, though you are evil, know how to give good gifts to your children, how much more will your Father in heaven give the Holy Spirit to those who ask him!"** (Luke 11:13).

If your prayer life is being slowed down by guilt, begin each prayer with a confession of your sins. Treasure Scripture's words of forgiveness given to you freely by grace. Call on the Father, *your* Father, to send the Spirit *he himself promised.*

Don't be afraid. He loves you unconditionally.

It will be okay if we make it okay

Jason Nelson

I want you to feel better at the end of this devotion. It will all be okay. God is in control. And you are a link in the chain of people who will make it okay. You have some declaring to do. You can cut this page out or write something yourself and send it to your pastors, elected officials, or anyone who is also a link in the chain. They have responsibilities. They get paid to do things in our behalf. Representative leaders make it okay when they put their thinking caps on and agree to do things God would like.

I won't judge you if you kick back in your recliner and pray for someone else to do something. I do it myself. But sometimes I try to influence events like I am trying to right now. What does it mean to be salt and light or yeast that leavens the whole doughy mess? So I've sent emails to officeholders and newspaper editors and had lunches with pastors because they are responsible for the messes in church and state. They work for you because **"you are a chosen people, a royal priesthood, a holy nation, God's special possession, that you may declare the praises of him who called you out of darkness into his wonderful light"** (1 Peter 2:9). So if you want to feel better, praise God by declaring what he expects from those who serve you.

Volunteer firemen

Pastor Mark Jeske

Most of us have a schizophrenic sense of justice. We personally like to live in the land of grace, a land where God treats us (but only us) with compassion; mercy; understanding; and, of course, complete forgiveness. We want all other evildoers punished to the full extent of the law. They deserve it! Act now, Lord!

Near the end of his brief ministry, Jesus was making what was essentially his death journey, traveling to Jerusalem for the last time. He knew with dreadful clarity the cross that awaited him there. He sent his disciples on ahead through the region of Samaria to line up food and lodging. They were rebuffed, and the disciples, stinging with indignation, were furious: **"When the disciples James and John saw this, they asked, 'Lord, do you want us to call fire down from heaven to destroy them?'"** (Luke 9:54). They got a scolding from the Master.

We are not equipped to judge other people. We barely know ourselves and our own hearts, much less that of anybody else. Only God knows who truly deserves what; only God knows where there is hope and who may yet turn to faith; only God knows the times for patience and the times for judgment. He sure doesn't want us raining down fire and brimstone on anybody.

Your and my job is to proclaim God's mercy in Christ and help people see the urgency. We'll let God do the judging.

Use your words to heal

Linda Buxa

"Shut your mouth; you are so disrespectful."

"Your tiny brain just can't handle it."

"Come on, guys, let's start boxing and punching him in the face."

"How old are you, kid? Where did you learn to speak in such a mewling, yet accusatory tone?"

These are actual comments that I pulled off Facebook and Twitter the day I wrote this devotion.

I bet you've read these words—or worse. And, if we're honest, we've probably all said some of them (or something else hurtful) at some point too. Sticks and stones may break my bones, but words will never hurt me is simply a lie.

Words do hurt. Today, children and adults carry the scars from being called names. While Jimmy Kimmel may have celebrities read Mean Tweets about themselves, I bet it's not always easy to laugh off hurtful comments. The Bible means it when it says, **"Careless words stab like a sword."** But there's more to that passage. It says, **"But the words of wise people bring healing"** (Proverbs 12:18 GW).

God's good news tells you how valuable you are; that you are treasured by him; that you are so valuable to him that he punished and killed his only Son instead of punishing you, all so that you could be in his family. Now it's not only a privilege; it's your purpose to pass along that healing message to other people.

Why am I still broken?

Pastor Mark Jeske

Perhaps you've heard church sermons portraying how wonderful the Christian life is. Perhaps you've heard thrilling testimonies from people whose lives were transformed by the gospel. Perhaps you've bought and read Christian self-help books that guarantee personal change. But perhaps also you're frustrated because your personal miracle still hasn't happened. You still fall into the same-old sins; you still drag around the same-old fears, failures, and guilt. You ask yourself, "Why am I still broken?"

Don't panic. It's not just you. St. Paul himself articulated the internal struggle that many of us feel:

"Although I want to do good, evil is right there with me. For in my inner being I delight in God's law; but I see another law at work in me, waging war against the law of my mind and making me a prisoner of the law of sin at work within me. What a wretched man I am!" (Romans 7:21-24). The only place he could find relief was in the comforting message of the forgiveness of our sins through Christ.

We won't be completely healed and transformed until we get to heaven. In the meantime, we exist in a state of perpetual spiritual warfare, afflicted by our own weaknesses and daily assaulted by the devil. But Christ's victory is real, and it is complete. He gives us *his* victory, and through faith we can claim it even while groaning.

Soon, soon comes the Triumph. Hang on!

Evidence of the Spirit: Faithfulness
Pastor Mark Jeske

"My word is my bond." Sometimes I laugh when I hear that. I think, "Yeah, right." Painful experience has taught me that some people's promises are no good. I don't want to lend them money, believe their stories, or depend on them for anything. They aren't *faithful.* They are driven by other impulses—maybe laziness, insecurity, fear, or greed—but they aren't faithful.

"The fruit of the Spirit is . . . faithfulness," says St. Paul (Galatians 5:22). To be *faithful* means that you say what you mean and mean what you say. You don't need to cross your heart and swear on a stack of Bibles because people know you tell the truth. You are loyal to your friends and family, don't betray confidences, and keep your promises. You pay your debts. You don't pretend to like people and undercut them later. Your boss loves your work because you deliver on your assignments. You don't lie to him or her, don't make excuses, and don't blame other people.

Faithfulness is a Spirit-fruit. That means we are trained and inspired from the Spirit's words in Scripture, and we are strengthened by the Spirit's indwelling in our hearts and minds. While it's true that unbelievers can show examples of faithfulness, when people claiming to be believers in Christ are unfaithful, it makes all Christians look like frauds and poseurs. Our faithful words and actions are evidence that our faith in Christ is real.

Your reputation is at stake. Christ's reputation is at stake.

Nothing to crow about

Jason Nelson

I have a question for anyone who knows anything about chickens. How long does a rooster live? I have new neighbors who raise chickens as a hobby. They have a rooster, and I want to put him in a roaster. He starts up first thing in the morning and goes on all day long. His hens must really be something because this guy is a crowing maniac. I walk regularly for over a mile one way and can still hear his ear-piercing cackle at the other end. How can he keep that up? Don't chickens ever get laryngitis?

But now I have newfound sympathy for St. Peter. How awful to have the guilt of your worst sin forever associated with the sharp, penetrating crowing of a rooster! Four gospels (Matthew 26, Mark 14, Luke 22, John 18) tell us that Peter denied knowing Jesus three times as he heard a rooster crow at least twice. I doubt the rooster stopped there. What went through Peter's conscience every time he heard a rooster crow?

I've spent time with people who were nearing the end of their lives and wanted to talk. They had haunting guilt. It was Satan's last attempt to get them to deny Jesus. They needed to confess their worst sins one last time and be reassured that those sins were forgiven. I pray when I get to that point, Jesus will come quickly and remind me that my roosters have nothing to crow about.

Did you hear?

Linda Buxa

I'm getting better as I get older and wiser, but I have to confess that I used to love sharing gossip. And I loved hearing gossip. Oh, I didn't think it was gossip. We were just sharing information . . . or venting . . . or asking for a prayer request.

What's insidious about gossip is that it looks pale in comparison to other "bigger" sins. After all, no one ever goes to a 12-step meeting and says, "My name is <fill in the blank>, and I'm a gossip."

Let's not deceive ourselves. We may not be ingesting gossip literally, but it's just as addicting. After all, **"the words of a gossip are swallowed greedily, and they go down into a person's innermost being"** (Proverbs 18:8 GW).

God wants you to use your words to build up other people. Instead, we give into the temptation to gossip. Gossip makes rumors sound like truth. Gossip hurts a friend's reputation. Gossip talks about people behind their backs to make fun of them. Gossip puts people down. Gossip laughs when other people hurt. Gossip is like sugar-covered poison. It tastes good, but it makes your heart and soul sick.

"With the tongue we praise our Lord and Father, and with it we curse human beings, who have been made in God's likeness. Out of the same mouth come praise and cursing. My brothers and sisters, this should not be" (James 3:8-10).

Today's a good day to be reminded.

Evidence of the Spirit: Gentleness

Pastor Mark Jeske

When I was in seventh grade, I started a fight on the playfield. We were playing football, and a player on the other side knocked me down with a perfect block. I jumped to my feet with fists balled up and swung. Isn't it funny, sad funny, how long-lasting anger memories can be? I can also remember long-ago events in which someone hurt me. Even if we later thought of ourselves as friends, I never forgot the pain, and so I will never fully trust that person again.

Anger and angry talk are family and home de-stroyers. When you go off, you may soon calm down and forget what you said. "I didn't mean it," you say. "I was only venting." But the family member who was the victim of your name-calling will have a knife in his or her back forever. A wife whose husband put down her looks will never feel pretty again. A husband whose wife treated him like a child will never stand tall again.

Here's a better way: **"The fruit of the Spirit is . . . gentleness"** (Galatians 5:22,23). Watch your mouth! Words said in anger can never be unsaid. You don't have to eat words that never made it past your teeth. The angrier you are, the less your brain is functioning. Speak softly. Ask questions. Listen harder. Keep a muzzle on your temper—nothing good ever came from a blowup.

Assume the best in people, not the worst.

A pure heart
Sarah Habben

It was 1967 in South Africa. Louis Washkansky, a middle-aged grocer, had only weeks to live. His heart was flabby and scarred and failing fast.

Then a young woman named Denise was fatally struck by a car. Her family donated her heart. And Dr. Christiaan Barnard attempted the "surgical equivalent of Mount Everest": the first successful heart transplant. Six hours later, Louis' new heart was in place. An electric current was applied. Louis' heart leaped . . . and began to beat.

Denise's gift gave Louis an extra 18 days of life before pneumonia claimed him.

Three thousand years ago in Jerusalem, King David was crushed by the spiritual state of his heart. Every heartbeat condemned him. Coveting. Adultery. Murder. Cover-up. His eternal future depended on one thing: a gift of mercy. He begged God for a transplant.

"Create in me a pure heart, O God" (Psalm 51:10).

A doctor might give our hearts a thumbs-up, but God sees something different, something dire. He sees a heart like King David's: bloated by ego, scarred by sin, failing to meet God's holy standards. What can we do? When our hearts condemn us, we can only fall on God's mercy and beg God to give us new hearts.

And that's what he does. In a wondrous exchange, he removes our rotten hearts and implants the pure heart of his Son. Jesus carried our foul hearts to the cross and died because of them. We are blessed with Jesus' heart through faith. We will live forever because of that gift.

october 28

Three ways to date
Pastor Mike Novotny

Whom should a Christian date? Many single Christians wish a God-fearing, funny, compatible, thoughtful, beautiful person would plop down from heaven. But it's not always that simple. So, whom should you date? If you are seeking God with your heart, your soul, your mind, your strength, your wallet, your worship, your body, your babies, your everything, perhaps the key to dating is to find someone who is seeking the same God.

Imagine it this way. You're holding hands with your new special someone and up there's Jesus. And you want to run to him, to seek him, to be near him. But Mr. Special doesn't like Jesus. He kind of likes calling his own shots, deciding for himself what's right and wrong, true or not. Picture your pulling this way and his arm pulling that way. Or imagine your man just standing there. He's not against Jesus, but he's not really for Jesus. He won't try to drag you away, but he's not running toward him. Picture trying to drag him to Jesus. Or imagine holding hands and running to Jesus, in love and toward the One who is love. Seeking God together. He might be new to church. She might not know Peter from Paul. But now you have one common direction. Sound beautiful? It is.

Remember Jesus' amazing words: **"But seek first his kingdom and his righteousness, and all these things will be given to you as well"** (Matthew 6:33). That's the wisdom God wants you to remember when you set up your next date.

Don't be discouraged
Pastor Mark Jeske

King Hezekiah faced one of world history's most severe tests of leadership. The rampaging Assyrian armies and their king, Sennacherib, had laid waste to and annexed all the lands north of Israel. Now they were mopping up the last Israelite resistance and preparing for the siege of Jerusalem that would end Israelite history.

Hezekiah consulted the Lord and then had a powerful message for the shaking and quaking Israelites: **"'Be strong and courageous. Do not be afraid or discouraged because of the king of Assyria and the vast army with him, for there is a greater power with us than with him. With him is only the arm of flesh, but with us is the LORD our God to help us and to fight our battles.' And the people gained confidence from what Hezekiah the king of Judah said"** (2 Chronicles 32:7,8).

"Do not be afraid? What? What?? Are you mad, O king? We are massively outnumbered and are down to our last couple of walled cities." But Hezekiah was not mad. Sennacherib had only human armies going for him. At this particular time, at least, Israel had the Lord on its side. No contest. The angels of death moved through the Assyrian camps and slaughtered 185,000 troops. If you are enjoying God's favor, protected by his hosts, carrying out his agenda, trusting in his providing, there is no force on earth that can stop him.

Or you.

Judah needed a reformation
Pastor Mark Jeske

Satan hates God and he hates God's children. He also loathes the church, that network of believers that holds to God's words and promises. In every generation in every century, he attacks both the content and authority of the Word of God, and he attacks church leaders who manage the outward gatherings with particular ferocity.

In the sixth and seventh centuries B.C., Satan had particularly significant success destroying the spiritual integrity of Judah's religious leadership: **"A horrible and shocking thing has happened in the land: The prophets prophesy lies, the priests rule by their own authority, and my people love it this way. But what will you do in the end?"** (Jeremiah 5:30,31). The priests and prophets failed miserably in their most important task: to safeguard the content and authority of God's saving Word. Judah needed a reformation.

That same crisis became the platform for the great Protestant Reformation that erupted after 1517. The same two issues were at the heart: what has God said, and how do I know it's true? Frankly, the church will always need reforming because Satan won't leave us alone. He will attack Christ and Scripture in every generation, ours included, ours especially.

You are part of the solution. The church doesn't belong to the clergy. It belongs to you, the people. Hold your "prophets and priests" accountable for their messages. Make sure that Christ is at the center and that the Scripture is held in the highest esteem as the inerrant and infallible Word of God himself.

Prophets should be messengers, not authors

Pastor Mark Jeske

The Protestant Reformation that was launched, more or less, by Martin Luther's tacking of 95 debate theses to the Wittenberg town bulletin board was only one of many reformation efforts over the millennia. The central issue of all spiritual reform is to redirect people to the fundamentals of the faith: what is God's message, and how do you know that?

Jesus predicted that there would be false Christs and false prophets in every era. His sad prophecy has proven true. Satan cannot resist prompting people to tamper with the Word and to substitute their thoughts (and his thoughts) and then pass them off as divine revelation. We must not let that happen on our watch. Man's word must never replace God's Word: **"'I am against the prophets who wag their own tongues and yet declare, "The LORD declares." Indeed, I am against those who prophesy false dreams,' declares the LORD. 'They tell them and lead my people astray with their reckless lies, yet I did not send or appoint them'"** (Jeremiah 23:31,32).

Satan will mess with you at some point—perhaps he is doing a number on you right now. How do you know what to think? What's right and what's wrong? What in our culture is from heaven and what's from hell? How can I hear the true voice of God?

Hang onto your Bible. Read your Bible. Then you'll *know* for sure.

november

Whatever you do, whether in word or deed,
do it all in the name of the Lord Jesus,
giving thanks to God the Father through him.

Colossians 3:17

Do angels really exist?

Pastor Mark Jeske

The existence of angels is a matter of faith. Doubtless because of strict orders from God, they do not reveal themselves except in very special circumstances. They are stealth agents who do their best work quietly and invisibly.

People who don't believe that the Bible is factual will find talk of angels to be superstitious nonsense, sort of like believing in fairies in *Peter Pan*. On the other hand, people who have come to faith in God and who have come to trust and accept the Bible as factual will have much more information to go on. Though there may be no visual or scientific evidence for angels and their work, the biblical writers were given information from God that gives detailed accounts of what is going on behind the scenes in the spiritual world.

God created them at the beginning of time, at some point during the creation week, and he made tens of thousands of them. They are creatures of spirit, speed, holiness, intelligence, and power. They have names, curiosity, emotions, and the ability to communicate. They exist to worship the Lord before his throne, carry out God's agenda on earth, and protect and care for God's children: **"Are not all angels ministering spirits sent to serve those who will inherit salvation?"** (Hebrews 1:14). Some angels will carry the believers to their heavenly home. Others will be tasked to round up unbelievers for their destiny of damnation.

Do you believe in angels?

Is there really a devil?

Pastor Mark Jeske

Charles Darwin's 1859 theories on natural selection and survival of the fittest initiated a large-scale abandonment of the Bible's teachings on creation. Among the many casualties of this radical revolution of thought is the disappearance of the idea that the evil in our world was brought by a fallen angel, Satan, the devil.

The fact that so many people today don't believe in the devil unfortunately does not make him disappear. In fact, his work gets easier when he and his demons can work undetected. The Bible opens a window so that you and I can see what is really going on in the universe. The trouble began with a revolt in heaven: **"Then war broke out in heaven. Michael and his angels fought against the dragon, and the dragon and his angels fought back. But he was not strong enough, and they lost their place in heaven. The great dragon was hurled down—that ancient serpent called the devil, or Satan, who leads the whole world astray. He was hurled to the earth, and his angels with him"** (Revelation 12:7-9).

Since he couldn't overcome God and the good angels, led by St. Michael, Satan turned his fury on God's children, and he persuaded them to join his conspiracy of evil. Christ's death on Calvary delivered a mortal blow to the old serpent, but he's still alive, still urges on his demons, and is still actively seeking to persuade humans to commit spiritual suicide and join him.

Beware!

Is there really a hell?
Pastor Mark Jeske

You wouldn't get the idea that many people today take the concept of hell very seriously. "Aw, hell!" is a common statement of general disgust and disappointment. The word is also used to denote admiration: "That kid is a hell of a linebacker!" Or scorn: "Go to hell!" But it seems to me that when people use the word in those ways, they aren't thinking about the reality of enduring God's angry judgment and punishment for all eternity.

Skeptics don't want to accept the reality of anything that they can't see, sense, or measure. So far in God's plans nobody has ever emerged from hell to describe the experience for the living. But there are two powerful witnesses to the reality of judgment and hell that cut deep even into agnostic and atheistic hearts. One is conscience. Every man, woman, and child on earth knows basic right and wrong and knows the taste and weight and fear of guilt.

The second is the Word of God. Even when people say they don't believe it, inside they know it's true. They just don't want to submit to it. God's Word is very clear, painfully clear, on what is going to happen when people die and when all are gathered before the Judge. He will say to those on his left, **"Depart from me, you who are cursed, into the eternal fire prepared for the devil and his angels"** (Matthew 25:41).

Use the word *hell* as the Bible does. Mean it when you say it. Thank Jesus for saving you from it.

Is there really a heaven?

Pastor Mark Jeske

There is good news here on the skepticism front— polls consistently show that more people believe in the existence of heaven than hell. Hurray! Unfortunately, though, it seems as if the great majority are universalists—they assume that everybody has a right to enter heaven upon death. Have you ever in all your life attended a funeral where the presider or obituary reader didn't assume the soul of the departed was in heaven? But God's Word is clear—only those who repent of their sins and believe and trust in Jesus Christ as their Savior will enter.

Scripture has much to say about the beauty and peace and joy that await us. What a comfort for people whose earthly lives have been hard. I am really looking forward to heaven, but my anticipation is as nothing compared with people who have ALS, spina bifida, severe depression, or Parkinson's: **"I saw the Holy City, the new Jerusalem, coming down out of heaven from God, prepared as a bride beautifully dressed for her husband. And I heard a loud voice from the throne saying, 'Look! God's dwelling place is now among the people, and he will dwell with them. . . . He will wipe every tear from their eyes. There will be no more death or mourning or crying or pain'"** (Revelation 21:2-4).

The Holy Book whose story began with God's creation and mankind's miserable fall concludes with the restoration of all the believers. Heaven is our ultimate destination.

Look up! Live with heaven sparkling in your eyes.

Friendship is hard
Linda Buxa

It began in kindergarten when every student in my daughter's class was called "friend." While the teacher attempted to develop the essential character traits of kindness and empathy, you could already hear the phrase, "You can't be my friend if . . ." followed by "you talk to her" or "you sit by him" or whatever other standard five-year-old children set.

As we all live through our teenage years, we realize that friendships just get harder. They fluctuate rapidly, thanks to drama, mean people, clothing styles, interests, or the popular group. By the time we reach adulthood, it almost seems that we don't expect to call many people "friend."

We'd like it to be easier, but friendship is hard—because we're all working with sinful people (including ourselves). So when I think about being Jesus' friend, I think it might be easier. After all, he's perfect. What's so hard about being his friend? Well, to be his friend, he turns our focus back to the people around us: **"My command is this: Love each other as I have loved you. Greater love has no one than this: to lay down one's life for one's friends. You are my friends if you do what I command"** (John 15:12-14).

That makes friendship even harder! To be called Jesus' friend, we love others completely, sacrificially. We give, even when we're hurt. We put aside our self-centeredness in order to serve. We lay down our lives because our friend Jesus laid down his.

Twin hounds

Sarah Habben

Who's hounding you lately? Is your boss bugging you for that report? Is your mom following you around with an armload of dirty laundry? Is a certain some-body not taking a hint when you don't text back?

Or maybe *what* hounds you is far worse. Maybe depression nips at your heels. Maybe age or illness or temptation is panting just over your shoulder and all you feel is bone-deep weary.

But turn around. Open your faith-filled eyes and take a second look. What's hounding you?

"Surely your *goodness* and *love* will follow me all the days of my life, and I will dwell in the house of the LORD forever" (Psalm 23:6).

The verb *follow* in Hebrew could be translated here as "hound." What's hounding you? God's goodness and mercy, that's what. The twin hounds of his goodness and love pursue you relentlessly, even on days when you ignore or forget them. These loyal companions ac-company you down every road—down Stressful Street and Heartache Highway and Weary Lane. And when life's challenges have you cornered with seemingly no way out, Goodness and Love are there holding your real enemies at bay, not Mom armed with your smelly socks but Satan and his henchmen, Sin and Death.

When hard things hound you, turn around. There at your heels is God's goodness. His mercy. His cross. *Especially* his cross. On that wooden cross, Goodness rescued you. Love forgave you. Satan was disarmed. And heaven's doors were opened wide so that you can dwell in God's house forever.

Work the dirt
Pastor Mark Jeske

Are you a farmer? If not, ask one about his soil. Farmers are very concerned about the productivity of their land and will spend a lot of energy and money to prepare it and tend it. They will plow it under in the fall; disc it in spring; remove stones heaved up by frost; and then after planting they cultivate, spray, fertilize, and water. You need to work the dirt to produce a crop.

Jesus lived in a time when the vast majority of his listeners were connected directly to agriculture; thus many of his stories and parables had farm themes. One of his most famous illustrated the way in which the Word of God took root in people's hearts: **"The seed on good soil stands for those with a noble and good heart, who hear the word, retain it, and by persevering produce a crop"** (Luke 8:15).

It is a bitter reality that the Creator's tender request for a personal relationship with his creatures can bounce off their hearts the same way perfectly good seeds bounce off an asphalt road. People need to work the dirt when they hear the Word—pay attention, show respect, take it seriously, humble themselves, accept God's rebukes, and believe God's forgiving love.

In your private devotional reading of your Bible, screen out distractions, quiet your mind, and let God speak to you. In church, do your best to process your pastor's message without critiques and forensics judging.

Work the dirt so the Word can produce its fruit in your life.

Last days

Pastor Mark Jeske

In human history, as narrated for us in the Bible, there were a few colossal events with worldwide significance that marked major eras. God's majestic creation week launched the human story. The great flood, which only Noah's family endured, was the end of an era and a new beginning, though human civilization soon turned sour and violent. The formation of a special family through Abraham and Sarah might be called the Age of the Patriarchs. The exodus and giving of the covenant through Moses on Mt. Sinai ushered in the era of God's intense focus on the nation of Israel.

The last of the great ages began with the coming to earth of Jesus Christ, the Son of God. Scripture calls this era the last days: **"In the past God spoke to our ancestors through the prophets at many times and in various ways, but in these *last days* he has spoken to us by his Son, whom he appointed heir of all things, and through whom also he made the universe"** (Hebrews 1:1,2).

All of God's saving work has now been completed in Christ. Nothing remains but to set the Spirit loose through Word and sacraments to touch as many people as possible before the final trumpet is sounded. "Last days" can also hint at the very end of history, as the physical universe will begin to disintegrate immediately prior to the triumphant return of Christ the Judge.

The next era will be life in heaven itself. Are you ready? Are you excited?

I'm not what I used to be

Pastor Mark Jeske

When you're young, life's possibilities seem endless. You may be broke, indebted even, but you've got time. Plenty of time. You've got energy to burn. Whatever you don't know, you can learn. Whatever you don't have, you can get. Then all of a sudden you're a senior citizen. How did that happen so fast?

Seniors sometimes don't see their golden years as all that golden. Bad back, knees, or hips provide a steady baseline of daily pain. Dumb investments or a run of bad luck leave you with far less retirement money than you envisioned. Memory, agility, and energy diminish. That youthful optimism turns into sour self-pity. Confidence morphs into complaining. "I'm not what I used to be" is shorthand for "I feel useless."

But consider the story of Anna. **"There was also a prophet, Anna. . . . She was very old; she had lived with her husband seven years after her marriage, and then was a widow until she was eighty-four. She never left the temple but worshiped night and day, fasting and praying"** (Luke 2:36,37). Inspiration! This senior saint didn't stay home feeling sorry for herself and what she couldn't do anymore. She did what the Lord still enabled her to do. She could still worship, fast, and pray. The Lord richly rewarded her vigilance and positive attitude—she was allowed to recognize her infant Savior in the arms of his mother, Mary.

Is there a senior in your life who could use your help in finding significance today?

When nothing is everything
Sarah Habben

In your relationships with one another, have the same mindset as Christ Jesus: . . . He made himself nothing" (Philippians 2:5,7).

The president adjusted his pants to squat before his 14 cabinet members. The secretary of agriculture squirmed uneasily. The president smiled, then carefully removed Mr. Agriculture's shiny leather brogues. Then his navy dress socks. The feet within looked like they hadn't seen the sun in a good while. Didn't smell great either. But the commander in chief cradled Mr. Agriculture's bare toes and lowered them into a basin of water.

Cut! That scene won't play on a Hollywood screen anytime soon. It isn't realistic. It wouldn't complement our tough foreign policies. No commander would act like such a *nothing.*

But *nothing* is the status that Christ chose. Our Commander in Chief, in very nature God, did not work his rank to his own advantage. Instead, he made himself *nothing.* Not just a foot washer, not just the Roman soldiers' buffoon, but a criminal on death row. He obediently served and suffered and died to make us sinful, selfish *nothings* into his brothers and sisters.

And now *nothing* is our beautiful vocation. Not because we are worthless, but because Christ made us priceless. As we interact in the checkout line, at parent-teacher meetings, at church and work and in our homes, we share Christ's mind-set. We put others first. We cheerfully shed our "rank" and rights. We wash feet (or floors or clothes or dishes), knowing that we serve our Servant Savior.

In him, *nothing* is everything.

Difficult people: In the mirror

Jason Nelson

If everyone you know is difficult to deal with, here's a heads up. Take a look in the mirror. The most difficult person of all is staring back at you. Under the wrong circumstances, I can be every kind of difficult person there is including some beast no one has ever seen before. Every personality type has a dark side. It shows itself when we are stressed, in pain, afraid, or depressed. Then we face the difficulty of dealing with ourselves.

King David may be the most self-aware person in the Bible. He tells us more about his own good traits and bad behavior than anyone I can think of. When you catch yourself being difficult, read Psalm 139 and start where David did: **"You have searched me, Lord, and you know me. . . . You are familiar with all my ways"** (verses 1,3). And be willing to take your self-examination as far as he did: **"Search me, God, and know my heart; test me and know my anxious thoughts. See if there is any offensive way in me"** (verses 23,24). Then be ready for God to love you enough to send someone to point out your offensive ways.

Yeah, I'd like to be the stallion ahead of the stampede, the big lion of the pride, the front goose in the formation, the alpha male of the pack; but what I need to be more often is just one of the sheep of the Good Shepherd. Then I'll be much less difficult to deal with.

Difficult people: The butterfly

Jason Nelson

Some people are difficult to deal with because they act like butterflies. These are lovely folks who enjoy soaring on the updraft of whatever intrigues them. They are generally pleasant, nonconfrontational, agreeable, and fragile. They are frustrating to deal with because you never know which way they're headed or if they will stay on course until they get there. Butterflies shouldn't be pinned to a desk and pressed behind a glass where they can be inspected by supervisors. Butterflies need freedom. They need space to move in the direction of their inspirations.

Butterflies also need boundaries in order to have productive lives and make contributions to society. They need assistance in developing self-discipline. We can help them appreciate that God sets boundaries for all people with things like regular seasons (Psalm 74:17). He does it so there will be order in our world and in our individual lives. Boundaries are expressions of God's love because they outline the pleasant places through well-tested norms and procedures. Playing by the rules can help butterflies have a delightful existence (Psalm 16:6) and avoid a big crash.

If you have a butterfly in your family, company, or school, learn to enjoy them. Try to capture the value of their creativity without damaging their wings. Establish limits but make them very broad so your butterflies can do what they do best—fly. But you can't leave the door wide open, or they'll be gone.

Difficult people: The bull

Jason Nelson

Some people are difficult to deal with because they act like bulls. They intimidate others to get what they want. It's a power play. They bully people they think won't challenge them. Here is old wisdom for dealing with bulls: **"A soft answer turneth away wrath: but grievous words stir up anger"** (Proverbs 15:1 KJV). A calm response to a bull doesn't need to be a weak one. You don't want to bellow back at a bull, and you don't want to turn your back on a bull. But bulls will back off when they see your strength.

During my career, I faced down some bulls. Sometimes I didn't see them coming, and they blindsided me. I learned to ask raging bulls, "What have I done to offend you that you are treating me this way?" That usually invited some calm. Bulls threatened to sue me, pull their kids from my school, and report me to ecclesiastical authorities because they thought I was coloring outside the lines. I learned to say, "I am always willing to meet with you and discuss your concerns and try to arrive at a solution. But do not threaten me." A bull hung up on me once, so I called her right back and asked her never to do that again. Another bull kept criticizing this, that, and the other thing, so I finally asked him, "Can your ministry stand up to the kind of scrutiny you are putting my ministry under?" I never heard from him again.

Difficult people: The fox

Jason Nelson

Some people are difficult to deal with because they act like foxes. They're always working an angle. They are driven by self-interest. There's always a hidden agenda. They grin, but you can't trust what's behind it. Deceit is a regular part of their *modus operandi*. It's sad, but you can never trust a fox. If you do, it will likely come back to bite you.

Solomon was fed up with the damage foxes caused. He said, **"Catch for us the foxes, the little foxes that ruin the vineyards, our vineyards that are in bloom"** (Song of Songs 2:15). The only way to effectively deal with foxes is to catch them in the act. Don't try to catch one by yourself. It is essential to have witnesses to discussions and transactions. Verbal agreements with foxes are worthless because foxes manipulate the circumstances around them. Insist that foxes produce evidence to back up their claims. Rumors are not evidence. Make foxes go on the record, and be willing to go on the record yourself if you need to challenge one.

Herod was a political hack and was jealous of Jesus. He was out to get the Messiah. Jesus called him out publicly: **"Go tell that fox, 'I will keep on driving out demons and healing people today and tomorrow, and on the third day I will reach my goal'"** (Luke 13:32). It's very hard to deal with foxes, and there is often a price to pay.

Difficult people: The toad

Jason Nelson

This may seem unkind, but some people are difficult to deal with because they act like toads. They're just there. They blend in with their surroundings, and you have to almost step on them to get them moving. When they do jump, it's not very far. And the poor things have warts. They don't distinguish themselves in any noticeable way. Frogs croak, but I have no idea what noise toads make or what they contribute to an ecosystem. Toads need a shot of enthusiasm, and they may need to get it from you.

Never underestimate the power of transferable energy. Motivated people can help unmotivated people get moving. Just about everyone responds to encouragement from an upbeat person. There must have been some toad whisperers in Corinth. The Macedonians were moved to give generously by the example of generous Corinthians. Paul commented on the transference: **"Your enthusiasm has stirred most of them to action"** (2 Corinthians 9:2).

Toads aren't happy about their toadyness either. They have feelings too. Soaring with the eagles may be unattainable, but they might like to try to keep up with the frogs. So, **"be kind and compassionate to one another, forgiving each other, just as in Christ God forgave you"** (Ephesians 4:32). Remember, **"love is patient, love is kind. It does not envy, it does not boast, it is not proud"** (1 Corinthians 13:4). It's not about feeling superior. It's all about picking up the toads.

Happy Jesus?

Pastor Mark Jeske

Jesus seems terribly earnest, doesn't he? Driving out demons, teaching crowds of people for many hours at a time, scolding his disciples for being such blockheads, healing the sick, debating with Pharisees and religious teachers, and withdrawing for intense spiritual quiet time with his Father—all these activities portray how seriously and intensely he took his three-year ministry. Do you suppose he ever smiled? Was Jesus ever happy?

Fortunately Scripture answers that question for us: **"At that time Jesus, full of joy through the Holy Spirit, said, 'I praise you, Father, Lord of heaven and earth, because you have hidden these things from the wise and learned, and revealed them to little children. Yes, Father, for this is what you were pleased to do'"** (Luke 10:21).

God does feel emotions. And although Jesus was often disappointed by the lack of faith and spiritual progress in his followers, he at other times rejoiced at the signs of faith and spiritual progress in his followers! The Father's wonderful Word and Spirit made those things happen. Those same emotions wash through his heart as he tracks your life. Our failings do make him sad, and we should consider the impact on him when we are tempted to sin. But our repentance, faith, worship, and acts of service bring him joy.

As you read these golden words from the Word, I imagine that he's smiling at you right now.

Punishment pays for your sin

Linda Buxa

At Sensō-ji, the oldest Buddhist temple in Tokyo, there's a shrine to Kume no Heinai. An expert swordsman of the 17th century, Kume killed many men in sword-fighting duels. Later, he lived at Sensō-ji, performing devotions and Zen meditation, praying for the souls of those he killed. As a dying request, he asked his followers to carve a statue of him and bury it near one of the temple's gates. This way, countless people would step on it, which he felt would help atone for his sins.

People in the 21st century do this too. On their deathbeds, they wonder if there is really a way they could actually be forgiven. Their pasts haunt them and their secret sins weigh on them. They are guilty, anxious, and stressed about how they have screwed up not only their pasts but afraid it will affect their eternal futures. This is why they need to hear that there is no punishment or condemnation, all because Jesus took the punishment for them. Now **"unlike the other high priests, he does not need to offer sacrifices day after day, first for his own sins, and then for the sins of the people. He sacrificed for their sins once for all when he offered himself"** (Hebrews 7:27).

P.S. It's not just the dying who feel this way; it's the living too. Share the message of forgiveness with them now too!

Joy in hardship

Pastor Mark Jeske

This Thanksgiving it's not going to be particularly hard to have thankful feelings in my heart. The year has brought plenty of challenges and disappointments, to be sure, but my problems are relatively small. We still have our house, we were fed like clockwork, we were employed the full 12 months, and nobody in our family died young.

I wonder if I will have the prophet Habakkuk's grace when I face some real disasters: **"Though the fig tree does not bud and there are no grapes on the vines, though the olive crop fails and the fields produce no food, though there are no sheep in the pen and no cattle in the stalls, yet I will rejoice in the Lord, I will be joyful in God my Savior"** (Habakkuk 3:17,18).

I wonder if my generally cheerful spirit can take serious adversity. I wonder if my worship life would grind to a halt if I blamed God for taking away major supports of my life. My father's generation was much more churchgoing than today's, and they had to survive a decade-long catastrophic financial depression and World War II. Perhaps not all hardships are bad if they make us realize our dependence on God. Perhaps losses of material things might inspire us to value more our spiritual treasures in Christ.

Perhaps seeing the earth for the broken place it really is will move us to lift up our eyes and long for heaven.

What every dude desires

Pastor Mike Novotny

Every wife's plan should be to satisfy her man. No, the male supporters of Time of Grace did not pay me to say that. In the beginning, when God made marriage, he had a plan for every wife to satisfy her man. Listen to this: **"The Lord God said, 'It is not good for the man to be alone. I will make a helper suitable for him'"** (Genesis 2:18). Told you. God created the first ever wife to satisfy her man. How so?

Well, what help did her husband need? He needed help seeking God. That's why God made woman. The woman, unlike all the animals, had a soul that sought God, a soul divinely designed to seek God and be supremely satisfied in him.

Wives, what your husband needs is not a home-cooked meal or a new truck or more sex. What he needs is God. That's the only thing that will satisfy his soul. And we husbands forget how to be happy so quickly. We get tricked into thinking if only we had more (fill in the blank). And we waste our lives pursuing what won't satisfy. But you can help us. Help us see the glory and power and plan of God. Help us see our worth, no matter what our net worth. Help us see our riches in heaven. Help us remember everything is temporary, but God's mercy endures forever. Because what every dude desires is God. That's how a wife can help her husband live happily ever after.

Five words
Sarah Habben

Here's a great thought to begin and end your day: "I am baptized into Christ." Those five words can drown five thousand doubts.

Can it be? That trickle of baptismal water you once received couldn't wash a dirty dinner plate. Yet it cleansed your sin-soiled heart by the power of God's Word!

That same saving power was at work during Noah's flood. Before God pulled the plug, he designed an ark to save the faithful few. The evil that threatened Noah's faith was flushed away. But the same floodwater safely buoyed the faithful in the ark. **"In it only a few people, eight in all, were saved through water, *and this water symbolizes baptism that now saves you also.* . . . It saves you by the resurrection of Jesus Christ"** (1 Peter 3:20, 21).

The dribbles of baptismal water on your forehead are long dry. But Baptism's power is present tense. When temptation swims your way with gleaming teeth, think: "I AM baptized into Christ." Baptism drowns your desire to swim with the sharks. When you doubt God's forgiveness, think: "I AM baptized into Christ." You are no longer God's enemy. You are his child, safe and warm in the ark of Christ. When Satan whispers, "How can you be sure you're saved?" remember, "I AM baptized into Christ." Your baptismal water—with the power of God's Word—flows from the flood of grace at Jesus' cross and tomb. That grace, poured on you at your baptism, will never dry up.

I am baptized into Christ. Five words to drown five thousand doubts.

The glory of grandparenting
Pastor Mark Jeske

Grandparenting is great. (Full disclosure: I do not know that from personal experience. I base that assertion on the empirical evidence of the many hundreds of grandparents I know who can barely control their delight at having a chance to be with their grandchildren.)

Grandparents pack their refrigerator door with pictures of their grandkids. They remember every birthday and will send cards and gifts. They will drop what they're doing when a grandbaby is born and spend a week helping out the new parents. They will provide respite childcare to give the frazzled parents a breather. If they live reasonably close, they may watch the toddlers one or two days a week to lighten the cost of childcare.

"Children's children are a crown to the aged" (Proverbs 17:6). They really are. Grandchildren make us oldsters feel young again. How we miss our own children's youthful energy, shrieks of laughter, simplicity of spirit, emotional honesty, and eagerness to learn. Just think how much priceless wisdom jumps across two generations when kids spend time with grandparents.

I will always remember my maternal grandmother. She never was given an education higher than seventh grade; she never operated a motor vehicle, went to the beauty shop, had a mani-pedi, or wore a pair of slacks in her life. But I consider her one of the strongest influences in my life. She made time for me.

She made me feel important. You know, like one of her crowns.

Everybody knows your name

Pastor Mark Jeske

Remember the theme song from the TV sitcom *Cheers*? Everybody feels a need to belong somewhere. That's what made the *Cheers* tavern so much fun—it was a place where everybody knows your name, where everybody's glad you came, a place where you are accepted just as you are. You don't have to pretend to be somebody else.

When you are trying to bring someone back into the faith who has been slipping away for a long time, you are not alone in your efforts. Your congregation is a valuable ally. God made people to need other people. We need to know that somebody is interested in us, cares about how we're doing, knows and loves our children, and is always there for us. We need a place where we can get involved and serve and use our gifts and talents, a place where everybody knows our names.

Here's what a happy church fellowship looks like: **"Selling their possessions and goods, they gave to anyone as he had need. Every day they continued to meet together in the temple courts. They broke bread in their homes and ate together with glad and sincere hearts, praising God and enjoying the favor of all the people"** (Acts 2:45-47).

Aren't you glad you have a place like that? Social capital is wealth too. This is the warmth and love that awaits the people whom you are trying to bring back. Appreciate those dear people and use them!

P.R.A.Y.

Pastor Mike Novotny

Most of my prayers sounds like this: "Dear God, AAAAAAAAAAAAA! In Jesus' name. Amen."

I should explain. I think of prayer as having four steps—Praise. Repent. Ask. Yield. (P.R.A.Y.) But my prayers tend to jump to and stay focused on the third step—Ask. "Dear God, please bless this and fix that and be with them." How about you? Do you focus on the Ask when you pray?

Peter offers an encouragement to not skip the Praise. He begins, **"Praise be to the God and Father of our Lord Jesus Christ!"** (1 Peter 1:3). Before asking for God to fix his friends' suffering, Peter pushes his friends to praise God in the midst of their suffering.

Here's why—Once we praise, our prayers change. Once we spend quality (and quantity!) time saying good things about God's love, God's power, God's holiness, God's wisdom, God's control, God's presence, and God's character, our prayers evolve. We immediately start to Repent: "God, you are so good to me, yet I chose to do something bad against you . . ." And we Ask: "God, if people only knew how good you are, doctor visits and medical bills and loneliness couldn't stop their joy. So open their eyes to know you better!" And we Yield: "God, you know everything and you want what's best for me, so I trust you. I'm asking for this, but your will be done."

Can I challenge you for the next 24 hours to begin every prayer with a word of Praise?

Your alive and well and for-sure future

Pastor Mike Novotny

There is, perhaps, no more misunderstood word in the Bible than *hope*. In English, the word *hope* is used for any random wish, no matter how far-fetched the odds. "I hope to be cancer free." "I hope to become a grandparent soon." "I hope it doesn't snow in Wisconsin on the Fourth of July!"

But the Bible has a radically different definition for *hope*, a definition that can make you really, really happy today. Listen to Peter's words: **"Praise be to the God and Father of our Lord Jesus Christ! In his great mercy he has given us new birth into a living hope"** (1 Peter 1:3). A living hope. *Living* means not dead. Alive and kicking. *Hope* means a for-sure future, a guaranteed tomorrow. So *living hope* means "an alive and well and for-sure future." Something incredible is going to happen for sure! It's alive and well and on its way! You and I as children of God may not have it just yet, but we will soon and very soon. And it will make us so happy!

Do you know the living hope of every Christian? The **"inexpressible and glorious joy"** of being with God (1 Peter 1:8). Being with God forever will make you so happy that you will jump and dance and shout and worship. If the angels, who have never been forgiven of a single sin, have spent thousands of years praising their place in the presence of God, just imagine what we will feel when we see the face of the One who saved us from sin so that we could be born again into the family of Jesus!

Why did Jesus cross the road?

Linda Buxa

Our neighbor called my husband to let him know that one of our chickens crossed the busy road and spent the day with their horses. (You can insert your own "chicken crossing the road" joke here.)

When we got home that night, we discovered that same chicken didn't come back to the coop (like chickens normally do). So at 8:45 P.M., my daughter and I grabbed flashlights and headed over to look for it. We searched in the pine trees until we finally found it about 6 feet up. I held the flashlight while my daughter made her way through thick boughs and broken branches, getting scratched up, until she finally reached up to grab it. It flapped and flapped its wings, not wanting to come down, but she held on. She carried it back across the road, where we put it in the coop with the rest.

You know what? Jesus did the same for humanity.

When Adam and Eve sinned, they crossed the road, separating themselves from God—and we couldn't bring ourselves back. So the Father sent his Son to earth to recover us. Jesus found us, even when we didn't want to be found. **"But God demonstrates his own love for us in this: While we were still sinners, Christ died for us"** (Romans 5:8).

Then he rose from the dead, effectively carrying us back across the street to safety.

And someday he'll come back and carry us all the way to our eternal home.

Why do we cross the road?

Linda Buxa

You didn't think I could get two devotional thoughts out of a save-the-chicken adventure, did you? Oh, but I did!

After Jesus completed his rescue mission—by paying for our sins on the cross and rising again from the dead—he ascended into heaven to prepare a place for us. While he's doing that, he put the people who believe in him on his search-and-rescue team. Now, out of thankfulness for our rescue, we go out looking for others who are separated from him.

In a story (also called a parable) about who God wants invited to heaven, he says, **"'Go out quickly into the streets and alleys of the town and bring in the poor, the crippled, the blind and the lame.'**

"'Sir,' the servant said, 'what you ordered has been done, but there is still room.'

"Then the master told his servant, 'Go out to the roads and country lanes and compel them to come in, so that my house will be full'" (Luke 14:21-23).

Jesus went to prepare not only your place in heaven but a spot for other people too. They won't know about this spot, though, unless we go look for them and invite them in. We might get scratched up a little in the process. They might put up a fuss, and it might get a little discouraging. But hang on! Because there's nothing sweeter than bringing someone back home with you.

Thankful for my baptism

Pastor Mark Jeske

Some of you can remember your baptism as though it were yesterday because perhaps it was yesterday. For others it's a faint memory of a long time ago, and for still others there's no memory at all because it took place at a very young age. But whether your certainty of Baptism comes from personal memory or from a yellowing certificate, signed by people you dearly love, isn't it a joy to reflect that it's a done deal?

Somebody else was surely involved in helping you to that point. Some Christian friend or family member persuaded you to ask, just like the Ethiopian in his chariot asked the evangelist Philip. Or maybe your godmother held you in the family's traditional, long, white christening gown. We can be thankful for these wonderful people who wanted to share their Savior with you.

Most of all we can be thankful for Christ's priceless gift itself. **"All of you who were baptized into Christ have clothed yourselves with Christ"** (Galatians 3:27). Baptism is pure grace. It is 100 percent God's doing. It isn't magic water, of course—the power source is God's Word working through the water, and that Word has clothed you with Christ, i.e., the holiness of Christ. It marks the day in which you were officially adopted into God's family. Cherish that day and its significance—there's a lot of hope and comfort there to sustain you throughout your life.

Perhaps there's another person in your life who needs this experience?

Thankful for my Bible

Pastor Mark Jeske

You and I have access to God's wonderful Word pretty much whenever we want it, in inexpensive printed editions as well as online on demand. We have not only one English translation but *many.* We have study Bibles, concordances, atlases, commentaries, and encyclopedias virtually and in print. From the casual attitude so many of us show toward Bible reading and Bible study, you wouldn't conclude that we deeply respected the terrible sacrifices people made to bring us the Word.

William Tyndale dared to translate the Bible into English in the 1520s. For this he was denounced as a heretic by the bishops and his books were burned. He was betrayed and seized in Antwerp, strangled, and burned at the stake in 1536. The very best way to honor this martyr and all who suffered to bring the Bible to their people is to read it and know it as our dearest earthly treasure. Jesus used its power to fight off the devil's temptation: **"It is written: 'Man shall not live on bread alone, but on every word that comes from the mouth of God'"** (Matthew 4:4).

Be a Bible reader not just to compete better at historical trivia or to do a piece of unpleasant work as a good and meritorious deed. The Bible is your lifeline to Jesus Christ. Satan will do everything in his power to cut that cord. Don't let him. Enjoy the Word. Learn the Word. Grow in the Word. Apply the Word. Live the Word.

Thankful for the Lord's Supper
Pastor Mark Jeske

It's pretty hard to be mad at people you're eating with. There's something about breaking bread with people that promotes intimacy, understanding, bonding, and camaraderie.

It's no surprise that the Savior chose the warmth of the supper table for one of his most important parting gifts to his disciples and to all believers. Taking two ordinary foodstuffs found all over the world, Jesus linked the ordinary with the extraordinary, earth with heaven, and created a sacrament. Simple bread and wine, eaten and swallowed by believers, would become the vehicles for the very body and blood that were offered on the cross in payment for the sin of the world: **"He took a cup, and when he had given thanks, he gave it to them, saying, 'Drink from it, all of you. This is my blood of the covenant, which is poured out for many for the forgiveness of sins'"** (Matthew 26:27,28).

Baptism is intended as a one-time act, our formal adoption into God's family. Lord's Supper is intended as a repeated activity, assuring sinners that the forgiveness of their sins is still valid. When people hear the Word of God spoken, they can always (mistakenly) assume that it is meant for others. When the body and blood are placed in their mouths, there can be no mistake about who is loved and whose sins are forgiven.

Thank you, Jesus, for being this close to me. Thank you for the gift of yourself.

Thankful for heaven

Pastor Mark Jeske

Call it the "light at the end of the tunnel" effect. Isn't it amazing how much adversity we can stand if we can see an end to it? if we see that something really positive will come out of it? if the short-term sacrifice results in long-term gain?

I am thankful for heaven, and not just heaven someday. I am thankful for heaven right now because I have the sure knowledge that I am loved, forgiven, and immortal. St. Paul took a lot of abuse in his long ministry, but the bright glow ahead pulled him forward: **"I consider that our present sufferings are not worth comparing with the glory that will be revealed in us"** (Romans 8:18). The stooped and frail elderly will stand up straight. The muscles of people with fibromyalgia will never shriek with agony again. The blind will never again be in the dark 24/7. The deaf will hear and make music. Amputees will regain their limbs, and my friends with disabled legs will run like deer.

We don't have to get everything now. So much of the pressure on our lives is the terror that we're running out of time, have limited resources, and feel cheated if we don't get all the experiences other people have. I am thankful for heaven, where time, friends, and adventures will have no limits.

After our first week there, you and I will say to each other, "Totally worth everything to be here."

december

She gave birth to her firstborn, a son. She wrapped
him in cloths and placed him in a manger, because
there was no guest room available for them.

Luke 2:7

Who, me? Proud?

Pastor Mark Jeske

The 13th chapter of 1 Corinthians is justly famous. It is a brilliant and poetic exposition of the meaning of true love, biblical love, Christ-like love. You have undoubtedly heard it read and applied at a Christian wedding ceremony.

The great risk to a quick reading of this legendary passage, however, is that it states philosophic abstractions that you can cheerfully agree with but that have no impact on your life whatsoever. For example, **"Love is . . . not proud"** (1 Corinthians 13:4). You would concur—"It sure isn't." But here's the point of St. Paul's powerful essay—is it true of *you*? That *you* are not proud? Do the people around you see evidence of vanity and arrogance in your life?

Pride is a deadly sin. It seduces us into thinking that we are better than others, that we are worthy of God's favor, that we deserve a ticket to heaven. Pride feeds our egos, stoking an interest only in what revolves around *us*. It is impossible for people with pride sickness to assume the attitude and posture of a servant, the posture that Christ adopted and that he invites us to share.

Repeat after me: "I am a foolish sinner who would be sunk without my Savior's mercy. Forgive me, Jesus, for my proud words and actions. It is better to serve than be served. How can I make someone else feel important today?"

Heroes of Christmas: Zechariah

Pastor Mark Jeske

When people say they were speechless after some shock, their silence probably didn't last very long. In a minute or two they opened up with a torrent of talk. One of my Christmas heroes really was speechless—he literally was struck dumb by God to ponder the powerful angelic message that he didn't believe.

The poor man may have thought that he would never utter another word as long as he lived. He submitted to God's discipline without bitterness. But when the miracle child appeared, just as the angel Gabriel had promised, he showed to all, and to his God, that he fully grasped the great role his infant son would play in preparing the world for Mary's even greater Son: **"Then they made signs to his father, to find out what he would like to name the child. He asked for a writing tablet, and to everyone's astonishment he wrote, 'His name is John'"** (Luke 1:62,63). Giving his baby the name the angel had foretold was a silent testimony that showed understanding, obedience, and trust in God's revelation. God smiled from heaven and released his servant's tongue.

What glorious praise then came out of his rusty mouth! The "Song of Zechariah" in Luke chapter 1 is an outburst of poetic faith and joy that his child would herald the ministry and work of Jesus Christ, the Savior of the world.

When you read Zechariah's story, your heart will jump for joy too.

A key to stronger faith?

Pastor Mike Novotny

According to a study done by the University of Georgia, there is something that can revolutionize your relationships. After surveying five hundred married people, the study revealed that being financially solid and learning healthy communication habits are important for couples, but not nearly as powerful as . . . praise. Couples who praise one another grow so close that they can deal with other issues, like debt and miscommunication.

Do you think the same thing would work with God? Peter does. He writes, **"Praise be to the God and Father of our Lord Jesus Christ!"** (1 Peter 1:3). Peter, who is writing to a group of suffering, persecuted Christians, knows the key to revolutionizing their faith is praise (and he'll spend the rest of his book giving them good reasons to do it!).

So what could you praise God for today? Perhaps you could start with who God is. He is holy—as pure goodness, he will never do anything to you that is not good. He is eternal—he will never die, grow frail, leave you, or forsake you. He is wise—he knows the perfect solution to the problem that keeps you up, the perfect words to say at the perfect time in the perfect way. He is gracious—he loves you even when you give him no reason to.

Are you looking for a stronger faith? There's a simple way to get there. Praise God!

Wiggle on out
Sarah Habben

My first friend in Antigua was 70-year-old Junie James. Blind for years, Mr. James still made it to church every Sunday where we shared a pew. Once, when I confessed I was having some difficulty adjusting, he said, "Here in Antigua we say, 'Wiggle on outta dat'—like a worm wiggling out of a hole." Mr. James was telling me not to get stuck in my dark hole but to persevere. Eventually I'd see the light.

Barely two months after we met, Mr. James slipped and fell on his concrete floor. He hit his head and died.

Mr. James' funeral took place after a night of rain. The soil in the cemetery was like glue. It took six rubber-booted gravediggers 45 minutes to cover the coffin. Not even a worm could "wiggle on outta dat" mud.

There is pain at a Christian funeral. We are struck dumb by the finality of box and dirt and dark, dark hole. We are stunned by death's greed. We weep.

But there is joy at a Christian funeral too. Faith wiggles on out of despair. It rises to the light of truth: that **"Christ has indeed been raised from the dead, the firstfruits of those who have fallen asleep"** (1 Corinthians 15:20). Jesus paid the wages of our sin. He rose from death. He will pull his forgiven children from death's sleep. No grave can hold us. No hole is too dark or too deep. In Christ, we will wiggle on out of death and awaken to eternal life.

Jesus: The Lord saves

Pastor Mark Jeske

Over the years I've wondered why God so often chose to communicate with people through dreams. For instance, it was in his sleep that a young carpenter named Joseph discovered that his fiancée, Mary, was going to become the mother of the Savior of the world. Maybe God chose the means of a dream video so that Joseph would believe it. After all, everything is possible in our dreams, even the incarnation of God himself. The last thing God wanted was a wide-awake Joseph arguing with him (as had Zechariah the priest) that his magnificent plan was not possible.

The angelic night messenger even provided Joseph the name the royal baby was to be given: **"She will give birth to a son, and you are to give him the name *Jesus*, because he will save his people from their sins"** (Matthew 1:21). Interestingly enough, this was not a new name, minted for this unique occasion. In Hebrew it is the same as that of Moses' successor. Jesus' name in Hebrew was *Yehoshua*, a variant of Joshua. Its splendid meaning: "The LORD saves."

The great composer Johann Sebastian Bach would often put the initials J.J. at the top of a manuscript for a new composition (*Jesu Juva*, Latin for "Help me, Jesus"). That name to him represented not only his salvation from hell but also the One who would help him from day to day.

May the name of Jesus always sound sweet to your ears.

Every ending is a new beginning
Jason Nelson

Lately, I've been getting my devotions to my editor about a year in advance. I am amazed at how quickly time passes and how soon I can read them published. Older people say this a lot, but time really does fly. If you are young and thinking, "I have lots of time to do what I need to do," I have two things to say to you: "Ha! Ha!" Get busy now preparing for everything coming down the road because the end of the road is approaching faster than you think.

Friend of Jesus, no matter what painful or wonderful endings you marked in the past year, please watch for the early signs of new beginnings. Seize them as opportunities for you and God to develop together. Think about what the Bible teaches about life, appreciate God's love for you, gather up bits and pieces of experience, and put them in a file named "lessons learned." Then keep it handy.

And pray the prayer of fresh starts: **"Lord, you have been our dwelling place throughout all generations. Before the mountains were born or you brought forth the whole world, from everlasting to everlasting you are God. Satisfy us in the morning with your unfailing love, that we may sing for joy and be glad all our days. May the favor of the Lord our God rest on us; establish the work of our hands for us—yes, establish the work of our hands"** (Psalm 90:1,2,14,17).

Who, me? Touchy?

Pastor Mark Jeske

I sure can see the problems caused by other people's hair-trigger tempers. One of the members of our church council went off on me once for no good reason. It took a huge investment of energy, patience, love, and time to restore the relationship. What I'm not so sure about is whether the people around me think I'm touchy. Touchy? *Moi?*

"Love is . . . not easily angered," says St. Paul in 1 Corinthians 13:4,5. It sure isn't. The real question is whether or not you and I are easily angered. Why do we do that? Because anger is fun in a way, at least at first. The adrenaline rush makes us feel really alive. Because we feel indignant and righteous and have to teach other people a lesson not to mess with us. Because we all secretly long to be wild and free, letting out the beast within. It is hard work to show restraint when upset. Because emotional outbursts are a way of controlling a situation, knocking others off-balance and maybe even intimidating them into trying to soothe and placate you by giving you what you want.

Scripture teaches us that our anger does not bring about the righteous life that God requires. Rather than revealing what's wrong with other people, our outbursts usually show the weaknesses in us—insecurity, self-absorption, and a bitter spirit. God's patient love for us inspires us to seek to understand others rather than rush to judgment.

Assume the best in others' hearts instead of leaping to conclude the worst.

Our best defense

Jason Nelson

Years ago I was on jury duty. I spent three days in a courtroom listening to arguments in a civil case. The plaintiffs charged the defendant with damaging their livelihood and business by claiming to own part of what they thought was their property. The plaintiffs were humble people whose attorney was pretty disorganized and wore a rumpled suit. The defendant was a confident businessman, and he had a slick lawyer. The evidence required us to render a verdict in favor of the defendant. But we felt bad about it. We had sympathy for the plaintiffs, but their case was weak. In our deliberations, we noted that the defendant mounted a good defense because he had a better lawyer.

I have been in court other times. I was called to testify in a custody case for a student I was counseling. I had to appear before a judge to get disability benefits. I don't like courtrooms because I'm afraid if I say the wrong thing, I will get myself in trouble. According to the letter of the law, we are always in God's courtroom. And we should be uneasy about being there if we choose to represent ourselves. **"But if anybody does sin, we have an advocate with the Father—Jesus Christ, the Righteous One. He is the atoning sacrifice for our sins, and not only for ours but also for the sins of the whole world"** (1 John 2:1,2).

Heroes of Christmas: Elizabeth

Pastor Mark Jeske

When God wants to do something big, he sends one person. When he wants to do something *really* big, he begins his preparations before the champion's birth and even selects a childless older couple who have grieved over their infertility. Abraham's wife, Sarah, was given a miracle son, Isaac; Manoah and his wife were given a miracle son, Samson; and Zechariah's "barren" wife, Elizabeth, became pregnant with John the Baptist.

Elizabeth is a Christmas hero. Women know that the risk of childbirth both to mother and baby increases as the mother gets older. She may have had doubts about her ability to carry out her mission. Then she received a visit from her much younger relative Mary, who had even more amazing news. But Elizabeth, filled with the Holy Spirit, already knew about Mary's extraordinary unborn baby: **"But why am I so favored, that the mother of my Lord should come to me?"** (Luke 1:43).

This is why Elizabeth is such a hero. She believed the unbelievable. Why? Because it was logical? No. Because it was convenient or lucrative? No. It's because she believed the Word of God. You have her same dilemma—God invites you too to believe the unbelievable, that eternal and almighty God himself, in the second person of the Trinity, took on human flesh in order to save us from eternal damnation. He invites you to believe that through him you receive forgiveness, favor, and immortality.

What a Christmas present!

What every wife wants

Pastor Mike Novotny

What does a woman want? As a dude, I would be completely unqualified to answer that question. But I'm a Bible dude, so I actually know. Husbands, future husbands, brothers who have sisters, are you ready to write this down?

Guys, what every woman wants is . . . God. Remember back in the beginning when God created the first woman. What did he do first? He created the man and then gave the man his Word. The Word about worship, about the garden, about God. This is what it means for the husband to be **"the head of the wife"** (Ephesians 5:23). He is the leader in the seeking-God project! His job is to share the Word with his wife, to tell her about God, to grab her hand and lead her to the source of eternal love.

Flowers are fine, but only God never wilts; his grace never falls like dead petals on the kitchen table. Marble countertops are great, but only God is the rock that can support her soul through stress and kids and cancer. Vacations are fun, but only Jesus can give rest to her soul, a rest she doesn't have to work for, pay for, a rest that never ends. Deep in her heart is a longing to be loved, and God will always love her; a longing to do something that matters, and God promises every cup of water she gives to the kids in Jesus' name will not be forgotten. We are temporary men who can give temporary gifts. But, by God's grace, we can lead her to the eternal God. That's really what a woman wants.

Two wrong notes

Linda Buxa

At my daughter's Christmas concert, she was playing a hymn for everyone to sing along. The program said there were two stanzas to sing. She thought there were three. So when everyone else stopped singing, she played two chords of the third stanza—and quickly stopped.

As we were walking out to the car, she only talked about those two chords—even though she had played four songs that night. I asked, "Why is it that out of all the right notes you played, you only think about the two that you weren't supposed to play?"

She replied, "Those are the two that people noticed."

We can understand her reaction, can't we? We all know that one mistake can ruin our perception of a performance.

So it makes sense that one sin ruined perfection too. All it took was one sin from Adam and Eve and the rest of us were infected. **"For just as through the disobedience of the one man the many were made sinners, so also through the obedience of the one man the many will be made righteous"** (Romans 5:19).

This is why we need Christmas. The baby in the manger came to be fully and completely obedient to his Father—to play all the right notes (without playing extra). Then, after he took the punishment for our failures, he gave us the credit for his performance. Now we are righteous—right with God.

And we can have a Merry Christmas.

Lay down love

Sarah Habben

These days, marriage is about as popular as powdered wigs. Divorce abounds; cohabiting is the norm. Part of the problem is that godly love has lost its seat to worldly passion. If passion opens its hungry mouth and roars, feed it whatever it wants! But if passion fades, so does your obligation.

Godly love is different. **"This is how we know what love is: Jesus Christ laid down his life for us. And we ought to lay down our lives for our brothers and sisters"** (1 John 3:16).

Love isn't something you fall in and out of. Love is a laying down. Godly love pinnacled on the cross when Jesus laid down his life for us, his enemies.

But Jesus also loved us by leaving heaven to live with us. By losing sleep to pray for us. By skipping supper so he could touch a few more hearts. By befriending the uncool and unclean. Each deliberately placed tile of Jesus' love creates a beautiful new foundation for our lives as spouses or singles. His love covers the ugly laminate of our past mistakes.

Best of all, his love gives us the power to act in kind. We can lay down our lives and, maybe harder than that, our unruly passions in order to serve others. We who are single can love by zealously guarding the virginity of our special someone. We who are married can love by choosing to give (and forgive) without keeping count.

Christ Jesus, make your love my passion. Amen.

God's secret agents are everywhere

Pastor Mark Jeske

God has an army of human servants who do his will and do their part to carry out his agenda. We usually assume that these are the active church members who study the Word and engage in public worship, right? In other words, church people.

But we don't know the half of what God has going on. He has connections with people beyond our ability to track and identify. Scripture has quite a few stories of God's secret agents in very unpredictable places. For instance—a pharaoh of Egypt. Seriously! Did you know that a pharaoh named Necho was receiving direct instructions from God himself? What?

This led to the (seemingly) absurd scenario where an Egyptian needed to lecture an Israelite king who should have known better about not getting in the way of God's plans: **"Necho sent messengers to him** (i.e., King Josiah)**, saying, 'What quarrel is there, king of Judah, between you and me? It is not you I am attacking at this time, but the house with which I am at war. God has told me to hurry; so stop opposing God, who is with me, or he will destroy you'"** (2 Chronicles 35:21). Somehow this Egyptian had been drafted into God's plans, had believed in the truth of his instructions, and had obediently carried them out.

Doesn't that give you a sense of wonder at what God may be up to right under your nose? His secret agents are everywhere!

Unity in the community

Pastor Mark Jeske

We live in an age of bitter disunity. Our national politics are shrill and rough. Political parties gerrymander districts to make them permanently safe for their party candidates. Social media that allows people to hide behind screen names has become a forum for abusive shaming and trolling. The business world is a jungle. Salespeople poach each other's clients. People fake injuries in order to sue "deep pocket" companies and their insurers. Homeowners and big companies stiff their contractors.

Every difference between people—gender, race, age, ability/disability, ethnic background, religious beliefs, economic level—becomes a political wedge issue to divide us against each other. All these behaviors have the same sickness at the core—the worship of self. People want money, power, and pleasures for themselves and their tribe, and they don't care on whom they step to get what they want.

There is another way, a better way—to think of the common good instead of just me/me/me. We have a mighty heavenly helper for that noble goal: **"In Judah the hand of God was on the people to give them unity of mind to carry out what the king and his officials had ordered, following the word of the Lord"** (2 Chronicles 30:12). Money and power are terrible motivators for people to yield and sacrifice. But God's love can help us transcend our divisions and actually care about people.

Let's pray today that the hand of God will be upon us.

The confessions of a man

Jason Nelson

I have a confession. It's hard to be a man. I'm sure it's hard to be a woman too, but I can't speak to it. Maybe one of my female colleagues could cover that topic. I'm just glad I never had to give birth. Most of the things God says about men and women in the Bible apply to both no matter which one he is addressing. And when God gets pointed with men, he is often tailoring a message toward our weaknesses. Fathers are more likely than mothers to exasperate their children because they are men. And it's hard to be a man.

The script for manliness is bent toward brutishness because men wrote it. We get a pass for being crude and smelly that women don't get. We would like to think we are bigger, faster, stronger, but most ladies I know are tougher than I am. They would never start a fight or a war nor believe they have a mandate to finish it. Men have a history of thinking it is the order of the universe that we should dominate everything. And we can struggle to be cooperative when we don't.

And then there is the God-man, Jesus Christ. Men have profaned his name too often and failed to seek real manhood in him. Religion is for women and children, right? Not at all.

I have grown to admire the men who have patterned their lives after Jesus.

Heroes of Christmas: Mary

Pastor Mark Jeske

Zechariah and Thomas were doubters in the gospel stories. Mary was not. She is a hero not so much because of what she *achieved*, but because she *believed*. Her faith in God's clear Word enabled her to serve God's agenda in the way he designed for her.

When Gabriel appeared to her with the extraordinary message that she was going to bear a child as a virgin, she didn't argue, "Sir, what you just described is biologically impossible, you know. Do I have to explain human biology to you?" When she heard the importance of her child, she didn't shirk the burden, as if to say, "I don't want that for my life."

Here's what she did say: **"I am the Lord's servant. . . . May your word to me be fulfilled"** (Luke 1:38). Her faith enabled her to walk a hard road. She and Joseph were poor; now they would be poor with a needy baby. In her ninth month she had to make the hard journey from her home in Nazareth all the way to the town of Bethlehem. And one day Mary would have to witness the torture and execution of her precious Son. The prophet Simeon had told her what being the mother of the Savior would cost her: "A sword will pierce your own soul." Not literally, of course. But she was going to hurt as though it had.

Mary believed the unbelievable. This Christmas, God invites you to do it too.

Don't harass the sheep

Linda Buxa

Sometimes I think Christians are so busy pointing out everything that's wrong with the world that we become jerks for Jesus. The words we say are full of condemnation and contempt. Instead, when we look at the world, I'd hope that our attitude is like that of Jesus: **"When he saw the crowds, he had compassion on them, because they were harassed and helpless, like sheep without a shepherd"** (Matthew 9:36).

So often we get arrogant, pointing out what's wrong with "them," that we end up harassing the sheep instead of having compassion on them.

Really, what Jesus condemned the most was when the legalistic church leaders made so many rules and made it so hard for people to come to faith that the people just gave up. Faith seems unappealing when people believe they will never measure up to the rules.

Instead, today, when Jesus tells you to go out into the world and take the good news, speak the truth out of love for Jesus and love for the people you're talking to. Take his message of forgiveness and redemption to the people who live differently than you do and who need to know that following Jesus is about knowing the good news, not about following all the rules.

Let the Holy Spirit work through the words you speak. Let him be the one to change people's lives as they are transformed by faith—in his time.

And, whatever you do, don't harass the sheep.

I feel goaded by guilt
Pastor Mark Jeske

Do you know what it's like never to feel that what you do for somebody else is enough? Or good enough? Are you insecure about the affection you have from your family? Do you find yourself trying to earn people's approval but never get it? Do you suspect that people are only pretending to be nice to you, but really they despise you for all your shortcomings?

Worse—are you ashamed of things in your past, and your efforts to make amends just never seem to make the guilt go away? Are you too embarrassed to pray and ask for things, knowing that you don't "deserve" them?

If you said yes to two or more of those questions, here's your problem: you're too obsessed with yourself. *Of course* you have shortcomings. That's why you and I need a Savior. The way out of your guilt hole is in making Jesus Christ the center of your life and the Prime Mover of your agenda and rationale: **"Christ's love compels us, because we are convinced that one died for all, and therefore all died. And he died for all, that those who live should no longer live for themselves but for him who died for them and was raised again"** (2 Corinthians 5:14,15).

Jesus Christ has forgiven you unconditionally and completely. Guess what? You can forgive yourself. Since he loves you, it doesn't matter how other people treat you. Since he likes you, you can choose to like yourself.

Give a eulogy today!

Pastor Mike Novotny

Do you know what a eulogy is? In Greek, it simply means, "a good word." We often equate eulogies to funeral speeches, but such praise doesn't have to wait until the wake. It can happen today.

I think of Bethany's eulogy. When her father turned 50, Bethany gathered 50 eulogies, 50 good words of praise about the kind of man her father was and the kind of deeds her father had done. I wasn't there for his party, but I can only imagine how that daddy felt when his little girl read her eulogies. And I can only imagine how reading those "good words" made her appreciate her father even more.

No wonder Peter writes, **"Praise be to the God and Father of our Lord Jesus Christ!"** (1 Peter 1:3). Peter knows the power of praise, of giving a daily eulogy, not for the dead but for the living God, the exalted King who calls himself our Father and we his dear children. Peter encourages us today to think of 50 thousand reasons why God is worthy to be praised, blessed, exalted, magnified, glorified, and lifted up. Unpack what words like *grace, mercy, salvation, forgiveness,* and *peace* mean. List the blessings that prove God is worthy to be praised. If you take time to praise God today, your Father won't be the only one moved. Your heart will be too.

Thanks anyway
Jason Nelson

It seems like Paul is expecting too much from us in his letter to the Philippians. In chapter 4 he presses a talking point straight out of the book of spiritual correctness: *No matter what, be thankful.* With the Thessalonians, Paul made a rational argument: **"Give thanks in all circumstances; for this is God's will for you in Christ Jesus"** (1 Thessalonians 5:18). We should be thankful because God wants us to be thankful. His will is done and that's that. But with the Philippians, Paul makes it a matter of the heart. Gratitude is an expression of a spirit that is uplifted from what we choose to remember about the people we love. **"I thank my God for all the memories I have of you"** (Philippians 1:3 GW).

That's how grief yields to gratitude at the grave of a loved one, because we remember the spark that person brought to our lives. The hell that is war and the violence of terror are no match for the eternal flame that fallen compatriots lit in our hearts. I would be very thankful to pass into the next life with the recollection of the angelic faces of my grandbabies on my mind.

Paul was thankful not to be what he used to be. The Lord Jesus appeared in his life and converted him from being a hater to being a lover of God and God's people. The memory of Christ's love turned chains, hardship, and martyrdom into opportunities for Paul to say, "Thanks anyway."

Evidence of the Spirit: Love

Pastor Mark Jeske

Sometimes God is really, really obvious in his work. He once demonstrated his terrible wrath over human sin by sending massive amounts of water to the earth's surface, covering it completely and ending all terrestrial life except for Noah's floating zoo barge. He once demonstrated his compassion and power by feeding the equivalent of a basketball arena full of people with just five small loaves and two fish.

But God more often is really, really subtle in his work, and that is an offense to some. They want more flash, more bang, more miracles, more power—something! God is utterly unmoved by people's demands for a show. Instead, he seems to prefer manifesting his working by the godly behaviors of his believers. We are God's ambassadors who speak for him but also his handiwork, quiet but powerful *and visible* evidences of the Spirit's indwelling.

Scripture calls these godly behaviors "fruits of the Spirit," and the fifth chapter of Galatians lists nine of them. The first may be the most powerful of them all: **"The fruit of the Spirit is love"** (Galatians 5:22). Love is the *unconditional* giving of worth and importance to another person. Jesus Christ is the gold standard, giving up his life to give us life.

It is our first purpose on earth to love God and to make other people feel valuable. When this day is over, will anyone have noticed at least one example of the Spirit-fruit of love in what you said and did today?

Who, me? Grudges?

Pastor Mark Jeske

"As far as the east is from the west, so far has he removed our transgressions from us" (Psalm 103:12). How I love the comfort of that Scripture passage. How I love knowing that my record of moral failings, my idolatries, lies, and omissions, disappear from God's book of deeds like shaking up an Etch A Sketch. What a relief it is to believe, to *know*, that my meeting with God personally when I die won't bring his disgust crashing down on my head.

So why do I hang onto old hurts the way I do? Love **"keeps no record of wrongs,"** says St. Paul (1 Corinthians 13:5). It sure doesn't. The real question is whether or not *you and I* keep a record of wrongs. I think I know why I persist in doing that. Remembering other's faults is a cheap way for me to feel superior. If I refuse to forgive, I can imagine that I hold the moral high ground. A grudge is like an asset—if I forgive, I give up the issue as a weapon to use for my advantage. I might need that weapon in a future argument.

Jesus told a parable once about an unmerciful servant who had been forgiven an immense debt but who then turned on a fellow servant for a relative pittance. Today is the day for you to dump the anger bag, shake out all the IOU grudges you've been hoarding, and release your fellow sinners from your judgment.

Heroes of Christmas: Joseph

Pastor Mark Jeske

Joseph is a Christmas hero. God's beautiful rescue plan for the human race really put this dear man through some changes. He had great plans for his life: he was building his carpentry business and planning a wedding with Mary, his fiancée. Then came the news that she was pregnant, and he knew he was not the father. How crushed his heart! How fallen his hopes!

Get this—God could have explained everything to him at the same time as Mary, but he didn't. He allowed him to think that Mary had been unfaithful. God let him sweat: **"Because Joseph her husband was faithful to the law, and yet did not want to expose her to public disgrace, he had in mind to divorce her quietly"** (Matthew 1:19). It was only then that God sent another angel messenger to explain about the miraculous conception and the identity of her astounding Baby. Joseph believed the unbelievable. How that must have blown his mind—"I'm going to be the stepfather of God!"

The presence of God in human flesh in their arms didn't make their lives easier, however. The little family had to flee Judea from the murderous rage of King Herod, and Joseph then had to try to find a way to feed them in exile in Egypt, far away from his tools and customers. For all he knew, he would never be able to return.

But in faith he allowed God to use him for his saving plan. He's a hero to me.

Christmas Eve

When Christmas is hard

Linda Buxa

Is it hard for you to sing the song "Joy to the World" right now?

Maybe you're facing a layoff or handling a family crisis. Possibly it's chronic or sudden illness or the fallout from addiction. Maybe your arms are lonely from infertility or divorce or widowhood.

This time of year, it seems you're expected to ignore your pain, slap a bow on it, and smile. But how will your life ever be merry and bright when your world is shaking, when your heart is breaking, and when you cry yourself to sleep? How will you ever sing "Joy to the World" when you're under spiritual attack?

Mind if I tell you how? You'll be able to sing "Joy to the World" because it wasn't written for when Jesus came the first time. It was written for when Jesus comes the second time. It was written to remind you that the miserable things of this world are temporary. Thanks to Jesus, who came the first time to live and die for you one time, you now get to live with him for all time.

So this Christmas Eve, if it's hard, go ahead and grieve. But **"do not grieve like the rest of mankind, who have no hope. For we believe that Jesus died and rose again, and so we believe that God will bring with Jesus those who have fallen asleep in him"** (1 Thessalonians 4:13,14).

The baby in the manger is your hope. All will be well.

Christmas Day

Two-way Christmas traffic

Pastor Mark Jeske

Of the many, many astonishing features of the events of the first Christmas, one of the most astounding is how few people noticed anything at all. Mary's emergency childbirth in the stable was attended only by Joseph and the other animals. Nobody in the packed inn wanted to risk losing a bunk for the night, so Joseph probably didn't even bother asking for help.

The chosen shepherds, working late in their favorite Bethlehem fields, were the only viewers of a heavenly light show that you'd think half the world would have seen. But even though the human audience for God the Son's stunning entry in the flesh onto our planet was small, it doesn't mean that not much was happening.

On the contrary. There was massive two-way traffic between earth and heaven that night, some going up and some coming down: **"Suddenly a great company of the heavenly host appeared with the angel, praising God and saying, 'Glory to God in the highest heaven, and on earth peace to those on whom his favor rests'"** (Luke 2:13,14).

Peace came to earth that night. Not the ceasing of warfare or crime. Those two evils will plague us till judgment day. No, a better peace—God turning a smiling face to all believers because of his Son. And starting that night, the glory-praises for the great Incarnation will rise for all ages from the throats of people and angels.

Let me hear you say, "Glory to God!"

The loyalty of a husband

Jason Nelson

I have a friend who studied art and design. He says, "The eye is drawn to a vertical line." That's the temptation men face when they meet women who are revealing a little too much of what their mamas gave them. Eye contact, gentlemen!

Women are God's art. Men have noticed their beauty and reproduced the female form in stone, on canvas, in celluloid film, and in their minds. Sometimes it's respectful, and sometimes it's just plain wrong. In real time, male/female interactions can produce sexual tension. And they can test a husband's love and honor for his wife. Where do you look? What should you think? What do you say? And what are you willing to buy if she is selling something? It all depends on where your loyalties lie.

It's interesting that a single man gave the best advice for marriage: **"Husbands, go all out in your love for your wives, exactly as Christ did for the church—a love marked by giving, not getting. Christ's love makes the church whole. His words evoke her beauty"** (Ephesians 5:25-27 MSG). It takes a loyal husband a lifetime to extol his wife's beauty and keep her self-image whole. God forbid any man should ever break something so beautiful. Gentlemen, it is a good feeling to have a long marriage and be able to say, "This is my wife. She's still everything I'm looking for."

From compost to kings

Sarah Habben

People from many nations call Antigua home. But they don't all share the Antiguans' love for salt fish and *sous*. When expats travel off-island, they purchase the food they crave. My Greek friend fills her suitcases with 20 liters of olive oil. The Syrians next door stock up on tahini. We stuff ours with nuts. At customs, suitcase lids are lifted and goods are taxed. The hassle and cost are worth it for things that are highly valued. Nobody would go through the bother for boxed mac and cheese.

Now lift the lid of your heart. It probably looks a lot like mine. Packed with good intentions as stale as cardboard, with words that glow an artificial color, with "godly" actions as flaccid as overcooked noodles. Who could value hearts like these?

Christ does. Christ about whom angels sing:

"You are worthy . . . because you were slain, and with your blood you purchased for God persons from every tribe and language and people and nation. You have made them to be a kingdom and priests to serve our God, and they will reign on the earth" (Revelation 5:9,10).

Christ craves a relationship with sinners. He thought nothing of the hassle and cost but traveled to earth to purchase us with his blood. That precious blood transforms us from compost to kings. Believers from around the globe are his precious gifts to God. And when God looks inside our hearts, he doesn't recoil in disgust. He sees Christ. He sees believers who delight to serve him—not just in heaven, but right now.

The Christmas truce

Jason Nelson

World War I was one of the deadliest conflicts in human history. New weapons were used in old-style combat. Enemy forces dug in right across from each other and then tried to blow each other to kingdom come. But it was quiet on Christmas Eve 1914, because one side decided to decorate its trenches for Christmas. The other side did the same. Before long the men were meeting in no-man's-land singing carols, exchanging souvenirs, and wishing each other a merry Christmas. Then the fraternizing ended and the hostilities resumed.

We commemorate the very first Christmas truce by kneeling around a baby in primitive Pampers because we believe he is the Prince of peace. Of course, he brought peace between us and God. Absolutely, we give glory to God in the highest for that in itself. But what about the rest of it? Can't we make the Christmas truce last a little longer? Can't we sustain the miracle of Christmas another day or two? We won't need to stockpile ammo if we are looking to make peace, if we are praying for peace on earth and expressing goodwill toward others because of the Christ Child. The angels weren't just being sentimental because it was Christmas Eve when they sang: **"Glory to God in the highest heaven, and on earth peace to those on whom his favor rests"** (Luke 2:14). They were declaring the transforming effect Jesus can have in our hearts and in our world.

So maybe the guy who leaves his Christmas lights up all year round isn't just too lazy to take them down. Maybe he is declaring a truce.

Evidence of the Spirit: Peace

Pastor Mark Jeske

Do you have any "drama mamas" in your life? You know who they are—they thrive on conflict and tension. They love gossip (rebranding it as "news about friends"). They draw energy from arguments and fights. Perhaps since they are unhappy themselves, they selfishly want to drag others into their swamp of negativity.

It's not hard to thrive on conflict—you just surrender to the devil's pull. Arguing can be fun in a way—there's a big charge of adrenaline and you feel alive. You feel morally or intellectually superior to someone else. If you had the foresight to recruit cheerleaders in advance, you have a posse with which to rehash the conflict, chalk up wins, and recap your best lines. But not a one of these things brings happiness, not a one builds real friendships, and not a one of them comes from the Spirit.

You know why not? Because **"the fruit of the Spirit is . . . peace"** (Galatians 5:22). The Spirit of God teaches us a whole new set of behaviors: to defuse instead of intensifying tension . . . to listen first, listen again, and talk later . . . to think the best of people until proven otherwise . . . to look for things to praise in people rather than ridicule . . . to find more joy in reconciling two people than in provoking and enjoying a fight . . . to choose to be genuinely happy for other people's achievements.

If Christ is the Prince of peace, then I guess his followers should strive to be Dukes and Duchesses of peace.

Hear it; live it

Pastor Mark Jeske

The Christian faith that has come to you and me is a massive inheritance, complex and rich. But that very volume and complexity can get us so distracted with peripheral things that we lose the main thing.

Linguistic scholars can analyze and catalog the Bible's Greek and Hebrew vocabulary; anthropologists can relate the Bible's stories to scientific discoveries of other ancient civilizations; archeologists can dig for ancient religious artifacts; historians can track the spread of the church; architects and engineers can devote lifetimes to studying historic places of worship; musicians can immerse themselves into the myriad styles of church music that have come down to us. Art scholars can specialize in Christian imagery and media.

All those are wonderful things, but they are no substitute for the core activity that Jesus himself described on one of his journeys: **"Blessed rather are those who hear the word of God and obey it"** (Luke 11:28). All the scholarly discoveries in the world are no replacement for connecting to Christ through the Word. Knowledge won't save you on judgment day. Only Christ will.

I hope that you put energy and talent to work in building the church—maintenance, bookkeeping, food preparation, human care, music, outreach, and organizing for services. Just make sure that the main thing is always your main thing. Listen to your Savior's voice; absorb it; take it to heart; trust him completely; arrange your life according to what he has said.

Hear. Read. Believe. Do.

Look back
Sarah Habben

Tick. Tock. There are more than 30 million seconds in a year. How many of those 30 million moments of the year do you still cherish? How many do you wish you could undo? How many have simply pulled away from the curb of memory like a string of indifferent taxis?

Tick. Tock. Soon the new year will ease into the station. We don't know what she carries, but we know her carriages are full. Contentment. Anxiety. Joy. Pain. Failure. Triumph. Birth. Death.

Are you ready?

You will be, if you stand on the platform of Psalm 77:11: **"I will remember the deeds of the Lord; yes, I will remember your miracles of long ago."**

Asaph, the psalmist, had his eyes fixed on a far more distant horizon than the year gone by. He had been feeling snubbed by God. Despair kept him awake at night. But then he recalled his Sunday school lessons, "the miracles of long ago." The God who had "forgotten" Asaph was the same God who had split the Red Sea to lead his flock from slavery, who had fed and clothed them in the desert of their lives. Asaph needed hope for tomorrow. So he turned around and locked his eyes on the past.

As you head into a new year, remember *this* miracle of long ago: God gave his Son for you. You are no longer a slave to sin. Your misspent moments are forgiven. The Promised Land of heaven awaits.

Look back. And head into the future with hope.

Devotions for Special Days

"Good" Friday

Pastor David Scharf

"In the same way the chief priests, the teachers of the law and the elders mocked him. 'He saved others,' they said, 'but he can't save himself! He's the king of Israel! Let him come down now from the cross, and we will believe in him'" (Matthew 27:41,42).

Ironically, the religious leaders kind of had a point. Jesus came not to save himself but to save us humans! Jesus came not for his benefit but for our benefit. Jesus stayed on that cross not because it was helpful for him but because it was VITAL for us!

So we are filled with awe on this day. Imagine! God loves you and me so much that he's willing to go to the cross for us! God loves us so much that he's willing to lay down his life for us! And the devil can try to lead you and me to doubt, to wonder if God really loves us, but the cross drives those doubts away. Look! Jesus is up there! He's up there for you! He's up there because he loves you!

And, oh yeah, let's be clear; if he had wanted to come down, he had the ability to do so. And that makes it all the more beautiful. He did all this—went through all this suffering—willingly. That's how much he loves you; that's how much he loves me.

No wonder we call this Friday, "Good."

Convinced by witnesses

Jason Nelson

The resurrection wasn't proved by forensic science. The empty tomb gave up only so many clues. Those on the scene came to different conclusions when they saw the evidence. Mary Magdalene thought the tomb was empty because a gardener moved the body to clean up the place. The presence of angels didn't establish the fact for others. Thomas had to see it for himself. But over time many came to believe Jesus rose from the dead because the testimony of witnesses was so convincing.

That is the irony of Easter. The pretext for killing Jesus was based on just enough false testimony by a few witnesses to make the case against him. But it was the convincing testimony of a growing number of witnesses that established the fact he was alive. It was the only case the apostles needed to make. **"God has raised this Jesus to life, and we are all witnesses of it"** (Acts 2:32).

That is also the legacy of Easter to us. The case for Jesus never rests. Many are still not convinced. We are called to testify by Jesus himself who lives on high and in our hearts. **"But you will receive power when the Holy Spirit comes on you; and you will be my witnesses in Jerusalem, and in all Judea and Samaria, and to the ends of the earth"** (Acts 1:8).

I'm ready. Jesus is alive and well. I have seen it myself.

Mother's Day disappointment

Diana Kerr

Woodrow Wilson meant well when he made Mother's Day a national holiday, but he probably didn't anticipate how Mother's Day would become a day for some people to feel bummed out.

Motherhood comes with a lot of high bars, and Mother's Day brings extra attention to our hurts. We set the bar too high for our own moms, and we who are moms ourselves also set the bar too high for how we want to be *treated* as moms. I'm guilty on both accounts.

Every year around Mother's Day I hear moms lament, "No one got me anything." "My husband planned nothing." "I didn't even get a break from my usual mom duties on MOTHER'S day."

Around my first Mother's Day, I found myself battling a little discontent too and realized I need to let people off the hook.

God pointed out this truth about me that I bet is true about you too: My discontent with other people usually stems from spiritual dysfunction. If human relationships delight me, great, but when they don't, I can still be okay. Why? Simple: God is more than enough.

So when you feel disappointed with your mom (or any other person) or about how you're treated as a mom, let's pray that God helps us echo David's words with overflowing contentment: **"Because your love is better than life, my lips will glorify you. I will be fully satisfied as with the richest of foods; with singing lips my mouth will praise you"** (Psalm 63:3,5).

Father's Day

You are your children's refuge
Linda Buxa

King David is known as being a "man after the Lord's own heart."

So when his son King Solomon wrote in Proverbs 14:26, **"Whoever fears the Lord has a secure fortress, and for their children it will be a refuge,"** we can guess he was writing based on his own experience of being raised by a father who respected, praised, and worshiped the Lord.

Fathers, this proverb is just as true for your children today as it was three thousand years ago.

But maybe you don't feel like quite the hero of faith that legendary David was. It's easy to think of the ways you've failed, isn't it? Well, don't forget that Solomon wrote these words even though he knew his father had had an affair with a married woman and sent her husband into battle to be killed. After that, David married her and she eventually became Solomon's mom.

David was a sinful, forgiven man after the Lord's own heart. Whatever your sins, you are also a forgiven man after the Lord's heart. With your heavenly Father as your secure fortress, you are passing along an inheritance of faith to your children. As you pray with them, teach them about integrity, talk with them about God's promises, and remind them over and over about grace. You are giving them a safe place to hide as they face the world's relentless attacks.

Wear white

Sarah Habben

It's Labor Day in the United States. A day that honors the contributions of the working person. The bittersweet "last" day of summer. And, if you follow fashion custom, your final day to wear white.

In the 1950s, showing up to work in white seersucker after Labor Day was fashion suicide. But even today, there are plenty of folks (hi, Mom) who will tuck away their whites until next summer.

The book of Revelation has something to say about wearing white. In John's vision of heaven, an elder asked, rhetorically, **"These in white robes—who are they, and where did they come from?"** And then he said, **"These are they who have come out of the great tribulation; they have washed their robes and made them white in the blood of the Lamb. Therefore, they are before the throne of God and serve him day and night in his temple; and he who sits on the throne will shelter them with his presence. 'Never again will they hunger; never again will they thirst. The sun will not beat down on them,' nor any scorching heat. For the Lamb at the center of the throne will be their shepherd; 'he will lead them to springs of living water.' 'And God will wipe away every tear from their eyes'"** (Revelation 7:13-17).

This Labor Day, as you put your workaday woes momentarily behind you, as you pause before reentering the hurry-scurry of fall, look to the Lamb at the center of the throne. Your Savior renews you. Your labor is blessed because of Jesus.

He dresses you in white.

Thanksgiving Day

Overlooked blessings

Jason Nelson

"Whoever can be trusted with very little can also be trusted with much" (Luke 16:10).

Thanksgiving Day is dedicated to honoring God for the blessings we have in common. Many of these are obvious because they are big in our lives. We make them bigger in order to celebrate the day. A savory feast, great deserts, and a nice nap in a warm house remind us to appreciate our daily bread even when it's a little more bland.

But it is really the accumulated effect of little things that make our lives rich and full. Abundance is rarely delivered in one big package. God tends to give it to us a piece at a time. Great blessings materialize as we are faithful with lesser ones. We end up with so much by sweating the small stuff and making the best use of very little.

And some blessings are inconspicuous because of their absence. Thank God if we had little illness this year or fewer unexpected repairs. Thank God if tension at work was way down and we had less inner turmoil. Thank God we all got to drive more because we paid less for gas.

As we join hands around the table to thank God for things that are hard to miss, let's also be grateful for the very little things we have been given that are easy to overlook.

About the Writers

Pastor Mark Jeske has been bringing the good news of Jesus Christ to viewers of *Time of Grace* in weekly 30-minute programs broadcast across America and around the world on local television, cable, and satellite, as well as on-demand streaming via the internet. After Easter 2019 he will be passing his television main speaker role to Pastor Mike Novotny. Pastor Jeske is the senior pastor at St. Marcus Church, a thriving multicultural congregation in Milwaukee, Wisconsin. Mark is the author of several books and dozens of devotionals on various topics. He and his wife, Carol, have four adult children.

Pastor Mike Novotny has served God's people in full-time ministry since 2007 as a pastor in Madison and now Appleton, Wisconsin. He also serves as a speaker for *Your* Time of Grace video devotions and will be the main speaker of the *Time of Grace* television program after Easter 2019. Mike loves seeing people grasp the depth of God's amazing grace and unstoppable mercy. His wife continues to love him (despite plenty of reasons not to!), and he often prays that Jesus would return before his two daughters are old enough to date.

Linda Buxa is a freelance writer and Bible study leader. She is a regular speaker at women's retreats and conferences across the country, as well as a regular blogger and contributing writer for Time of Grace Ministry. Linda is the author of *Dig In! Family Devotions to Feed Your Faith* and *Parenting by Prayer.* She and her husband, Greg, have lived in Alaska, Washington D.C., and California. They now live in Wisconsin, where they are raising their three children.

Pastor Matt Ewart and his wife, Amy, have been blessed

with three young children who keep life interesting. Matt is currently a pastor in Lakeville, Minnesota, and has previously served as a pastor in Colorado and Arizona.

Sarah Habben resides in Antigua, where her husband, Dan, became a missionary in August 2017. Since their arrival, Sarah has spent a lot of time sweating, slapping mosquitoes, dodging hurricanes, and adjusting to life in the Caribbean after 18 years in Alberta, Canada. She has four daughters, three of whom are in uniform on the island and one who is at Luther Preparatory School in Watertown, Wisconsin. Sarah is the coauthor of *The Bloodstained Path to God* (2012, Northwestern Publishing House) and the author of *The Mom God Chose: Mothering Like Mary* (2015, Northwestern Publishing House).

Diana Kerr is a certified professional life coach on a mission to help go-getter Christian women break free from overwhelm and design their time and life for what matters most. Diana lives in Milwaukee with her husband, Kyle, and their son, Harrington. Visit dianakerr. com to learn more about Diana and explore her free tips and resources on intentional living.

Pastor Daron Lindemann is pastor at a new mission start in Pflugerville, Texas. Previously he served in downtown Milwaukee and in Irmo, South Carolina. Daron has authored articles or series for *Forward in Christ* magazine, *Preach the Word*, and his own weekly Grace MEMO devotions. He lives in Texas with his wife, Cara, and has two adult sons.

Jason Nelson had a career as a teacher, counselor, and leader. He has a bachelor's degree in education, did graduate work in theology, and has a master's degree in counseling psychology. After his career ended in disabling back pain, he wrote the book *Miserable Joy:*

Chronic Pain in the Christian Life (2007, Northwestern Publishing House). He has written and spoken extensively on a variety of topics related to the Christian life. Jason has been a contributing writer for Time of Grace since 2010. He has authored many Grace Moments devotions and several books. Jason lives with his wife, Nancy, in Wisconsin.

Pastor David Scharf served as a pastor in Greenville, Wisconsin, and now serves as a professor of theology at Martin Luther College in Minnesota. He has presented at numerous leadership, outreach, and missionary conferences across the country. He is a contributing writer for Time of Grace and a speaker on the *Your* Time of Grace video devotions. Dave and his wife have six children.

About Time of Grace

Time of Grace is for people who want more growth and less struggle in their spiritual walk. The timeless truth of God's Word is delivered through television, print, and digital media with millions of content engagements each month. We connect people to God's grace so they know they are loved and forgiven and so they can start living in the freedom they've always wanted.

To discover more, please visit timeofgrace.org, download our free app at timeofgrace.org/app, or call 800.661.3311.

Help share God's message of grace!

Every gift you give helps Time of Grace reach people around the world with the good news of Jesus. Your generosity and prayer support take the gospel of grace to others through our ministry outreach and help them find the restart with Jesus they need.

Give today at timeofgrace.org/give or by calling 800.661.3311.

Thank you!

49733913R00215

Made in the USA
Columbia, SC
28 January 2019